The Colorado

Smart Shopper

JANET SIMONS

The Colorado
Smart
Shopper

Useful Words Publishing
Denver, Colorado

Dear Readers:

Is *your* favorite store here?
If not, we'll put it into the next edition of
The Colorado Smart Shopper.
We need to hear from you! If you've got an
addition, correction, complaint or comment,
drop us a line:

Janet Simons
The Colorado Smart Shopper
Useful Words Publishing
Suite 100
1015 S. Gaylord Street
Denver, CO 80209

To order a copy of *The Colorado Smart Shopper,* send a
check for $12.95 to the address above. Colorado residents,
add 95¢ for sales tax. As an incentive to order direct,
there is no charge for shipping and handling.
Make checks payable to Useful Words Publishing.

Copyright © 1995 by Janet Simons

Published by:
Useful Words Publishing
Denver, Colorado

Printed and bound in the United States of America.

ISBN 0-9645635-0-9

Cover design by Heidi Edwards.

Editing by D&D Editorial Services.
Interior design and typesetting by DAW Editorial Services.

Contents

Introduction

In January 1991, the first Shop Smart column appeared in the *Rocky Mountain News*, and it has run . . . well, almost every weekday since then. This book—your guide to "smart shopping" in Colorado—was inspired by the experiences I've had writing that column, and some of the material in this book originally appeared in a slightly different form in the *Rocky Mountain News*.

In four years, the Shop Smart column has weathered many changes due mainly to the loyalty of its readers, who call and write with suggestions and flock to the stores that are featured in it. I'm grateful to each of you, as well as to the *Rocky Mountain News*, whose muscle provides the column's visibility, to a loyal and supportive editor, Mary Winter, and to Marty Meitus, who first had the idea that I was the right person for this particular assignment.

In the fall of 1994 came the radio show, the *Smart Shopper*, on Newstalk 63 KHOW. I never saw myself as a "radio personality," so I owe a debt to station manager David Baronfeld, who did. As I find my broadcasting voice on this powerful radio station, listeners are tuning in. The *Smart Shopper* is a call-in show that airs on Saturday evenings from 6 to 7 p.m. It has provided a new opportunity for me to respond directly to consumer questions, to offer suggestions and, most important, to listen and learn.

This book, though, is meant to fill a need that neither the column nor the radio show can completely satisfy. The value of books is that you hold them in your hands (as you are doing with this one now) and thumb through them. Without knowing what you're looking for, you suddenly find new, useful information. And a book can be more immediate than either a newspaper column or a radio show because its breadth makes it possible for *you* to choose the information—not me.

In fact, I've organized this book with you, the shopper, in mind. The entries are grouped by type of store and also grouped by type of merchandise; in addition, there's an index. Whether you're looking to see if your favorite brand is represented at a factory outlet mall, where to find a good deal on sweat shirts or if there's a MacFrugal's in your area, you will be able to get the information—quickly, easily and accurately—from *The Colorado*

Smart Shopper. The accuracy, of course, will be somewhat compromised by the passage of time—as stores open and close and change their phone numbers, names and price structures. But, the book is, as we go to press, as accurate and thorough as we mere humans can make it.

This book has been a thought ever since the first time a reader of the Shop Smart column called me at the *Rocky Mountain News* to ask, "where was that place that had the _____?" You can fill in the blank—"one hundred roses for $10," "boys' sports jackets," "inexpensive flannel boxer shorts," "cheap panty hose," "factory-return refrigerators," "consignment clothing for men". . .

"What Colorado needs," I thought, "is a place to look up this stuff."

A book! And, since it was already my job to gather the information, I couldn't think of a better person than me to write it.

There's a long haul between gathering information and producing a book, however, and that's where the owners of D&D Editorial Services and DAW Editorial Services came in. Without nearly a year of totally unselfish and completely professional effort from Deborah Lynes and Darice Whetstone, this book would have remained nothing more than a good idea. Thanks, too, to Patty Hodgins and Sherry Stevens for much appreciated editorial assistance. All four of them made this book possible.

Although some aspects of a book are immediate, others aren't. Once information is printed, there's no changing it. That's why there are phone numbers in this book. Always call ahead to make sure the store you're hoping to visit is still in business. (Phone numbers change, too, of course. So if you get one of those irritating messages saying the number is no longer in service, check with information before you give up entirely.) I learned this the hard way when I took a day off with the kids recently to visit the Bugle Boy factory outlet in Castle Rock. It's not there anymore. The one in Longmont has closed, too. This happened right at press time and, although I tried to correct the several entries in the book that were affected, I realize the book can never be perfectly up to date. We wasted an afternoon. Call ahead and be a smarter shopper than the Smart Shopper.

Speaking of phone numbers, a huge chunk of the phone numbers in Colorado (and in this book) were due to change just as we were going to press. In 1995, Colorado is getting its third area code. The way I read this is that "303" phone calls outside the local Denver metro calling area become "970" phone calls. Except for Longmont. That remains "303"—we think. We tried to update all the phone numbers in this book to reflect that change. In practical terms, the old area codes are still good until October 1; dial wrong, and the calls will transfer automatically.

The final three people who need to be thanked are my husband, Alan Brandt, and our two children, Rachel and Reuben. Thanks, Alan, for never complaining about the crankiness, late nights or long-distance telephone bills. And thanks, kids, for hardly ever grumbling and for bragging about me to your friends.

—Janet Simons

Section 1

Categories of Stores and Sales

Discount Department Stores and Membership Warehouses

They have it all: clothing for men, women and children; pillows; suitcases; toys; in some cases, like Outlet World, even major appliances. *Never* assume that something won't be at one of these places. We've bought Gucci shoes at Tuesday Morning, bar stools at Sam's Club, Seder plates at TJ Maxx. You just don't know what you'll find; so if your normal route takes you near one of these places, check it often. And if you happen to be passing by, surrender to your sense of adventure.

Just a few words of caution. With the exception of the membership warehouses, which get their discounts out of massive and odd-lot purchasing and bulk packaging, most of the merchandise at these places has already been on sale. "Suggested retail" may bear no relationship to the actual price in another store. Clothing, equipment, furniture or other non-perishables may be damaged, returned, discontinued, past-season, seconds or outdated. Purchase carefully and check warranties and return policies. And don't get too excited. If you don't really need it, it's not a bargain.

Bigg's Hypermart

10001 Grant St., Thornton, 252-4447

24 hours daily. Closed Christmas Day.

You can find anything under one roof here—groceries, clothing, electronics, housewares, appliances, toys, cosmetics, seasonal items. Unlike many of the places in this listing, Bigg's is not a clearance center but is rather a discount center, similar to the new Super K Kmart stores.

Burlington Coat Factory

12455 E. Mississippi Ave., Aurora, 367-0111; 3100 S. Sheridan Blvd., Denver, 937-1119; 400 E. 84th Ave., Thornton, 287-0071; 7325 W. 88th Ave., Westminster, 431-9696; 545 N. Academy, Colorado Springs, (719) 597-8505.

*10 a.m. to 9:30 p.m. Monday through Saturday; 11 a.m. to 6
p.m. Sunday.*

In addition to coats, Burlington Coat Factory sells a full range of
clothing for men, women and children; accessories; baby
equipment; linens; housewares; gifts; luggage; and closet
accessories. Shoes are sold only at the Bear Valley store.
Discounts range from 10% to 50%. Inspect any purchases
carefully; return policies at Burlington Coat Factory are very
restrictive.

The Half Price Store

14400 E. Alameda Ave., Aurora, 340-4300.

*9:30 a.m. to 9:30 p.m. Monday through Saturday; 9:30 a.m. to
7:30 p.m. Sunday.*

The first branch of this national chain in Colorado carries
clothing, shoes, housewares, toys, children's clothing, accessories,
holiday supplies, colognes, perfumes and more. All merchandise
is marked half the original suggested retail price, and there are no
seconds. But remember, "suggested retail" is a phrase that doesn't
mean much. Jeans were advertised here at $15 to $18; you could
find them on sale for that at Mervyn's, Sears, Penney's
Montgomery Ward or the Levi's and Bugle Boy factory outlet
stores.

Hibbard & Co.

17 S. Tejon St., Colorado Springs, (719) 635-2525

*10 a.m. to 5:30 p.m. Monday through Friday; 10 a.m. to 5 p.m.
Saturday.*

We include Hibbard's not because it is a discounter, although its
prices are generally modest, but because it is a Colorado Springs
institution. The store hasn't changed much in appearance or
inventory in living memory. The floors are wooden, some ceilings
are tin, merchandise is displayed on huge oak tables, sales are
concluded by sending a customer's money to central accounting
via a pneumatic tube system, and the elevator has an accordian-
like door still manned by an elevator operator! Also you won't
want to miss the wonderful time clock at the back of the first

floor near the Notions Department. The store has a variety of merchandise, including a great housewares section, clothing for men and women, linens and notions. If you fear an item (say, a plastic rain hat or woman's nightcap) may not be manufactured anymore, check here first before abandoning all hope. This marvelous store, which should be added to the historic site preservation list if it's not already on it, is a museum to retailing.

Kmart

Throughout Colorado. Check the *Yellow Pages* under Department Stores for the location near you.

8 a.m. to 10 p.m. daily.

If you're a browser who doesn't require much attention, Kmart is a great place to browse. It's a particularly good place to find good deals on non-perishable food items, such as salad dressing and spices, and for picnic supplies, such as plastic plates and paper tablecloths. Kmart's new Super K stores are "hypermarkets," where you can buy anything from apples to washing machines. Check the Wednesday food flyers if you've got a Super K near you. They usually have one outrageous bargain, just to lure people inside.

MacFrugal's Bargains and Close-outs

10 W. First Ave., Denver, 722-7667; 8125 Sheridan Blvd., Arvada, 429-7844; 15351 E. Hampden Ave., Aurora, 680-0310; 779 Peoria St., Aurora, 344-5322; 1951 S. Federal Blvd., Denver, 936-2799; 10575 W. Colfax, Lakewood, 202-1140; 5085 N. Academy Blvd., Colorado Springs, (719) 598-5554; 1990 S. Academy Blvd., Colorado Springs, (719) 591-7494. For information on others locations, call (800) 800-9992. (Be ready with the ZIP code for the area you need.)

9 a.m. to 9 p.m. Monday through Saturday; 11 a.m. to 7 p.m. Sunday.

MacFrugal's is similar to a small department store—it has a little of everything. Among the items you can find good deals on are rugs; framed pictures; dried-flower arrangements; baby clothing; toys; small accessories such as scarves, socks, slippers and gloves;

pantyhose; office products; personal care items; and seasonal items such as Halloween costumes and Christmas decorations.

Marshall's

8555 W. Belleview Ave., Denver, 973-2133; 15151 E. Mississippi Ave., Aurora, 337-3845; 7550 Wadsworth Blvd., Arvada, 431-7483; 1875 28th St., Boulder, 449-1997; 3650 Austin Bluffs Pkwy., Colorado Springs, (719) 598-8333.

10 a.m. to 9 p.m. Monday through Friday; 10 a.m. to 8 p.m. Saturday; noon to 6 p.m. Sunday.

These stores carry a full line of clothing for men, women and children, and you can frequently find designer labels, including Ralph Lauren Polo and Liz Claiborne, at about half of what you'd pay at department stores. Marshall's stores also have outerwear, accessories, housewares, jewelry and shoes.

Outlet World

550 E. 84th Ave., Thornton, 286-6800.

10 a.m. to 9 p.m. Monday through Saturday; 11 a.m. to 6 p.m. Sunday.

Montgomery Ward used to have a scratch-and-dent clearance center for furniture and appliances in the warehouse district, as Sears still does. But Ward's got onto the discount bandwagon and opened Outlet World in the North Valley Mall. There are still scratched dishwashers, discontinued love seats, odd dining room chairs and mismatched mattress–and–box spring pairs—and everything is covered by manufacturers' warranties. You'll also find shoes, linens, coats, underwear, housewares—virtually anything you'd find at a Montgomery Ward Store—but in broken sizes and models—and later.

Phar-Mor

6795 W. 88th Ave., Westminster, 431-1383; 401 W. Girard Ave., Englewood, 762-0629.

8 a.m. to 10 p.m. Monday through Saturday; 9 a.m. to 7 p.m. Sunday.

Phar-Mor's merchandise selection includes greeting cards, office and school supplies, non-perishable food, paper goods, storage systems, toiletries and over-the-counter drugs. There's always an additional discount on something, and Pharmor doubles manufacturers' coupons. It's also about the cheapest place in town to rent videotapes.

Price Club

1471 S. Havana St., Aurora, 750-2118; 7900 W. Quincy Ave., Denver, 932-1810; 6400 W. 92nd St., Westminster, 650-1366.

10 a.m. to 8:30 p.m. Monday through Friday; 9:30 a.m. to 6 p.m. Saturday; 11 a.m. to 5 p.m. Sunday.

In addition to its regular discounts, Price Club occasionally has amazing bargains. We once found a package of 40 Fuji AA alkaline batteries for $8.99—that's 20¢ each. Is it better to join Price Club or Sam's Club? We did an item-by-item comparison between them and found price differences to be negligible. Selections differ somewhat, though. If you're thinking of joining, you can check it out by stopping by a store and asking for a one-time pass or by going in with a friend who's a member. Price Club memberships cost $35 a year, for which you get two membership cards. If you use the membership frequently it will eventually pay for itself. Join the club you think you'll use most frequently. It's probably the one that's nearest your house.

Ross Dress For Less

98 Wadsworth Blvd., Lakewood, 233-1700; 1070 S. Sable Blvd., Aurora, 369-7693; 5910 S. University Blvd., Littleton, 797-2980; 5110 N. Academy Blvd., Colorado Springs, (719) 528-5211.

9:30 a.m. to 9 p.m. Monday through Saturday; 11 a.m. to 7 p.m. Sunday.

Selections are so similar among Ross, TJ Maxx and Marshall's that it's hard to say something different about each of them. On any given day, the merchandise will depend largely on what the buyer found a good deal on. It could be anything, so check. Ross, too, gets good labels, including Chaus and Christian Dior.

Sam's Club

7350 W. 52nd Ave., Arvada, 420-8401; 1400 S. Abilene St., Aurora, 745-8081; 505 S. Broadway, Denver, 722-2152; 4827 S. Wadsworth Way, Littleton, 971-0136; 7817 Park Meadow Drive, Littleton, 799-3905; 715 S. Academy Blvd., Colorado Springs, (719) 597-2311.

10 a.m. to 8:30 p.m. Monday through Saturday; 11 a.m. to 6 p.m. Sunday.

The average Sam's Club carries 3,500 different items, but consistency of the selection can be a problem (as it can be at Price Club). There's a little bit of everything, including food, paper goods, office supplies, clothing, housewares, furniture, electronics, luggage and gift items like books, jewelry and perfume. Here's one difference between Sam's Club and Price Club: the Sam's Club on South Broadway is making an effort to bring in kosher meat. It already carries (and sells) lots of Empire kosher chicken at approximately half the price it sells for in the supermarkets. Sam's Club memberships cost $25 a year; $35 if you buy two membership cards.

Target

Throughout Colorado. Check the *Yellow Pages* under Department Stores for the location near you.

8 a.m. to 9:30 p.m. daily.

Target's Sunday flyer is favored reading material in our house; when Target has a sale you can't beat it. We surveyed school-supply prices on a week when Target was running a sale, and it emerged as the surprise winner, even against Office Depot and Office Max, which offer low-price guarantees. By the way, a survey of shopper habits a while back found that Target is the first place most people go when they're looking for children's clothing. It's also a great source for maternity clothes and really cheap kids' shoes and boots.

TJ Maxx

2350 S. Parker Road, Aurora, 671-8757; 700 16th St., Denver, 892-6020; 98 S. Wadsworth Blvd., Lakewood, 238-3540; 8996 W. Bowles Ave., Littleton, 979-3404; 5901 S. University Blvd., Littleton, 794-5921; 7647 W. 88th Ave., Westminster, 425-7495; 3949 Palmer Park Blvd., Colorado Springs, (719) 574-7103.

9:30 a.m. to 9:30 p.m. Monday through Saturday; noon to 6 p.m. Sunday. Downtown Denver: 9:30 a.m. to 7 p.m. Monday through Saturday.

We think fond thoughts of TJ Maxx because it brought discount shopping back to downtown Denver at a time when it was badly needed—right after the downtown Woolworth's closed. You can find almost anything here at discount, including clothing for men, women and children, housewares, accessories, jewelry and shoes.

Tuesday Morning

8270 W. 80th Ave. (the Meadows Center), Arvada, 422-9994; 7400 E. Hampden Ave., Denver, 488-9940; 4301 E. Virginia Ave., Glendale, 333-8156; 15372 E. Alameda Parkway, Aurora, 695-4357; 12790 W. Alameda Parkway, Lakewood, 989-2792; 7562 S. University Blvd. (Southglenn Square), Littleton, 779-0328; 8996 W. Bowles Ave. (Bowles Avenue Marketplace), Littleton, 972-2155; 4800 Baseline, Boulder, 494-1535; 3520 N. Academy Blvd., Colorado Springs, (719) 596-1043; 222 Walnut St., Fort Collins, (970) 224-3432.

10 a.m. to 6 p.m. Monday through Saturday; til 8 p.m. Thursday; noon to 6 p.m. Sunday. Open only periodically. See Direct and Seasonal Sales.

The emphasis at Tuesday Morning is on gifts. If you've got a wedding to attend, it's a good place to check. If the couple you're shopping for is registered somewhere, go by the department store to get a feel for their color and design preferences. Then browse Tuesday Morning to see if there's something that complements the items they've chosen. It's not *just* gifts, though. They also have unpredictable selections of toys, clothing, luggage, linens, shoes—even food.

Wal-Mart

Throughout Colorado. Check the *Yellow Pages* under Department Stores for the location near you.

9 a.m. to 9 p.m. Monday through Saturday; 9 a.m. to 6 p.m. Sunday.

What's good about Wal-Marts: They've got good selection, good prices and better customer service than either Kmart or Target. What's bad about Wal-Marts: Often they're in the boonies. We live in the center of Denver, and the only time we ever shop at one is when we're in Avon, Glenwood Springs or the wilds of suburbia. This is good, though, if you're a rural or suburban shopper.

Factory Outlet Malls

Factory outlet malls are springing up all over the state. They're in Silverthorne, Durango, Castle Rock and Loveland, and a mall is on the drawing board for Georgetown. A lot of towns seem to view them as an economic panacea—one has even been promoted for the tiny Western Slope town of Fruita. As it turns out, the stores are subject to the same retail pressures (too much overhead, too few customers) as everyone else, and they close, too. But while this trend is hot, it may do to small independent retailers what hand-held calculators did to slide rules. So you might want to think about all its ramifications before embracing it completely.

For one thing, when you spend your money at these stores, you undercut the individual merchant down the street. Small retailers in particular have trouble competing with these guys, but department stores feel their impact, too, each time a family piles into a car and heads for Castle Rock rather than Joslins. When stores go out of business, they leave holes in neighborhoods, downtown centers and in malls (which, alas, are also our neighborhoods), contributing to the decline of the urban lifestyle.

We wouldn't want you to stay loyal to your local retailers just for the sake of loyalty. But it seems to us that conscientious shoppers can do as well at sales in town as they can at outlets that have marked down their merchandise by only about 30%, which is where most outlets start. Most of the items you find at outlets are, at some time during the average month, available at similar prices in your local mall. Outlet merchandise is usually six to eight months behind what the manufacturers are showing in the malls. The "suggested retail" on the price tag is what the item sold for then. And "suggested retail" is just that—a suggestion. It's a straw man for traditional retailers, who may keep an item at "suggested retail" for only a few weeks, if that long, before marking it down. Some items *never* sell at suggested retail.

Department stores and mall shops have clearances, too. You just have to catch the sales, and to do that you have to watch the ads and the Shop Smart column and be alert. And if you miss a sale, there are still lots of places where the past season's merchandise goes. Many items are just as cheap, or cheaper, at such stores as Ross, Tuesday Morning or Sam's Club as they are at factory outlets. If you know what something should cost before you shop, you can do just fine without leaving town. Next time you're in an outlet mall town, ask the locals where they shop. You may find that they come to your town.

A minor industry has sprung up consisting of magazines and books telling you breathlessly about how much money you can save at these malls, but don't expect miracles. Be aware that these publications are supported by factory outlet advertising money, so they're very promotional. The savings they tout are based on the assumption that you ordinarily pay suggested retail, which, of course, bargain-hunters don't do. And it's bargain-hunters who go to factory outlet malls. If you're really interested in outlet shopping, though, you may benefit from subscribing. There are some coupons in the back of *The Joy of Outlet Shopping* that are good in Colorado factory outlets (Corning Revere, L'eggs/Hanes/Bali, Nine West, Oshkosh B'Gosh, Trader Kids, The Ribbon Outlet). You'll get back the price of the magazine if you use them. To order, send $6.95 plus $1.50 for postage and handling to Joy, P.O. Box 17129, Dept. J6, Clearwater, FL 34622-0129.

If you can do well without leaving home, why go to factory outlet malls? For the sales, of course. When items go on serious closeout at factory outlets, it's hard for traditional retailers to touch the prices. Because agreements with retailers generally prohibit advertising by factory stores, you won't know what deals are available until you get there. The first thing to do when you arrive is to drive slowly or walk past the stores and look for sale signs in the windows. There are too many stores in the average mall for any mortal to cover on any one trip, so concentrate on the stores that interest you most. It may help make a list of stores and prioritize it. Then briefly survey each store in your personal top five. Through this process, you may reach one of those transcendent shopping moments when you realize that your child's size in Nikes is $5 a pair.

Moreover, if you're loyal to a certain brand or designer, armed with the phone numbers below, you can call the stores that represent your favorite and ask questions. Some outlets won't tell you anything over the phone, while others will even take phone orders and ship. (Shipping costs are added to the final price.)

Finally, factory outlet malls are great for people (many of them male) who don't have the interest, patience or stamina to shop regular sales.

Find out the rate of local sales tax, because it varies from town to town, and posted prices don't reflect it. If the rate is higher at the factory outlet mall than it is where you usually shop, that cuts into final savings.

Also, before you get into the car to travel to a factory outlet mall, look over the section of this book on Stray Factory Outlets. You may discover a factory outlet right down the street.

One additional word of caution. Although the promoters of this industry would like you to believe that these places do nothing but grow, some move or go out of business. The factory outlet mall trend developed very quickly, and any boom has potential for bust. At Silverthorne, for example, you will no longer find Aileen, Evan-Picone, Gitano, Greetings 'n' More, Members Only, Small World, Ribbon Outlet, Royal Doulton, Toys Unlimited or Wallet Works. If you're planning a long drive just to shop at one or two specific stores, call ahead to make sure they're still there.

Following is a list of the stores and their merchandise categories and phone numbers for factory outlet mall stores in Colorado that are open as of this writing. For more information on individual stores, check the listing under the store's merchandise category.

Finally, if you're planning a trip to the Grand Tetons or Yellowstone National Park, it may interest you to know that there's a group of factory outlet stores in Jackson, Wyo. (Benetton, J. Crew, London Fog, Polo Ralph Lauren). Headed for Utah? There are outlets near Zion National Park and in Park City. If you're going south, check the mall in Santa Fe—it has a Donna Karan outlet. If you're planning an eastward trip on Interstate 76, you may want to plan a stretch break in Nebraska at the Cabela's factory outlet in Sidney (see Sporting Goods). Or, if you're on Interstate 80, there are malls at North Platte and Gretna (exit 432).

The out-of-state factory outlet mall nearest Denver is in Colby, Kansas, about 200 miles away, just across the state line from Burlington on I-70. If you're headed that way, you may want to check the Polo Ralph Lauren outlet—it's a lot closer to anyplace in northeastern Colorado than Ralph's outlet in Durango. The area code for Colby is 913. At this writing, the stores there include: Aileen's, 462-2260; Barbizon Lingerie, 462-3069; Bass Shoes, 462-3360; Bugle Boy, 462-3310; B.U.M., 462-2667; Corning/Revere, 462-8289; Famous Footwear, 462-2213; Florsheim, 462-2213; Full-Size Fashions, 462-3070; London Fog, 462-7734; Polo Ralph Lauren, 462-3364; Prestige Fragrance, 462-8675; Socks Galore, 462-3828; Swank, 462-2667; Van Heusen, 462-7799; Welcome Home, 462-2227; Westport Ltd., 462-2221.

Castle Rock

With 110 stores, the factory outlet mall at Castle Rock is the biggest in the state. Castle Rock is also the factory outlet mall by far most accessible from the state's most concentrated population areas—the Denver metro area and Colorado Springs. From our house in southeast Denver, it's a half-hour drive. And here's one more major advantage—from Denver (or even Boulder) it's a toll-free phone call to any of the stores.

To get to the Castle Rock Factory Shops, take I-25 about 35 miles south from Denver to exit 184, Meadows Parkway. The mailing address is 5050 Factory Shops Blvd., Castle Rock 80104. For mall information, call 688-4494. Hours are 9 a.m. to 9 p.m. Monday through Saturday; 11 a.m. to 6 p.m. Sunday. Amenities include a playground (great for restless children), rest rooms and a food court (great for weary adults) that includes the Branding Iron BBQ, Burger King, Chinese Combo Express, Cinnamonster, Garden of Eatin', Subway, Taco Bell and Villa Pizza.

American Eagle Outfitters, 660-8390.
See Sportswear for Men and Women.

Adolfo II, 688-4130.
See Women's Clothing.

Aileen, 688-9530.
See Women's Clothing.

American Tourister, 660-8130.
See Luggage and Briefcases.

Ann Taylor, 688-3335.
See Women's Clothing.

Athlete's Foot, 660-3820.
See Shoes for Men, Women and Children.

Barbizon Lingerie, 688-5412.
See Accessories and Jewelry.

Bass, 688-3676.
See Sportswear for Men and Women; Shoes for Men, Women and Children.

Big Dog, 688-1831.
See Sportswear for Men and Women.

Book Warehouse, 688-8085.
See New Books.

Boston Traders, 660-0393.
See Sportswear for Men and Women.

Boston Trader Kids, 660-1973.
See Children's Clothing.

Britches Great Outdoors, 688-4596.
See Sportswear for Men and Women.

Brooks Brothers, 688-8894.
See Sportswear for Men and Women.

Bruce Alan Bags, 688-2920.
See Accessories and Jewelry; Luggage and Briefcases.

B.U.M. Equipment, 688-5050.
See Sportswear for Men and Women.

Cape Isle Knitters, 688-2281.
See Sportswear for Men and Women.

Capezio, 660-0797.
See Women's Shoes.

Carter's, 688-0648.
See Children's Clothing; Baby Necessities.

Casual Corner, 688-3818.
See Women's Clothing.

Champion Hanes, 688-6159.
See Sportswear for Men and Women.

Chicago Cutlery, 660-3303.
See Housewares, Gifts and General Merchandise.

Chico's, 688-2950.
See Women's Clothing; Accessories and Jewelry.

Colours & Scents, 660-4807.
See Cosmetics and Fragrances.

Colours by Alexander Julian, 660-3810.
See Menswear.

Corning Revere, 688-1551.
See Housewares, Gifts and General Merchandise.

Danskin, 660-9073.
See Women's Clothing.

Discount Entertainment, 660-8482.
No other listing. The outlet carries current and nearly current videotapes, audiotapes and compact discs at a 10% to 15% discount.

Dockers, 688-3717.
See Sportswear for Men and Women.

Duck Head, 660-9669.
See Sportswear for Men and Women.

Eagle's Eye, 660-0477.
See Women's Clothing.

Eagle's Eye Kids, 660-9810.
See Children's Clothing.

Etienne Aigner, 688-9650.
See Accessories and Jewelry; Women's Shoes.

Factory Brands Shoes, 660-3620.
See Shoes for Men, Women and Children.

Famous Brands Housewares, 660-8349.
See Housewares, Gifts and General Merchandise.

Fan Fair, 688-6665.
See Sports Team Paraphernalia.

Farberware, 660-2188.
See Housewares, Gifts and General Merchandise.

Fila, 688-2208.
See Sportswear for Men and Women.

G III, 688-8189.
See Outerwear.

Galt Sand, 660-0699.
See Sportswear for Men and Women.

Geoffrey Beene, 688-6968.
See Menswear.

Geoffrey Beene Woman, 660-1924.
See Women's Clothing.

Guess? 688-6588.
See Sportswear for Men and Women.

Gund, 660-4863.
See Toys.

Harry & David, 660-6651.
See Food.

Izod/Gant, 688-2393.
See Sportswear for Men and Women.

Jockey, 660-0880.
See Accessories and Jewelry; Sportswear for Men and Women.

John Henry & Friends, 660-3305.
See Menswear.

Jonathan Logan, 660-3848.
See Women's Clothing.

Jones NY Factory Finale, 660-2083.
See Women's Clothing.

Kid's Zone, 660-0212.
See Children's Clothing.

Kitchen Collection, 660-9396.
See Housewares, Gifts and General Merchandise.

Koret, 660-1740.
See Women's Clothing.

Leather Loft, 688-5836.
See Accessories and Jewelry.

L'cessory, 688-2792.
See Accessories and Jewelry.

L'eggs/Hanes/Bali, 688-6455.
See Accessories and Jewelry.

Leslie Fay, 688-2861.
See Women's Clothing.

Levi's, 688-6711.
See Sportswear for Men and Women; Accessories and Jewelry.

Maidenform, 688-8234.
See Accessories and Jewelry.

Marie Diamond, 660-9121.
See Women's Clothing.

Mikasa, 688-1109.
See Housewares, Gifts and General Merchandise.

Mother's Work Maternity, 660-2030.
See Maternity Clothes.

9 West, 660-9177.
See Women's Shoes.

Napier, 688-4515.
See Accessories and Jewelry.

Naturalizer, 660-9277.
See Women's Shoes.

Nautica, 660-6095.
See Menswear.

Nordic Track, 660-0100.
See Sporting Goods.

Olga-Warner, 660-1495.
See Accessories and Jewelry.

Oshkosh B'Gosh, 660-3378.
See Children's Clothing.

Outlet Marketplace, 688-7490.
See Sportswear for Men and Women.

Paper Outlet, 688-8150.
See Party, Holiday, Office and School.

Perfumania, 688-9711.
See Cosmetics and Fragrances.

Pfaltzgraff, 688-9246.
See Housewares, Gifts and General merchandise.

Prestige Fragrance, 660-8697.
See Cosmetics and Fragrances.

Ribbon Outlet, 660-3591.
See Home Accessories.

Robert Scott & David Brooks, 688-3275.
See Women's Clothing.

Rocky Mountain Chocolate Factory, 660-1320.
See Food.

Royal Doulton, 660-1601.
See Housewares, Gifts and General merchandise.

Russell, 660-1161.
See Sportswear for Men and Women.

SAS Shoes, 660-3822.
See Shoes for Men, Women and Children.

SBX, 660-1100.
See Sportswear for Men and Women.

Silverheels Jewelry, 660-0886.
See Accessories and Jewelry.

Socks Galore by Hanes, 660-8260.
See Accessories and Jewelry.

Sony, 660-9038.
No other listing. This outlet sells Sony electronic equipment at discount. Most has been returned and reconditioned; everything is factory warranted. No phone orders.

Springmaid/Wamsutta, 660-2070.
See Home Accessories.

Sunglass Outlet, 660-0780.
See Accessories and Jewelry.

Tanner, 660-8769.
See Women's Clothing.

Ties Etc., 660-0799.
See Accessories and Jewelry.

Tommy Hilfiger, 688-8877.
See Menswear.

Toy Liquidators, 660-9481.
See Toys.

Van Heusen, 688-3477.
See Menswear; Women's Clothing.

Victoria Creations, 660-3848.
See Accessories and Jewelry.

Villeroy & Boch, 688-1101.
See Housewares, Gifts and General Merchandise.

Wallet Works, 660-0190.
See Accessories and Jewelry; Luggage and Briefcases.

Welcome Home, 688-6689.
See Home Accessories.

Westport Ltd., 688-9281.
See Women's Clothing.

Whims/Sarah Coventry, 688-2690.
See Accessories and Jewelry.

Windsor Shirt, 688-2802.
See Menswear; Women's Clothing.

Woolrich Factory Outlet, 660-9580.
See Sportswear for Men and Women.

Durango

Durango is a long way from most of the population in Colorado,
but the group of factory outlet stores in this pleasant town is
worth a visit if you're traveling to the Four Corners area, say, for
a visit to Mesa Verde, for a skiing vacation at Wolf Creek or
Purgatory or just for diversion on your way home from the Grand
Canyon. And many, many folks go down for a ride on the
narrow-gauge railroad from Durango to Silverton. Ralph Lauren
put an outlet here because it's safely distant from competing
Denver retailers, and similar thinking probably went into the
placement of the Benetton outlet. Although the usual factory
outlets are certainly present, you also will find a few
southwestern Colorado manufacturers, such as Bula, that have
outlets only here. If there's a store in Durango and nowhere else
that interests you, you could try phoning to see if they ship. (Bula
does.)
     Most of the Durango stores are not in a mall but are
spread throughout town, with the highest concentration near the
railroad depot at Fifth Street and Main Avenue. The rest are along
Main or on the streets that intersect it, with stores on Sixth,
Eighth, Ninth and 14th avenues. At the opposite end of Main
Avenue from the depot there's a mall with seven outlets. This
listing includes street addresses, but giving clear directions for
Durango is complicated by the fact that, for example, there's a
corner of Third Avenue and Third Street. Once you're in town,
pick up a map at one of the stores. Shoppers shouldn't have any
trouble finding restaurants because the factory outlet area is
actually downtown Durango. Parents of restless children generally
wind up at McDonald's, which is visible from the highway and
has a huge indoor playground.

Because this mall isn't as centrally organized as the others, hours vary among stores. Summer hours are usually 10 a.m. to 9 p.m. Monday through Saturday; 11 a.m. to 8 p.m. Sunday. Winter hours are 10 a.m. to 8 p.m. Monday through Saturday; 11 a.m. to 6 p.m. Sunday.

Balizoo, 736 Main Ave., (970) 247-8194.
See Sportswear for Men and Women.

Bass Shoe, 1316 Main Ave., (970) 259-6483.
See Shoes for Men, Women and Children.

Benetton, 532 Main Ave., (970) 259-4431.
See Sportswear for Men and Women.

Bugle Boy, 1316 Main Ave., (970) 385-7890.
See Sportswear for Men and Women.

Bula, 145 E. Sixth St., (970) 259-1727.
See Sportswear for Men and Women.

Cape Isle Knitters, 1316 Main Ave., (970) 259-6604.
See Sportswear for Men and Women.

Capezio, 870 Main Ave., (970) 259-3335.
See Women's Shoes.

Durango Threadworks, 809 Main Ave., (970) 259-3783.
See Sportswear for Men and Women.

Izod/Gant, 558 Main Ave., (970) 247-1119.
See Sportswear for Men and Women.

Just a Second, 534 Main Ave., upstairs, (970) 259-2970.
See Sportswear for Men and Women.

L'eggs/Hanes/Bali, 1316 Main Ave., (970) 385-5232.
See Accessories and Jewelry.

Levi's, 1316 Main Ave., (970) 247-2925.
See Sportswear for Men and Women.

London Fog, 121 W. Eighth St., (970) 385-7546.
See Outerwear.

Polo Ralph Lauren, 110 E. Fifth St., (970) 259-2241.
See Sportswear for Men and Women.

Rocky Mountain Chocolate Factory, 519½ Main Ave., (970) 259-1408.
See Food.

Sequel Outdoor Clothing, 108 E. Fifth St., (970) 385-4421.
See Sportswear for Men and Women.

Sergio Tacchini, 528 Main Ave., (970) 385-4945.
See Sportswear for Men and Women.

Smelter's Coalroom, 801½ Main Ave., (970) 259-3470.
See Women's Clothing; Western Clothing and Cowboy Boots.

Socks Galore by Hanes, 1316 Main Ave., (970) 259-1727.
See Accessories and Jewelry.

Turtle Lake Clothing Co., 835 Main Ave., #108, (970) 247-0151.
See Women's Clothing.

Van Heusen, 1316 Main Ave., (970) 385-5001.
See Menswear.

Welcome Home, 1015 Main Ave., (970) 259-2827.
See Home Accessories.

Loveland

Colorado's newest factory outlet mall, Rocky Mountain Factory Stores, is off Interstate 25 at the Highway 34 exit, about 55 miles north of Denver and near the city of Loveland. For mall information, call (970) 663-1717. Mall hours are 10 a.m. to 9 p.m. Monday through Saturday; 11 a.m. to 6 p.m. Sunday. The mall opened with a Dairy Queen and a Burger King. A full-fledged food court is slated to open soon.

Aileen, (970) 663-2747.
See Women's Clothing.

Bass Clothes and Shoes, (970) 679-4606.
See Sportswear for Men and Women; Shoes for Men, Women and Children.

Big Dog, (970) 593-0313.
See Sportswear for Men and Women.

Bisou-Bisou, (970) 667-1705.
See Women's Clothing.

Boston Traders, (970) 667-3150.
See Sportswear for Men and Women.

Brooks Brothers, (970) 663-5460.
See Sportswear for Men and Women.

Bugle Boy, (970) 663-2213.
See Sportswear for Men and Women.

B.U.M. Equipment, (970) 593-0123.
See Sportswear for Men and Women.

Cape Isle Knitters, (970) 679-4608.
See Sportswear for Men and Women.

Casual Corner, (970) 669-5332.
See Women's Clothing.

Champion Hanes, (970) 667-5336.
See Sportswear for Men and Women.

Corning/Revere, (970) 669-2023.
See Housewares, Gifts and General Merchandise.

Dansk, (970) 593-0021.
See Housewares, Gifts and General Merchandise.

Eagle's Eye, (970) 593-0736.
See Sportswear for Men and Women.

Eagle's Eye Kids, (970) 593-0351.
See Children's Clothing.

Esprit, (970) 669-1324.
See Women's Clothing.

Factory Brand Shoes, (970) 593-0831.
See Shoes for Men, Women and Children.

Famous Brand Housewares, (970) 593-0226.
See Housewares, Gifts and General Merchandise.

Farberware, (970) 635-0262.
See Housewares, Gifts and General Merchandise.

Florsheim, (970) 962-9499.
See Men's Shoes.

Full-Size Fashions, (970) 593-0633.
See Clothes for Large Women.

Galt-Sand, (970) 593-0504.
See Sportswear for Men and Women.

Geoffrey Beene, (970) 667-2317.
See Menswear.

Harry and David, (970) 663-2990.
See Food.

Jockey, (970) 669-7002.
See Accessories and Jewelry; Sportswear for Men and Women.

Jones NY Factory Finale, (970) 669-8887.
See Women's Clothing.

Kitchen Collection, (970) 669-2661.
See Housewares, Gifts and General Merchandise.

Leather Loft, (970) 593-0535.
See Accessories and Jewelry.

Leathermode, (970) 593-0814.
See Accessories and Jewelry; Luggage and Briefcases.

L'eggs/Hanes/Bali, (970) 669-3777.
See Accessories and Jewelry.

Lenox, (970) 663-0879.
See Housewares, Gifts and General Merchandise.

Levi's, (970) 635-9333.
See Sportswear for Men and Women; Accessories and Jewelry.

London Fog, (970) 593-9851.
See Outerwear; Sportswear for Men and Women.

9 West, (970) 663-7004.
See Women's Shoes.

Oshkosh B'Gosh, (970) 635-9963.
See Children's Clothing.

Paper Outlet, (970) 593-0784.
See Party, Holiday, Office and School Supplies.

Prestige Fragrance, (970) 663-3186.
See Cosmetics and Fragrances.

Publishers Warehouse, (970) 593-0620.
See New Books.

Rockport, (970) 669-1204.
See Shoes for Men, Women and Children.

Rocky Mountain Chocolate, (970) 593-0106.
See Food.

SAS Shoes, (970) 635-9246.
See Shoes for Men, Women and Children.

Springmaid/Wamsutta, (970) 679-4600.
See Home Accessories.

Sunglass Hut, (970) 669-7584.
See Accessories and Jewelry.

Tommy Hilfiger, (970) 669-8877.
See Menswear.

Van Heusen, (970) 669-6667.
See Menswear.

Wallet Works, (970) 593-0733.
See Accessories and Jewelry; Luggage and Briefcases.

Welcome Home, (970) 593-0613.
See Home Accessories.

Westport Ltd., (970) 669-8903.
See Women's Clothing.

Silverthorne

The mountain town of Silverthorne is 70 miles west of Denver on
Interstate 70. Take exit 205; factory outlet malls are on both sides
of the interstate. Amenities are pretty slim. Barney's Cafe serves
the "Red Village" stores on the south side of the interstate. (The
colors will mean something to you when you pick up a brochure
at one of the stores.) There are two groups of shops on the north
side; Dote's Crepes and Coffee serves the north-of-the-interstate
"Blue Village," which is across Highway 9 from of the newest
group of stores, the "Green Village." Patrons of the Green Village
have to cross the street to Wendy's for refreshments.

You could get refreshment, though, just from the setting.
This has to be the prettiest factory outlet mall in the nation.

One could hope that a mall that seems to want the
business of parents, with some dozen stores featuring children's
clothing or toys, would take a page from Castle Rock's book and
erect a playground for impatient tots, especially considering the

recent closing of Toys Unlimited, which, in the past, had been able to provide cheap bribes for good behavior.

The factory outlet mall stores at Silverthorne offer a Preferred Client Card that provides discounts at several stores in the mall. Ask about it at the information booth before starting your shopping trip. If you can't seem to get one, stop by at Marisa Christina, and they'll sign you up.

The mailing address is 145 Stephens Way, Silverthorne, CO 80498. For mall information, call (970) 468-9440 or (800) 969-3767. Hours are 9 a.m. to 9 p.m. Monday through Saturday; 10 a.m. to 6 p.m. Sunday.

Adolfo II, (970) 468-7552.
See Women's Clothing.

American Tourister, (970) 468-7808.
See Luggage and Briefcases.

Anne Klein, (970) 262-1266.
See Women's Clothing.

Banister Shoe, (970) 468-8824.
See Women's Shoes.

Barbizon Lingerie, (970) 468-8056.
See Accessories and Jewelry.

Bass Shoe, (970) 468-2025.
See Shoes for Men, Women and Children.

Bass Clothing, (970) 262-2077.
See Sportswear for Men and Women.

Brands, (970) 468-9440.
See Sportswear for Men and Women.

Cape Isle Knitters, (970) 468-5338.
See Sportswear for Men and Women.

Capezio, (970) 468-9556.
See Women's Shoes.

Carole Little, (970) 262-1437.
See Women's Clothing.

Carter's Childrenswear, (970) 262-2238.
See Children's Clothing; Baby Necessities.

Champion Hanes, (970) 468-9462.
See Sportswear for Men and Women.

Colorful Images, (970) 468-6375.
See Home Accessories.

Colours by Alexander Julian, (970) 262-2476.
See Menswear.

Colours and Scents, (970) 262-2101.
See Cosmetics and Fragrances.

Corning/Revere, (970) 468-2721.
See Housewares, Gifts and General Merchandise.

Dansk, (970) 262-2267.
See Housewares, Gifts and General Merchandise.

Eagle's Eye Kids, (970) 262-2119.
See Children's Clothing.

Etienne Aigner, (970) 468-6455.
See Accessories and Jewelry; Women's Shoes.

Famous Brands Housewares, (970) 262-2267.
See Housewares, Gifts and General merchandise.

Fila, (970) 468-0232.
See Sportswear for Men and Women; Shoes for Men, Women and Children.

Galt Sand, (970) 468-0568.
See Sportswear for Men and Women.

Genuine Kids, (970) 262-2013.
See Children's Clothing.

Geoffrey Beene, (970) 468-5727.
See Menswear.

The Great Outdoor Clothing Co., (970) 262-0807.
See Sportswear for Men and Women.

Guess? (970) 262-9093.
See Sportswear for Men and Women.

harve benard, (970) 468-1338.
See Women's Clothing.

He-Ro Group, (970) 262-1944.
See Women's Clothing.

I.B. Diffusion, (970) 468-2288.
See Women's Clothing.

Izod/Gant, (970) 262-0667.
See Sportswear for Men and Women.

J. Crew, (970) 262-1612.
See Sportswear for Men and Women.

JH Collectibles, (970) 468-9023.
See Women's Clothing.

Jockey, (970) 262-1643.
See Accessories and Jewelry; Sportswear for Men and Women.

John Henry & Friends, (970) 262-2494.
See Menswear.

Jones NY Factory Finale, (970) 468-2609.
See Women's Clothing.

Leather Loft, (970) 262-0259.
See Accessories and Jewelry; Luggage and Briefcases.

L'eggs/Hanes/Bali, (970) 468-9563.
See Accessories and Jewelry.

Leslie Fay, (970) 468-9311.
See Women's Clothing.

Levi's, (970) 262-0133.
See Sportswear for Men and Women; Accessories and Jewelry.

Liz Claiborne; (970) 468-2484.
See Women's Clothing; Sportswear for Men and Women.

London Fog, (970) 468-5295.
See Outerwear; Sportswear for Men and Women.

Maidenform, (970) 468-5266.
See Accessories and Jewelry.

Marika, (970) 468-1515.
See Women's Clothing.

Marisa Christina, (970) 262-9322.
See Women's Clothing.

Mikasa, (970) 262-0715.
See Housewares, Gifts and General Merchandise.

Miller Stockman Western Wear, (970) 468-5133.
See Western Clothing and Cowboy Boots.

Naturalizer, (970) 262-5856.
See Women's Shoes.

Nike, (970) 468-6040.
See Sportswear for Men and Women; Shoes for Men, Women and Children.

9 West, (970) 262-2460.
See Women's Shoes.

Oneida Factory Store, (970) 262-0731.
See Housewares, Gifts and General Merchandise.

Oshkosh B'Gosh, (970) 262-2065.
See Children's Clothing.

Pfaltzgraff, (970) 468-9694.
See Housewares, Gifts and General Merchandise.

Prestige Fragrance, (970) 262-0319.
See Cosmetics and Fragrances.

Publishers Outlet, (970) 468-8417.
See New Books.

Rocky Mountain Chocolate Factory, (970) 468-9168.
See Food.

Russ, (970) 468-5036.
See Toys.

Samsonite, (970) 262-9495.
See Luggage and Briefcases.

Sassafras, (970) 468-2355.
See Housewares, Gifts and General Merchandise.

Silverheels Jewelry, (970) 262-0872.
See Accessories and Jewelry.

Socks Galore by Hanes, (970) 468-5500.
See Accessories and Jewelry.

Southern Cross, (970) 262-1180.
See Sportswear for Men and Women.

Sunglass Broker, (970) 262-1954.
See Accessories and Jewelry.

Van Heusen, (970) 468-0793.
See Sportswear for Men and Women.

Welcome Home, (970) 468-2739.
See Home Accessories.

Wemco Factory Store, (970) 262-1919.
See Menswear.

Windsor Shirt, (970) 262-0815.
See Menswear.

Ye Olde Family Name, (970) 468-2128.
See Home Accessories.

Stray Factory Outlets

Not all factory outlets are rounded up neatly into malls, where their presence is promoted by high-priced advertising and public-relations firms. Originally, all factory outlets were like many of the ones in this section. They came into existence so that manufacturers would have a place to sell their seconds, overruns and merchandise that hasn't moved in stores. These little bargain bazaars are frequently tucked into warehouses or previously unused corners of factories, and you can sometimes find yourself ducking under equipment or going into a dressing room and feeling the vibration of the heavy-duty sewing machines through the floor. If it's an outlet for a local company that makes food for wholesale distribution, you can smell the bread as it bakes and the nuts as they're roasted. Shopping at a true factory outlet can be a sensual experience.

When outlet shopping became a trend, lots of places opened outside of outlet malls and added "factory outlet" to their names. Many of them are just like the ones in malls, only they're not in malls, or they're in small, ancillary centers next to the big malls—like the Arrow and Bugle Boy outlets in Silverthorne, which might as well be part of the Silverthorne mall for all the difference it makes to most shoppers. Some of these places have subdued lighting and carpets and clerks who are better dressed than you'll ever be. These strays, which include hush-hush outlets like Donna Karan (see previous sentence), straggle all over the map. Here, too, are non-mall versions of factory outlets that are also in the outlet malls, such as Woolrich, which has an outlet in the mall at Castle Rock, and another one, listed here, in its factory in Broomfield. Perhaps the ones near the factories will feel more, well, sensual to you—and you may not have to drive so far.

Here's a listing of the ones we've been able to discover, with phone numbers. For information on individual stores, check the appropriate merchandise category.

Adler and York

7180 W. 38th Ave., Wheat Ridge, 234-0314.

See Women's Clothing.

American Olean Ceramic Tile Showroom

815 S. Jason St., Denver, 698-1400.

See Home Improvement.

Arrow Factory Store

167 Meraly Way, Silverthorne, (970) 262-1742.

See Menswear.

Atlas Luggage

2433 Curtis St., Denver, 292-0033.

See Luggage and Briefcases.

Australian Outback Collection Inc.

Showbarn Plaza, 27905 Meadow Drive, Evergreen, 670-3933.

See Sportswear for Men and Women; Outerwear.

Ava Kids

686 S. Taylor, Louisville, 666-1800.

See Children's clothing.

Avenrich Furniture

1863 Wazee St., Denver, 295-2834.

See Appliances and Furniture.

Basic Comfort

445 Lincoln St., Denver, 778-7535.

See Baby Necessities.

Boofers

2350 N. 95th St., Boulder, half a mile north of Arapahoe, 666-1883, 666-1884, 442-3334; 2425 Canyon Blvd., Boulder, 388-9830; The Total Look, 2120 S. Holly St., Denver, 758-6976.

See Children's Clothing, Special Needs, Women's Clothing, Clothes for Large Women, Maternity Clothes.

Boulder Sports Bag Company and Sportwaves

404 Baseline Road, Lafayette, 665-4122.

See Sporting Goods.

Boyer's Coffee

747 S. Colorado Blvd., Denver; 7295 Washington St., Denver; 6820 S. University Blvd., Littleton; 289-3345 for all three.

See Food.

Cabela's

Sidney, Nebraska, (800) 237-4444.

It's not really that far to Sidney. Heck, what's a 400-mile round-trip drive through scenic southern Wyoming for the real sporting goods fanatic?

See Sporting Goods.

Celestial Seasonings

4600 Sleepytime Drive, Boulder, 581-1202.

See Food.

The Chairman

1787 S. Broadway, Denver, 789-3710.

See Appliances and Furniture.

Chocolate Soup

7400 E. Hampden Ave., Denver, 741-6017.

See Children's Clothing.

Colorado Nut Company

730 S. Jason St., Denver, 733-7311.

See Food.

Current Factory Outlets

1250 S. Abilene, Aurora, 745-0525; 3550 S. Inca, Englewood, 762-9803; 5654 W. 88th Ave., Westminster, 427-2616; 3106 N. Stone Ave., Colorado Springs, (719) 630-7446; 425 S. College, Fort Collins, (970) 221-1176; 221 Summit Place, Silverthorne, (970) 262-9373.

See Party, Holiday, Office and School Supplies.

Dan Howard's Maternity Factory Outlet

2223 S. Monaco Parkway, Denver, 757-6070.

See Maternity Clothes.

Denver Boot Outlet

3795 Kipling St., Wheatridge, 425-6597.

See Western Wear and Cowboy Boots.

Discount Cabinets and Appliances

5969 Broadway, Denver, 292-9830.

See Furniture and Appliances.

Donna Karan Company Store

765 Anemone Trail, Dillon, (970) 262-2151.

See Children's Clothing; Menswear; Women's Clothing.

DV8 Sportswear

528 S. Broadway, Denver, 777-9275.

See Sportswear for Men and Women.

Echo Field

201 Steele St., Denver, 355-1480.

See Children's Clothing.

Entenmann's/Oroweat Thrift Stores

5050 E. Evans Ave., Denver, 691-6342; 9192 W. 44th Ave., Wheat Ridge, 424-1432.

See Food.

Esprit Direct

1200 Pearl St., Boulder, 447-9488.

See Women's Clothing.

Fieldcrest Cannon Bed and Bath Factory Store

10590 Melody Drive, Northglenn (Northglenn Mall), 280-2619.
See Home Accessories.

Gamine

1014 S. Gaylord St., Denver, 722-1629.
See Children's Clothing.

Hammond Candy

2550 W. 29th Ave., Denver, 455-2320.
See Food.

Impo Glaztile

860 S. Jason St., Denver, 722-4627.
See Home Improvement.

Jerry's Nut House

2101 Humboldt St., Denver, 861-2262.
See Food.

J-Rat Performance

1630 N. 63rd., #1, Boulder, 444-2779.
See Sportswear for Men and Women.

Leanin' Tree Inc.

6055 Longbow Drive, Boulder, 530-1442.
See Party, Holiday, Office and School Supplies.

Little Colorado

15866 W. Seventh Ave., Golden, 278-2451.

See Baby Necessities.

Madden Mountaineering

2400 Central Ave., Boulder, 442-5828.

See Sporting Goods.

Mountain Fashions

28005 Highway 74, Evergreen, 674-6220

See Sportswear for Men and Women; Western Wear and Cowboy Boots.

Nautica

765 Anemone Trail, Dillon, (970) 262-1615; Castle Rock Factory Stores, 660-6095.

See Menswear.

Nutorama Little Nut Hut

7174 Washington St., Denver, 289-2820.

See Food.

Out of the Woods

2590 Walnut St., Denver, 292-2012.

See Appliances and Furniture.

Pima Leather

2650 W. Second Ave., 936-0707.

See Appliances and Furniture.

Polo Ralph Lauren

Colby, Kansas, (913) 462-3401.

See Sportswear for Men and Women.

Quality Apparel Outlet

1485 S. Colorado Blvd., Denver, 756-6102; 5117 S. Yosemite St., Englewood, 290-0366.

See Menswear.

Quality Woodcrafters

212 Santa Fe, 534-6820.

See Appliances and Furniture.

Santa Fe Re-creations

Mercantile at Ojo, New Mexico State Highway 414 (off Highway 285), Ojo Caliente, New Mexico, (505) 583-9131.

See Outerwear; Western Wear and Cowboy Boots.

Sheepskin Factory

510 S. Colorado Blvd., Glendale, 329-8484.

See Accessories and Jewelry.

Ski Country Outlet

3065 S. Broadway, Englewood, 762-1720.

See Sportswear for Men and Women.

Stephany's Chocolates

4969 Colorado Blvd., Denver, 355-1522.

See Food.

Ultra Legs Hosiery

3489 S. Logan St., Englewood, 761-3705.

See Accessories and Jewelry.

U-Trau

1170 E. 49th Ave., Denver, 375-9620.

See Accessories and Jewelry.

Vollmer's Cheesecake factory outlet

4850 E. 39th Ave. Denver, 388-8393.

See Food.

Walter Drake & Sons

4510 Edison Ave., Colorado Springs, (719) 596-1882.

See Housewares, Gifts, and General Merchandise.

Women's Bean Project

2347 Curtis St., Denver, 292-1919.

See Food.

Wonder-Hostess Thrift Shops

6680 Wadsworth, Arvada, 420-0998; 1695 Peoria, Aurora, 360-7998; 80 E. 62nd Ave., Denver, 428-7431; 11805 W. Colfax, Lakewood, 238-6102.

See Food.

Woolrich

6900 W. 117th Ave., Broomfield, 469-5257.

See Outerwear; Sportswear for Men and Women.

Direct and Seasonal Sales

Some manufacturers don't have full-time factory outlets. Instead, when they have seconds or overruns to get rid of, they clear a corner of the warehouse or rent a vacant store and hold a sort of wholesale garage sale for one or two days. The merchandise may be laid out in boxes with hand-drawn signs on the sides. This translates into low overhead, and it means the deals can be amazing. Other direct sales are held by manufacturers' reps who are trying to get some cash for their samples or by retailers just starting out who aren't big enough to maintain a store.

A few nomadic sales are big deals, and they're widely advertised. Others do lots of publicity and are happy to put you on a mailing list if you give them a phone call. Still others are very elusive, and about the only way you can find out about them is to be tipped off by someone who's already on the mailing list, then go there and pay with a personalized check. That will usually get you on the mailing list for future sales.

These are some of the periodic sales we know about, and we hear about more than most people do. But we learn about new ones all the time, and even we are not on *all* these mailing lists. Nor can we really tell you a fool-proof way of getting on a mailing list—you're at the mercy of the company that's holding the sale. If there's a phone number, it can't hurt to call and ask. If there's only an address, it's because we couldn't get a phone number for you; you might write and hope for the best. Otherwise, after reading this, you'll at least have a better idea of what's out there. If you want to hear about the hush-hush sales, be sure to tell your friends you're interested. Maybe they'll ask you to come along next time they get a notification card in the mail.

With few exceptions, these are not regular stores. Some have no addresses listed because headquarters may be in someone's home. They have no regular store hours. Therefore, no hours are included in these listings. Under most (but not all) listings, though, you'll find a cross-reference where you can find more information.

Ava Kids

686 S. Taylor, Louisville, 666-1800.

See Children's Clothing.

Sales are held in Denver in May, August and November. In the past they've been at University Hills Mall, 2700 S. Colorado Blvd.

Boofers

2350 N. 95th St., Boulder, 666-1883, 666-1884, 442-3334.

See Children's Clothing, Special Needs, Women's Clothing, Clothes for Large Women, Maternity Clothes.

Clearances are held approximately quarterly in Boulder, most recently at the Depot, between 28th and 30th on Pearl Street. Sales in Denver, previously held at University Hills Mall, have been cancelled until the owner can find another location. (If you know about a good location in Denver for a warehouse sale, give her a call.)

Boulder Apparel Corporation

2108 55th St., Boulder, 444-3390.

See Sportswear for Men and Women.

Warehouse sales are held every two months, and each weekend during the holiday season.

DJB Enterprises

1390 S. Potomac St., Suite 136, Aurora, 696-9225.

See Home Accessories.

This is a mail-order company that sells fabric for home seamstresses.

Flooring Design Associates

3770 Paris St., Denver, 371-2929.

See Home Improvement.

Warehouse sale of remnant inventory in May.

Furniture Galleries Inc.

1601 E. Colfax Ave., Denver, 388-9273.

See Appliances and Furniture.

Public sale each summer.

Holiday Outlet

Robbie Peres, 660-4863.

Peres is an independent liquidator with good contacts among local manufacturers and warehousers. Call if you want to be on the mailing list for sales.

Imagine

Boulder, 443-5714.

See Children's Clothing.

Sales for back to school and holiday seasons, generally at the Depot in Boulder.

Imperial Headwear

5200 E. Evans Ave., Denver, 757-1166.

See Accessories and Jewelry.

Imperial Headwear recently closed its full-time factory outlet. Shortly after doing that, they had a weekend tent sale. They may do it again, so call and ask to be notified if that sounds interesting.

JNK/Birdlegs

1150A Speer Blvd., Denver, 436-9216

See Children's Clothing.

Sales in May and September.

Just Samples

8215 S. Holly St., Littleton, 843-0269.

See Menswear; Women's Clothing.

Sales are held once a month or so. The store's goal is to be open most of the time, and closed for only one week between sales.

Lowe Alpine Systems

620 Compton, Broomfield, 465-3706.

See Sporting Goods.

Sales in April or May and October or November are announced only in the newspaper *(Westword* and the *Boulder Daily Camera)*. There's no mailing list. Try calling just before a sale is due.

Mackenzie James & Co.

1804 S. Pearl St., Denver, 733-1987.

See Children's Clothing.

Sales in March, May, August and December.

Madison Exchange

100 S. Madison St., Denver, 320-0987.

Sales in mid- to late April, October and December.

The sales are on good-label clothing and accessories for men and women. These are samples, so sizes are in the small to middle range.

Merchandise Liquidators (Broadway Rose)

482 S. Broadway, Denver, 722-8611.

This independent liquidator is always on the lookout for a deal in men's and women's clothing to pass on to the public. Call to get on the mailing list.

National Western Stock Show

4655 Humboldt St., Denver, 295-1660.

See Western Wear and Cowboy Boots.

The National Western Stock Show dominates the Denver economy in January. If you live here and it's going on, it's worth the price of admission just to visit the retail exhibits, which feature an incredible variety of Western and non-Western merchandise.

Rocky Mountain Kids

Louisville, 665-4420.

See Children's Clothing.

Sales are very sporadic, but average once quarterly.

Sniagrab

Gart Sports Castle, 1000 Broadway, Denver, 861-1122.

Labor Day weekend.

Sniagrab is the sale that once rated a full-page color picture in *National Geographic*. (We didn't memorize the caption, but we like to think it was: "Fanatic Coloradans pray for snow as they prepare for their annual pilgrimage to the remote mountains.") Labor Day weekend is too early for snow, even in Denver. But if you can't think snow, think skis. The best strategy is to get copies of *Snow Country, Skiing* and other such magazines that offer consumer ratings on skis and ski equipment. Make a list of the equipment they rate as tops and look for that specific equipment when you go. Other sporting goods stores have adopted Gart's tradition of running a big sale on ski equipment for Labor Day. So, besides Gart's gigantic Sniagrab ("bargains," spelled backward), check for sales at Bevans Sports, 5002 E. Hampden Ave., and at the six metro Denver locations of Christy Sports.

Tuesday Morning

8270 W. 80th Ave. (the Meadows Center), Arvada, 422-9994; 7400 E. Hampden Ave., Denver, 488-9940; 4301 E. Virginia

Ave., Glendale, 333-8156; 15372 E. Alameda Parkway, Aurora, 695-4357; 12790 W. Alameda Parkway, Lakewood, 989-2792; 7562 S. University Blvd. (Southglenn Square), Littleton, 779-0328; 8996 W. Bowles Ave., (Bowles Avenue Marketplace), Littleton, 972-2155; 4800 Baseline, Boulder, 494-1535; 3520 N. Academy Blvd., Colorado Springs, (719) 596-1043; 222 Walnut St., Fort Collins, (970) 224-3432.

See Discount Department Stores and Membership Warehouses.

This national chain has made a marketing strategy out of what many small retailers and manufacturers do from necessity. It's open only periodically, mostly surrounding gift-buying holidays such as Christmas and Father's Day. Sales are scheduled to last about a month and half during the spring (mid-February to late March), two months during the summer (May and June), one month during the fall (mid-August to mid-September) and two and half months for the winter (mid-October through New Year's).

Museum Shops

Museum shops are wonderful places to look for unusual, inexpensive and educational items. Don't dismiss them. On a trip to Santa Fe, we bought an inexpensive piece of Indian pottery at a museum. The piece was later assessed at a higher price and better quality than pots that we'd paid much more for at exclusive gift shops. These shops are particularly worthwhile if you're a museum member, because most offer discounts to members. In some cases, membership in the museum is fairly inexpensive, and you'll be doing your part to support the cultural base for your city. Furthermore, museum shops are nonprofit; both memberships and purchases help support the museum.

There are too many museums in Colorado to list—more than 30 in the Denver metropolitan area alone—so they're not all here. Most museums, listed or not, have gift shops. If all you want to do is shop, call ahead to see if you must pay admission to the museum before you can get to the shop. At the Denver Art Museum and the Denver Museum of Natural History, for example, the shops are in a public area that does not require admission. Admission fees can add up; some are as much as $6 per adult.

And here's a tip. If you're traveling and you have a membership in a museum or zoo, ask if the place you're visiting has a reciprocal agreement that would give you free admission. Members of the Colorado Historical Society, for example, get free admission to museums run by the society throughout the state, including such remote destinations as Fort Garland and Trinidad. Members of the Denver Children's Museum may be able to gain admission to children's museums in other cities, or even other states.

Good museums are found throughout Colorado. One in Montrose pays tribute to Chief Ouray. There's a terrific new dinosaur museum in Fruita. Colorado Springs, Breckenridge, Pueblo and Grand Junction all have wonderful museums. (We spent happy hours at the Pioneer Museum in Colorado Springs during our formative years. Helen Hunt Jackson's daughter used to be a docent there, and she would chat about her mother's role in Colorado history—and the weather—for hours.) No time spent in a museum will be wasted, even if you don't buy a thing. If you're curious about a museum that's not listed, check your local *Yellow Pages.*

Anasazi Heritage Center

27501 Highway 184, Dolores, (970) 882-4811.

9 a.m. to 4 p.m. daily.

The Anasazi Heritage Center offers permanent exhibits on Southwestern archaeology and on the prehistoric Anasazi culture, including two 12th-century archaeological sites that are on the grounds. Its gift shop features books, replica pots, posters and videos; most items have something to do with native cultures of the Southwest.

Arvada Center for the Arts and Humanities

6901 Wadsworth Blvd., Arvada, 431-3939.

10 a.m to 4 p.m. Monday through Saturday.

Arvada Center's Art Market is a year-round version of the center's Holiday Market, which expands to take over the lower gallery in November and December. Look for items from local artists and artisans, including paintings, textile art, sculpture, jewelry, functional and sculptural pottery, holiday ornaments, handmade paper and more. The selection of merchandise is often coordinated with current performances or exhibits. The shop regularly carries books, cards, jewelry and ornaments. The Hmong textiles are especially nice. Many items are on consignment, so the selection varies.

Black American West Museum and Heritage Center

3901 California St., Denver, 292-2566.

10 a.m. to 2 p.m. Wednesday through Friday; noon to 5 p.m. Saturday; 2 p.m. to 5 p.m. Sunday.

This museum gift shop is especially proud of its collection of books about blacks and the American West. There are also audiotapes, t-shirts, dolls and other gift items. Although the museum keeps regular hours, if you want to browse in the gift store, it's best to call ahead and make sure it's open.

Buffalo Bill Memorial Museum

987½ Lookout Mountain Rd., Golden, 526-9367.

9 a.m. to 5 p.m. daily.

The Pahaska Teepee gift shop offers books, pottery, paintings, blankets, rugs and jewelry with Western or Native American themes.

Butterfly Pavilion and Insect Center

6252 W. 104th Ave., Westminster, 469-5441.

Hours not determined at time of publication.

The gift store for this nature center will be completed in the spring of 1995. The shop will carry the largest collection of butterfly- and insect-related items in the area. Call for more information.

Cheyenne Mountain Zoo

4250 Cheyenne Mountain Zoo Rd., Colorado Springs, (719) 636-2544.

9 a.m. to 4 p.m. daily.

The gift shop here has all kinds of animal-related items, including toys, stuffed animals, t-shirts, posters, books and jewelry. It's open even on Christmas.

Children's Museum of Colorado Springs

750 Citadel Drive East, Colorado Springs, (719) 574-0077.

10 a.m. to 5 p.m. daily; til 8 p.m. Wednesday.

The gift shop here is basically a toy store, with lots of model dinosaurs, dinosaur construction kits, magnets, calendars, magnifying glasses and other scientific and educational toys.

Collage Children's Museum

2065 30th St., Boulder, 440-9894.

2-5 p.m. Wednesday; 10 a.m. to 5 p.m. Thursday through Saturday; 1-5 p.m. Sunday.

The gift shop here has books and an especially nice selection of small, fun toys that sell for less than a dollar, so children can buy them with their own money.

Colorado Historical Society

1300 Broadway, Denver, 866-4993.

10 a.m. to 4:30 p.m. Monday through Saturday; noon to 4:30 p.m. Sunday.

This store has a wonderful selection of books on Colorado history and other Western subjects, and members get a 10% discount. You'll also find other items related to the pioneer era, authentic American Indian crafts and jewelry, period toys, etched glasses, scarves, tote bags, sand paintings, mugs, tea, t-shirts and sweatshirts.

Colorado Railroad Museum

17155 W. 44th Ave., Golden, 279-4591.

9 a.m. to 5 p.m. daily.

This railroad museum gift shop has more than 1,000 books on railroad history, as well as tie tacks, key fobs, belt buckles, coffee mugs and other gift items featuring logos from railroads of the past and present.

Colorado Springs Fine Arts Center

30 W. Dale St., Colorado Springs, (719) 634-5581.

9 a.m. to 5 p.m. Tuesday through Friday; 10 a.m. to 5 p.m. Saturday; 1-5 p.m. Sunday.

The store at this museum, tucked away near Colorado College, features greeting cards, posters, turquoise-and-silver jewelry, lots of crafts, art books for children and adults, rugs, books, note cards, art-show catalogs and more.

Colorado Springs Pioneer Museum

215 S. Tejon St., Colorado Springs, (719) 578-6650.

10 a.m. to 4 p.m. Tuesday through Saturday.

This shop features a comprehensive selection of books on the history of Colorado Springs, as well as such general gift items as silver jewelry, calendars, toys, note cards, stained glass, magnets and tiles.

Denver Art Museum

100 W. 14th Ave. Parkway, 640-2253.

10 a.m. to 5 p.m. Tuesday through Saturday; noon to 5 p.m. Sunday.

The DAM shop has recently moved into expanded space, and the volunteers who work at the store are very proud of it. There are a lot of items from all over the world, including statuary, masks, scarves, posters, cookbooks, art books, prints, greeting cards, exhibit catalogs and calendars. The jewelry is well priced and unusual. Also check the children's section. Members receive a 10% discount.

Denver Botanic Gardens

1005 York St., Denver, 331-4000.

9 a.m. to 4:30 p.m. daily; open til 8 p.m. when there are concerts.

The shop carries almost anything "gifty" that relates to plants—jewelry, painted china, magnets, potpourri, cards, bonsai, books, t-shirts, seed packets, spices, herbs and soaps. Many small items are quite inexpensive. Members of the Botanic Gardens receive a 10% discount on purchases more than $10. The Botanic Gardens also hosts various sales throughout the year. The Christmas sale is usually the weekend before Thanksgiving and the spring sale is on Mother's Day weekend. Other events include chili, rose and lily festivals.

Denver Children's Museum

2121 Children's Museum Drive, Denver, 433-7444.

10 a.m. to 5 p.m. Tuesday through Saturday; noon to 5 p.m. Sunday.

The emphasis at the Children's Museum is on science, including kits to help kids explore magnets, insects and the ever-popular dinosaur. There are also such marginally scientific toys as glow-in-the-dark stickers, Doodle Tops, gyroscopes, Tornado Tubes and Fickle Foam. A large group of items sells for $3 or less, and almost everything is less than $7. Museum members get a 10% discount.

Denver Museum of Miniatures, Dolls and Toys

1880 Gaylord Street, Denver, 322-1053.

10 a.m. to 4 p.m. Monday through Saturday; 1 p.m. to 4 p.m. Sunday.

This shop stocks great things for dollhouse lovers, including furniture and accessories such as dishes; there are also doll clothes, miniatures, ornaments, cards, coloring books, nesting toys, dolls (of course) and more. If you're looking for something very specific, such as figures from *The Wizard of Oz*, check with the collectors who volunteer for the shop here. If the shop doesn't have what you're looking for, chances are good that someone will know how to get it. If you want to visit the shop without paying admission to the museum, be sure to mention that fact at the entrance.

Denver Museum of Natural History

2001 Colorado Blvd., Denver, 370-6366.

9 a.m to 5:15 p.m. daily.

The shop at the Denver Museum of Natural History is one of the best places for gift shopping in the city, with a unique and carefully selected group of educational and decorative items—posters, artwork, toys, books, jewelry—some of which are museum quality. If you have a budding geologist in the family, check the mineral specimens. Good-quality specimens are inexpensive compared to prices at tourist rock shops. Some of the specimens have been made into bookends, and others are "just rocks." The shop offers a 10% discount for members.

Denver Zoo

2300 Steele St. (City Park), Denver, 355-7135.

Summer: 10 a.m. to 6 p.m. daily. Winter: 10 a.m. to 5 p.m. daily. Open holidays.

The zoo shop has many interesting and unusual items related to animals and nature as well as to current exhibits. If you or a friend have a collection (parrot mugs, turtle pins, ceramic rhinoceroses or whatever), check this place out. The shop also has a good selection of books about the natural world for children and adults.

Devil's Canyon Science Learning Center

550 Crossroads Court, Fruita, (970) 858-7282.

9 a.m. to 5 p.m. daily; closed holidays.

Dinamation International Corporation created the audiotronic animals at this center, which opened in the summer of 1994. Everything sold in the gift shop is dinosaur related, including replicas cast from fossils, kits, mugs, games, t-shirts, sweatshirts, posters, books and, of course, model and stuffed dinosaurs.

Forney Car Museum

1416 Platte St. (exit 211 from I-25), Denver, 433-3643.

9 a.m. to 5 p.m. Monday through Saturday; 11 a.m. to 5 p.m. Sunday.

If it's related to transportation, look for it here. There are books, novelties, posters, mugs, engineers' caps, railroad whistles, videotapes on railroad history and more.

Georgetown Loop Railroad

1106 Rose St., Georgetown, 670-1686; recording, 279-6101.

9 a.m. to 4 p.m. summer only; limited schedule during September.

Gift shops for the railroad are at the Silver Plume depot and at the Old Georgetown Station, 1106 Rose St., about a mile from the Georgetown boarding area. Merchandise includes lots of items with railroad logos, including t-shirts, engineers' caps, spikes, trains and jewelry, as well as mining-theme items, including geodes, gold dust and gold-panning kits. If you're a member of the Colorado Historical Society, you get a discount here.

Leanin' Tree Museum of Western Art

6055 Longbow Drive, Boulder, 530-1442.

8 a.m. to 4:30 p.m. Monday through Friday; 10 a.m. to 4 p.m. Saturday.

This listing is an exception to the others in this section because Leanin' Tree is a private, for-profit organization. If you're a fan of the Western art greeting cards made by Leanin' Tree, you'll enjoy the museum, which features the original art, including 200 paintings and two dozen sculptures. The shop sells a full selection of the company's cards, although at the same price ($1.50 apiece) they sell for elsewhere.

Metropolitan Museum of Art

3000 E. First Ave., Denver (Cherry Creek Mall), 320-8615.

10 a.m to 9 p.m. Monday though Friday; 10 a.m. to 7 p.m. Saturday; noon to 6 p.m. Sunday.

The stores run by the Met grew out of its catalog business—everything sold here or in the catalog is a reproduction of an item once displayed in the New York Metropolitan Museum. Items are chosen for their design quality and might include anything that's well designed—dishes, ornaments, address books, note cards, stained-glass pieces. And yes, if you're a member of the museum in New York, you get a 10% discount in this shop.

Museum of Western Art

1727 Tremont Place, Denver, 296-1880.

10 a.m. to 4:30 p.m. Tuesday through Saturday.

Fans of Western Americana who haven't visited this shop have missed a good selection of Navajo, Hopi and Zuni jewelry, framed prints and posters. The book selection includes new books as well as rare and out-of-print volumes. The museum makes a deliberate effort to keep quality high and prices low, and there's a 10% discount for members.

Nikola Tesla Museum of Science and Industry

2220 E. Bijou St., Colorado Springs, (719) 475-0918.

10 a.m. to 4 p.m. Monday through Friday; 11 to 4 p.m. Saturday.

The shop here includes general scientific books and lots of books on Nikola Tesla, an inventor whose year in Colorado Springs (1899–1900) brought major breakthroughs in his development of alternating current, radar, sonar, laser technology and logic circuits. In addition to books there are other souvenirs, including mugs and small items.

Paws Children's Museum

210 N. Santa Fe, Pueblo, (719) 543-0130.

11 a.m. to 5 p.m. daily.

This is a typical children's museum gift shop, featuring small scientific and educational toys as well as books.

El Pueblo Museum

324 W. First St., Pueblo, (719) 583-0453.

10 a.m. to 4:30 p.m. Monday through Saturday; noon to 3 p.m. Sunday.

This shop has a good selection of children's books, cookbooks and books on regional history and women's history as well as handcrafted silver jewelry, t-shirts and other gift items such as fry-bread mixes, mugs, calendars, paperweights and other souvenirs. Members of the Colorado Historical Society get a 10% discount.

Turner Museum

773 Downing Street, Denver, 832-0924.

Noon to 5 p.m. Monday through Friday; noon to 3 p.m. Sunday.

This little museum is dedicated to the works of British artist J.M.W. Turner. The shop sells books, note cards, postcards, prints and posters.

Special Needs

If you're learning to live with a wheelchair, a walker or an oxygen tank, you've got enough problems. Money shouldn't be one of them—but it will be. So here's how to save a little here and there as you buy the things you need.

Did you know that Medicare won't pay for a wheelchair until you've rented one for 13 months? Who knows this stuff? One person who does is Elliott Magalnick, owner of the Get Well Shop at 12028 E. Mississippi Ave., Aurora. And he's not the only one. Check with the businesses listed here. They've all shown an interest in meeting the needs of people whose needs are special. If this information isn't enough, stores that specialize in items for people with disabilities are listed in the *Yellow Pages* under such headings as Medical Supplies, Hospital Equipment and Supplies, Surgical Supplies, Oxygen Supplies, and Wheelchairs.

Boofers

2350 N. 95th St., Boulder, half a mile north of Arapahoe, 666-1883, 666-1884, 442-3334; 2425 Canyon Blvd., Boulder, 388-9830; The Total Look, 2120 S. Holly St., Denver, 758-6976; YouCan TooCan, 2223 S. Monaco Parkway, Denver, 759-9525.

Canyon Blvd.: 10 a.m. to 5 p.m. Monday through Friday; 11 a.m. to 4 p.m. Saturday. 95th St.: 10 a.m. to 6 p.m. Fridays; variable hours Monday, Wednesday and Saturday—call first. Total Look: 10 a.m. to 5 p.m. Monday through Friday; 11 a.m. to 4 p.m. Saturday; YouCan TooCan: 10 a.m. to 6 p.m. Monday through Saturday.

Boofers owner Priscilla Hendrickson has a Down's syndrome daughter, and she has designed her line of all-cotton clothing so it's easy for people with handicaps to get into and out of. The line is manufactured in Boulder. It's made for comfort, with no zippers, buttons or drawstrings, and for durability, from wonderful cotton-knit fabric purchased from the Absorba mill. Sizes range from preemie through adult. She takes phone orders. Boofers recently acquired the Estar line of women's clothing, which can be special-ordered to meet the requirements of people in wheelchairs or with other special needs. The women's Boofer line offers a wide variety of dresses and separates in all-cotton knit as well as washable sueded rayon and silk separates, sweaters and accessories. Normal prices range around $33 to $85; check the listing on Direct and Seasonal Sales to find out how to get it on clearance. People with special needs in Denver probably should call YouCan TooCan first (see listing below).

The Get Well Shop

12028 E. Mississippi Ave., Aurora, 752-2000.

9 a.m. to 5:30 p.m. Monday through Friday; 10 a.m. to 2 p.m. Saturday.

The Get Well Shop merchandise includes reachers, which are devices that enable people to pick things up without bending over ($12-$26); easy-to-use scissors ($17); foam that can be used to build up silverware, making it easier to grasp ($4.50 a yard); and Motus handle grips to make shovels and brooms easier to use ($6-$12). Adaptive equipment includes key holders and plate guards (rims that clip to the far end of plates so you can push your food against them). The store stocks blood pressure equipment and will teach people how to use it and works with three different prosthetic brassiere fitters for mastectomy patients. There are lots of products for feet, including heel cups and metatarsal pads. The shop also sells used equipment at reduced prices.

The Get Well Shop offers free home delivery for any order that adds up to $10 or more.

Gotcha Covered Gowns

Denver, 798-0178.

Gotcha Covered Gowns, made by Denverite Donna Mayhew, are attractive versions of hospital gowns, and they make good gifts for someone facing a long hospitalization. Mayhew also creates clothes and pillows under specifications she gets from physical therapists. The gowns sell for $17, $20 and $27. Mayhew can do custom orders for people who are in bed all the time.

King Soopers

Throughout Colorado's Front Range.

King Soopers will waive its $9 home delivery charge for virtually anyone with a legitimate physical limitation, including a hearing or visual impairment or a permanent or temporary disability. That means that if you just got out of the hospital with a broken leg, or you're confined to bed in the last months of pregnancy, you qualify. You will, however, pay $5 for the shopping fee. Seniors also receive free delivery.

Many King Soopers stores have pharmacies, and if you're buying medication for someone in a nursing home, talk to the King Soopers pharmacy near the facility. Although mail-order pharmacies promise inexpensive prices, I found that they were too far away, bureaucratic and impersonal to work for me. After trying and being frustrated by them, I've established a stress-free working relationship with the King Soopers near the nursing home that cares for my mother. If you're homebound, King Soopers pharmacies deliver free, and they're generally less expensive than other local pharmacies that do. They're also much more service-oriented than the discount mail-order places.

For groceries or non-prescription medical supplies, call King Soopers' TeleShopper, 778-5464, and explain the situation. There's also a TDD line for the hearing impaired: 744-9589. To reach a King Soopers pharmacy, check the phone book.

Love You Fashions

Thornton, 287-7001.

Nona Loser (it's pronounced Lesser) makes cotton-blend and linen-blend dresses with Velcro closings that are designed for women with arthritis or other joint-mobility problems. Among the stores that sell them are YouCan TooCan (see below); Cache's, 45 N. Main, Brighton, 654-0733; Velma's on the Bridge, 1675 Carr St., Lakewood, 237-4646; and Once Again, 6838 S. University Blvd., Littleton, 290-9329.

Saks Fifth Avenue—the Fifth Avenue Club

3000 E. First Ave., Denver (Cherry Creek Mall), 393-0476.

10 a.m. to 9 p.m. Monday through Friday; 10 a.m. to 6 p.m. Saturday; noon to 5 p.m. Sunday.

Although the Fifth Avenue Club was set up for the busy and well-to-do, membership in the Fifth Avenue Club at Saks Fifth Avenue in Cherry Creek Shopping Center is great for people with limited mobility or stamina who are serious shoppers. Members make an appointment by phone and explain their needs. Before the customer arrives, sales consultants go through the store pulling items from the customer's shopping list. While the customer is settled in a spacious private room, consultants bring the items in and offer assistance. Although no other store has a club, similar services are available from personal shoppers at Foley's, Joslins, Neiman Marcus and others (even Bed, Bath and Beyond). And, if you're not a big spender, Saks' personal shopper may suffice for you. (Perhaps I'm being too subtle. Here's the subtext: If you use the services of the Fifth Avenue Club, you need to make it worth their effort, so spend at least $2,000 a year at Saks.)

Walgreen Drug Stores

1111 S. Colorado Blvd., Denver, pharmacy, 758-8083, store, 758-8047; 6240 E. Colfax Ave., Denver, pharmacy, 321-0506, store, 321-0508; 2727 Palmer Park Blvd., Colorado Springs, pharmacy, (719) 634-3742, store, (719) 634-4746.

Always open.

What need could be more special than filling a prescription at 3 a.m. on Christmas morning? These three Walgreens are open 24 hours, 365 days a year. And the pharmacy on South Colorado Boulevard even has a drive-up window.

YouCan TooCan

2223 S. Monaco Parkway, Denver, 759-9525.

10 a.m. to 6 p.m. Monday through Saturday.

Martha Hansen, the owner of this new shop, has a long history working with adults who have physical limitations. She opened the store guided by the realization that people want a pleasant place to shop where the emphasis is on color and style, not on keeping the rows of bedpans shiny. There's lots of "easy-on" clothing for men and women, as well as adaptive devices such as built-up silverware, faucet extenders, special dishes, doorknob openers, card holders, reachers and writing aids. She has a desk and a table at the store so customers can try out merchandise before they buy.

YouCan TooCan will give free delivery for any order that amounts to more than $25.

Household
and Food

Appliances and Furniture

Furniture and appliances are big purchases, so proceed carefully. If your objective is an appliance, do some research in *Consumer Reports*. When you buy, keep your receipts. Ask lots of questions about the return policies, and get those policies in writing. Never submit to pressure from a salesperson. The item isn't going to walk out the door the minute you leave, and, if it is, why is the salesperson so insistent that *you* be the person who buys it? Be particularly careful about buying used appliances. And if you're thinking of renting, go to a reputable place that also leases furniture to businesses, not one that makes its pitch to individuals and families. Don't rent a TV set or a washing machine. If you have any credit at all, this is the time to use it. Unless you're renting only for a very short time, you may wind up paying for the item several times over.

Don't go shopping for furniture or appliances anywhere until you've made thorough use of a tape measure. Is that space wide enough for the refrigerator you're looking at? Deep enough? And don't forget to measure tall items that might not go through doorways and deep pieces that could block the opening of a window or door. If you're planning to take something up or down stairs, be sure you can turn whatever corners you need to turn, or you may find yourself in the position of a friend of ours, who sleeps on a box spring that has been sawed apart, bent and nailed back together.

We've included a couple of office furniture liquidating companies in this listing because they can be good sources for desks, bookcases or file cabinets at reasonable prices. But they can be even better sources for the furniture you don't think of when you think of offices. Most offices, for example, have coffee tables, pictures, lamps, end tables, occasional chairs and couches in their reception areas. They may have refrigerators, dinettes and microwave ovens in the break room. Sometimes used office furniture places wind up with those pieces, and because they're not part of the traditional fare, they may underprice them. So think creatively, and make a few phone calls.

There must be several hundred places to buy furniture and appliances in the Denver area, to say nothing of the state of Colorado. Obviously, this is not a complete listing. The only stores listed here are ones that have come to our attention or ones that are clearance centers or factory outlets.

A&A Quality Appliance

5995 E. Evans, Denver, 987-2266.

9 a.m. to 7 p.m. Monday through Friday; 9 a.m. to 4 p.m. Saturday and Sunday.

A&A is the warehouse-return outlet for General Electric appliances. Although there are usually a few inexpensive (but warranteed) scratch-and-dent items, this store's strength is that it gets top-of-the-line refrigerators and stoves that were display models or returned special orders. In other words, it's a good place to get a $1,500 refrigerator for $1,200.

American Furniture Warehouse

8501 Grant St., Denver, 289-4100.

10 a.m. to 10 p.m. daily.

This isn't a clearance center, but at 371,000 square feet, it *is* the largest single furniture store in the United States, and Jake's prices are usually pretty competitive. So if you're serious about shopping, you can see virtually anything under one roof here and get a good idea of what things are worth.

Amish Showcase

2670 E. County Line Road, Littleton, 843-9448.

10 a.m. to 8 p.m. Monday through Friday; 10 a.m. to 6 p.m. Saturday; 1-5 p.m. Sunday.

The furniture and accessories here are made by 10 Amish families in Illinois. The furniture, which is priced comparably to furniture that's not so lovingly crafted, is handmade of kiln-dried hardwoods and includes such items as entertainment centers and microwave cabinets, which the Amish, who shun modernity, would never use themselves. There are also tables, hutches, sleigh beds, rocking chairs, entry benches and spindle-back chairs, as well as candles, jams, jellies, pottery, wooden toys and quilts.

Aspen Office Furniture

777 Santa Fe, Denver, 534-0335.

8:30 a.m. to 5:30 p.m. Monday through Friday; 10 a.m. to 4 p.m. Saturday.

It sure isn't fancy, but this place is a good source for new and used desks, bookcases, lamps, storage cabinets, files, chairs or conference tables. Discounts range from 10% to 50% on new merchandise. The store carries furniture designed specifically for home offices. Aspen delivers, sets up, repairs and services the items it sells. Check the bargain basement, where you could get a used stapler for a buck or an orange office chair for $5.

Avenrich Furniture Manufacturing

900 S. Santa Fe Drive, Denver, 722-3056.

10 a.m. to 6 p.m. Monday through Saturday; noon to 5 p.m. Sunday.

Avenrich has been making sofas, chairs, loveseats and hideaway beds in Denver for 26 years. All furniture is made on the premises and sold factory-direct to the public. Sofas are custom-built to your personal specifications; if you're tall or short, or if a sofa has to go around a narrow staircase, let them help you. If you ask, they'll give you a tour of the factory. The showroom serves as a sort of three-dimensional catalog. If you're in the market for a leather sofa, ask these people about the difference between top-grain (which they sell) and splits. Furniture sold from the outlet is marked 50% of suggested retail.

Catholic Workers Used Furniture Plus

2306 Champa St., Denver, 296-4973.

9 a.m. to 5 p.m. Tuesday through Saturday.

Catholic Workers is a non-profit organization that offers inexpensive, practical items to people in and around the Five Points area. The store provides pick-up service for donated items and delivery service for large items, as well as furniture repair and refinishing.

The Chairman

1787 S. Broadway, Denver, 733-2100.

10 a.m. to 5 p.m. Monday through Friday; 11 a.m. to 4 p.m. Saturday.

This store is an outlet for Shafer Commercial Seating and other manufacturers, which means the chairs, although they're not all that much less expensive than chairs from other stores, are tough enough for restaurants. And that means they'll probably stand up to your 3-year-old until he's ready for college. If you really don't want to spend much but you really need something to sit on, tell owner Steve Farland. He may be able to find something ugly and cheap in the basement.

Cort Furniture Rental Clearance Center

600 S. Havana St., Aurora, 344-5114.

9 a.m. to 6 p.m. Monday through Friday; 10 a.m. to 5 p.m. Saturday.

Cort offers a wide selection of name-brand rental-return commercial and residential furniture at discount. Here's a place where you find a headboard for a queen-size bed for less than $50. They also get housewares, TVs, microwaves and VCRs, which sometimes go cheap in the clearance center. You could find a sofa and loveseat here for around $200.

Eclectic City

1787 S. Broadway, Denver, 733-2100.

10 a.m. to 5 p.m. Monday through Friday; 11 a.m. to 4 p.m. Saturday.

Eclectic City, which operates under the same roof as The Chairman (the owners are husband and wife), gets returned furniture and bric-a-brac from designers and show homes. There are some antiques and antique reproductions, and owner Barbara Farland offers free design advice.

Fred Schmid Clearance Center

1585 S. Colorado Blvd., Denver, 691-9495.

10 a.m. to 7 p.m. Monday through Saturday; noon to 5 p.m. Sunday.

This is a clearance center for Fred Schmid's 11 stores in the Denver metro area. There's an average 20% discount on scratch-and-dent, discontinued and one-of-a-kind items, including stoves, refrigerators, washing machines and electronic goods from many major manufacturers.

Furniture Galleries Inc.

1601 E. Colfax Ave., Denver, 388-9273.

9 a.m. to 5 p.m. Monday through Friday; 9 a.m. to 1 p.m. Saturday.

Members of the public are not allowed to buy directly from this wholesale showroom, where 100 manufacturers are represented. However, if you call, they'll put you on the mailing list to be notified for the public sale they have each summer.

Kacey Furniture Clearance Center

900 S. Santa Fe Drive, Denver, 777-6612.

11 a.m. to 6:30 p.m. Monday, Thursday and Friday; 9 a.m. to 5 p.m. Saturday; 11 a.m. to 5 p.m. Sunday.

All items are sold as is on a first-come, first-served basis. This is scratch-and-dent, showroom sample, discontinued or one-of-a-kind merchandise, and here it's generally about half the price of what it sells for in Kacey's other stores in Denver, Lakewood and Frisco.

Luxury Furniture Rental

1947 S. Havana, Aurora, 369-8640.

9 a.m. to 6 p.m. Monday through Friday; 9 a.m. to 5 p.m. Saturday.

This place exists to furnish corporate apartments. When the lease is up for the apartments, they take the furniture back to the store.

If it's in good shape it's re-rented. After several leasings, it's sold inexpensively. You could get a loveseat for as little $50 to $100, or a sofa-loveseat set for $250. Check the bargain basement.

Mail order furniture

Save big on furniture by phone ordering from discounters near High Point and Hickory, N.C., where 60% of American furniture is made. At Furnitureland South in High Point, for example, a Thomasville cherry dining table made to retail for $1,875 sells for $995. Such deals remain bargains even when the hefty cost of shipping is added. For fear of angering retailers, most of these places don't publish catalogs, so to shop by phone you must scout local stores to get model numbers and codes for preferred colors and fabrics. Double-check all the information with more than one store, because some retailers alter model numbers to foil shoppers who order from these places. When you call for prices, ask the salesperson to send copies of the manufacturer's brochure, wood samples and fabric swatches. For more information: Furnitureland, (919) 841-4328; Rose Furniture Co., (919) 886-6050; Nite Furniture Co., (704) 437-1491; Hickory Furniture Mart, (800) 462-6278; and Edgar B, (800) 255-6589, which has a catalog that costs $15.

Model Home Furniture

3265 S. Wadsworth Blvd., Lakewood, 986-7701.

10 a.m. to 6 p.m. Monday through Friday; 10 a.m. to 5 p.m. Saturday; noon to 5 p.m. Sunday; evenings by appointment.

Model Home Furniture offers pieces and accessories that once helped make showcases of homes built by most major local homebuilders, as well designer mistakes and custom samples—and they'll also special order. New furniture usually goes for about 40% less than suggested retail, and model-home pieces are priced by value. Prices aren't really all that cheap, but a persistent shopper may be able to find a decent deal.

Office Liquidators

5250 E. Evans Ave., Denver, 759-3375.

8:30 a.m. to 6 p.m. Monday through Friday; 10 a.m. to 4 p.m. Saturday.

The Office Liquidators store sells desks, chairs, credenzas, bookcases, computer furniture, file cabinets and wall systems cheaply because the company buys and sells furniture from offices that go out of business. It also sells new office furniture at below list price. Office Liquidators is a Denver-based business that deals mostly in American-made goods, and it offers private financing, delivery and follow-up service. The company's "Desk Doctor" service will come out to offices to repair desks or file cabinets.

Out of the Woods

2590 Walnut St., Denver, 292-2012.

7 a.m. to 4 p.m. Monday through Friday.

Oiled-oak bedroom sets, entertainment centers, dining sets, home-office furniture and bookcases are handmade on the premises. There's a small showroom, from which you can order custom pieces. The public that finds this obscure downtown place can get about 25% off what the items sell for in retail outlets.

Outlet World

550 E. 84th Ave., Thornton, 286-6800.

10 a.m. to 9 p.m. Monday through Saturday; 11 a.m. to 6 p.m. Sunday.

Montgomery Ward used to have a scratch-and-dent clearance center for furniture and appliances in the warehouse district, as Sears still does. But in the fall of '93, they got onto the discount bandwagon and opened Outlet World in the North Valley Mall. There are still scratched dishwashers, discontinued loveseats, odd dining room chairs and mismatched mattress-and-boxspring pairs—and everything is covered by manufacturers' warranties. But you'll also find shoes, linens, coats, housewares—virtually anything you'd find at a Montgomery Ward Store—but in broken sizes and models—and later.

Pima Leather

2650 W. Second Ave., Denver, 936-0707.

9 a.m. to 5 p.m. Monday through Friday.

Pima imports leather furniture from China and sells it to dealers throughout the country. They've formally closed their warehouse store, but they still sometimes have a few pieces for sale to the public. If you're shopping for leather furniture, call them and check.

Sears Outlet Store

701 Osage, Denver (near West Sixth Avenue and I-25), 892-8649.

8 a.m. to 5 p.m. Monday through Saturday; noon to 5 p.m. Sunday.

If you're not fussy about a dent on your appliances or a scratch on your furniture, check out the Sears Outlet Store. It features one- or two-of-a-kind demonstrators, floor samples and discontinued models. Everything is warranteed.

Shadow Mountain Interiors

1193 Highway 74, Evergreen, 674-4648.

9 a.m. to 6 p.m. Monday through Friday; 10 a.m. to 5 p.m. Saturday; noon to 5 Sunday.

An Evergreen-based artisan who works exclusively with Shadow Mountain Interiors crafts classic all-pine furniture to order, and the price is unexpectedly reasonable for custom pieces. You could pay around $650 for a straight-legged dinner table, and cocktail tables are around $350-$450. He'll make dressers, chairs, nightstands, consoles, headboards or virtually anything you can dream up.

Antiques, Auctions, Estate and Garage Sales

The *Denver Yellow Pages* has about 200 listings under Antique Dealers and another 40 or so under Antique Restoration. Obviously, that is the comprehensive listing—not this. But here are a few places we know about, have visited or have used, and we thought you might want to know about them, too. Also included are a few words about auctions, estate sales and garage sales.

& Etc. Antiques and Restorations

1065 S. Gaylord St., Denver, 744-0745.

9 a.m. to 5 p.m. Tuesday through Saturday.

The people at this little shop will come to your home, pick up damaged antiques and repair them. They do a great job, but they're not cheap. Before you engage them, take a cold look at the sentimental versus the actual value of the damaged piece.

Antique Mall of Lakewood

9635 W. Colfax Ave., Lakewood, 238-6940.

9 a.m. to 6 p.m. Monday through Saturday; noon to 5:30 p.m. Sunday.

This immense retail space (34,000 square feet) is divided among 126 vendors, so it's a great place to spend the day getting an education on antiques. And when you grow weary of turning over price tags and opening drawers, you can take a break at the on-premises restaurant, The Butter Churn. This is the only antique store in the metro area that's a member of the Better Business Bureau. The Antique Mall isn't a discount-oriented operation, but any place with this many vendors is bound to have a few who are willing to make deals.

Auctions

It's possible to get some great deals at auctions. In fact, that's where many flea-market folks get their goods. If you know what you're doing, you can find good antiques at auctions, too.

Edward "Andy" Anderson, the auctioneer at the Auction Center, 6361 E. 72nd Ave., Commerce City, (287-6173), is a reputable guy who has some suggestions for would-be bidders. He says you should call for inspection times and not bid on anything you haven't inspected in advance. Go knowing exactly what you will pay, and don't go beyond that price. Remain calm. It's the excitable people who wind up with truckloads full of broken water heaters. Finally, don't pay big money for some course that claims you can get rich by buying government surplus at auctions. You can learn all you need to know by reading up and focussing on the kind of merchandise you're going to bid on, going to a few auctions and paying attention.

And here's some advice from a friend who frequents auctions and has learned to spot the ones that—unlike the Auction Center—are a little shady. If the auctioneer seems to be deliberately ignoring bids, it could mean that the winner has been picked in advance. It might, theoretically, even mean that the winning bidder is a shill for the auction house, which wants to buy the merchandise cheap on consignment and resell it high.

Rest assured, however, that most auctions are honest. If you keep your head and are alert and well-informed, you can do as well at an auction as the most experienced bidder. Obviously, the Auction Center isn't the only auction house in town. For a complete listing, check the *Yellow Pages*.

Country Line Antique Shop

1067 S. Gaylord St., Denver, 733-1143.

11 a.m. to 5 p.m. Tuesday through Saturday.

If you're an old-fashioned lace-and-buttons-and-bows type, this store has some items that may appeal. Store owner Genna Morrow has taken the usable portions of worn or damaged antique patchwork quilts and made them into heart-shaped pillows, which are trimmed with vintage lace and buttons and range in price from $3 to $26, depending on the size. The

Country Line also stocks oak and pine furniture, antique garden accessories and other primitive oddments, such as pieces of fence.

Eron Johnson Antiques

1301 Wazee, Denver, 825-1178.

10 a.m. to 5 p.m. Monday through Saturday.

The 17th-, 18th- and early 19th-century furniture featured in this store ranges from primitive to formal, continental to American. There are no reproductions, but if you need a piece reproduced to match a set, for example, the people here can help you. You won't find discounts, but the store is worth mentioning because it's well-established, large (18,000 square feet) and reputable and because Eron Johnson has learned something during the 20 years he's been selling antiques in Denver.

Estate and garage sales

The rules for estate and garage sales are similar to the ones for auctions. Be informed, keep your head and be alert. You'll do best by narrowing your focus. If you collect perfume bottles or Monopoly games or Japanese prints, you'll know a good deal when you see it, so go directly to that merchandise.

At estate sales held in homes, kitchen ware, obviously, is most likely to be in the kitchen. So if you collect Depression glass, don't linger in the living room. After you've laid claim to the items you know best, look around with an open mind. Maybe there's a slightly damaged armoire you can pick up and repair. Just be sure you can do the repair yourself or you can live with the damage, or it probably isn't worth renting a truck or hiring a professional mover to get it home.

Be particularly cautious with needlepoint and Oriental rugs. Moth damage may be irreparable, and rugs are expensive to clean and repair. Fur coats are almost never worth buying. They probably haven't been properly stored and may be moth damaged.

It's often worthwhile to buy framed pictures at estate and garage sales. Although rare and valuable masterpieces don't generally turn up in such venues, look for frames. If you like a frame, discard the picture and use the frame for your own picture—it's almost always cheaper than having a frame made. Before you go, measure the pictures you need frames for—and take a tape measure with you to the sale.

If the owner is there or, in the case of estate sales, an heir, ask whether your purchase has a story behind it. Knowing some history will make the item that much more fun for you to own.

To get in touch with estate sales, one source to call in Denver is AMS Estate Liquidation. To hear a recorded announcement on sale content or location, call 377-0972 or 785-7388 weekly on Thursday, Friday or Saturday.

La Cache

400 Downing St., Denver, 871-9605.

10 a.m. to 4 p.m. Monday through Saturday.

This consignment shop handles quality estate-sale items: antique furniture, sterling, china, crystal. Twice a year, La Cache holds sales to clear away items on which the consignment period has expired. The store is staffed by volunteers, and all proceeds benefit the Children's Hospital.

Lili Marlene

2333 E. Ohio Ave., Denver, 744-7990.

9 a.m. to 3:30 p.m. Monday through Friday; 9 a.m. to 5 p.m. Saturday.

This place has been in business a long time doing something rather special. They'll custom design a lampshade for that special lamp and handcraft it. The price for this is not as high as you might anticipate.

The Olde Lamplighter

1521 Blake St., Denver, 595-3064.

8:30 a.m. to 4 p.m. Tuesday through Thursday; til 5 p.m. Friday; 8 a.m. to 3 p.m. Saturday; 8 a.m. to 1 p.m. Sunday.

We learned the hard way that it can cost almost as much to restore an antique as it does to buy one. But if it's your grandmother's lamp that's in pieces, maybe price isn't so important. Store owner David Gavin restored my grandmother's Gone-With-the-Wind lamp, and he did a fine job.

Red's Antique Gallery

5797 E. Evans Ave., Denver, 753-9187.

10 a.m. to 5 p.m. Monday through Saturday or by appointment.

Red's is a great place to start looking if you're thinking of buying antique or antique reproduction furniture, lamps or bronzes. There's 20,000 square feet of space featuring a little bit of everything, with a particularly wide selection of reproduced Remington bronzes. (You'll spot the place by the huge statues out front.) Co-owner Del Hurd is low key and willing to part with a wealth of information. Don't leave til you see Red's chair. This humongous piece provides an instant trip back to childhood—adults feel like 5-year-olds standing next to it.

Time After Time

5400 W. 38th Ave., Denver, 425-6865.

10 a.m. to 6 p.m. Monday through Saturday.

The neighbors love mother and daughter Charlene Roybal and Kelly Lucero, who took a derelict Victorian home in this old neighborhood and turned it into a cozy antique store. The deals are decent, too; decent enough that dealers occasionally stop by to find good prices on antiques, collectibles and old—but not quite antique—furniture.

Housewares, Gifts and General Merchandise

What can you say about a category where Junk-Tique is listed right after International Villa? It's a tough category to define. You want all your china to match, and you want it to complement your crystal—at discount? Try here. You want an Italian potato peeler? This is the place. How about a cheap plastic colander? You'll find that, too, in the various odd-lot stores where virtually anything might show up, but whatever it is, it's less than a buck. Perhaps more than any other category in the book, this one is for browsers. In general, if a store specializes in small, useful items and gifts—up to and including fine china, crystal and silver—try this category. For larger, decorative items, small appliances and linens, try Home Accessories. Careful though—there's a lot of overlap. If you don't find what you're looking for under one heading, try the other. The Dansk outlet has tablecloths as well as plates.

Chicago Cutlery

Castle Rock, 660-3303.

See Factory Outlet Malls for address, hours and directions.

This store has sets of Magnalite pots and pans, professional stainless steel, and three lines of Chicago Cutlery—Metropolitan, Cherrywood and Walnut. This is a "factory direct" store, and prices are between 45% and 60% lower than department stores.

China Warehouse

4919 E. 38th Ave., Denver, 377-0762.

10 a.m. to 4 p.m. Monday through Friday.

Mikasa china is sold at a discount here, but the store exists to sell the fine white porcelain that china painters use, including Limoges and German and Japanese imports.

Colorful Images

Silverthorne, (970) 468-6375.

See Factory Outlet Malls for address, hours and directions.

This is a gift store with clocks, knickknacks, teddy bears, cookie jars, canister sets and small pictures.

Corning Revere

Castle Rock, 688-1551; Silverthorne, (970) 468-2721.

See Factory Outlet Malls for address, hours and directions.

You can find discounts here of 20% to 70% depending on the product and local sales. Other than the discounts, one of the main reasons for shopping here is the selection of Corning, Pyrex, Corelle, Visions and Revere. There are items in these stores that you wouldn't ordinarily find locally—Corelle rice bowls, for example.

Dansk

Silverthorne, (970) 262-2267; Loveland, (970) 593-0021.

See Factory Outlet Malls for address, hours and directions.

Everything Dansk at 25% to 40% off department store prices. Dansk produces dishes, cookware, master series stainless steel, napkins, towels, tablecloths, flatware, crystal, glassware, barware and lots of other housewares.

Everything's a Dollar

Aurora Mall, Aurora; Buckingham Square, Aurora; Southwest Plaza, Littleton; Westminster Mall, Westminster; Crossroads Mall, Boulder; Chapel Hills Mall, Colorado Springs.

Mall hours.

Dime stores may be gone, but dollar stores are flourishing. In 1993, there were no Everything's a Dollar stores in Colorado. Now there are six. This fast-growing chain swept in from Milwaukee, and, unlike other odd-lot operations, settled in malls. Merchandise, all priced at $1, includes jewelry, personal care items, hardware, kitchenware, gifts, toys, novelties, food and lots of books, including hard-covers.

The Fair Variety Store

1116 Washington Ave., Golden, 279-1755.

9 a.m. to 5:30 p.m. Monday through Saturday; 10 a.m. to 3 p.m. Sunday.

The Fair Variety Store is an old-fashioned five-and-dime that carries a little bit of everything. Especially popular are notions, toys, "penny" candy and a dollar gift counter.

Famous Brands Housewares

Castle Rock, 660-8349; Silverthorne, (970) 262-0393; Loveland, (970) 593-0226.

See Factory Outlet Malls for address, hours and directions.

These are outlet stores for Lechters, a mall housewares store that has not made it to Colorado in any other form. Everyday prices at Famous Brands are usually lower than the sale prices at Lechters. The emphasis is on gadgets, and each store also carries wire organizers, cookware and bakeware, plastic storage systems, frames, glasses, plates, towels and place mats.

Farberware

Castle Rock, 660-2188; Loveland, (970) 635-0262.

See Factory Outlet Malls for address, hours and directions.

If you've always had a desire for a full set of Farberware stainless steel pots with aluminum-clad bottoms, here's your store. Discounts range from 20% to 50% off retail.

Half Price or Less

13960 E. Mississippi Ave., Aurora, 368-4841.

10 a.m. to 7 p.m. Monday through Friday; 10:30 to 7 p.m. Saturday; noon to 5 p.m. Sunday.

This store brings together a wide assortment of gifts and oddments, including calendars, wind chimes, t-shirts, crystal, toys, beer steins, children's jackets, novelties, stocking stuffers and housewares—anything owner Kenneth Long can buy cheaply enough to offer to the public at (you guessed it) half price or less.

Hibbard & Co.

17 S. Tejon St., Colorado Springs, (719) 635-2525

10 a.m. to 5:30 p.m. Monday through Friday; 10 a.m. to 5 p.m. Saturday.

We include Hibbard's not because it is a discounter, although its prices are generally modest, but because it is a Colorado Springs institution. The store hasn't changed much in appearance or inventory in living memory. The floors are wooden, some ceilings are tin, merchandise is displayed on huge oak tables, sales are concluded by sending a customer's money to central accounting via a pneumatic tube system, and the elevator has an accordian-like door still manned by an elevator operator! Also you won't want to miss the wonderful time clock at the back of the first floor near the Notions Department. The store has a variety of merchandise, including a great housewares section, clothing for men and women, linens and notions. If you fear an item (say, a plastic rain hat or woman's nightcap) may not be manufactured anymore, check here first before abandoning all hope. This marvelous store, which should be added to the historic site preservation list if it's not already on it, is a museum to retailing.

The International Villa

262 Fillmore St., Denver, 333-1524.

9:30 a.m. to 5:30 p.m. Monday through Friday; 9:30 a.m. to 5 p.m. Saturday; noon to 4 p.m. Sunday.

This local business, family-owned and service-oriented for 40 years, recently saw the writing on the wall and switched to a discount pricing structure. The store, which specializes in china, crystal, silver and flatware, offers all tabletop merchandise at 20% to 40% off retail prices. This change was made in an effort to remain a player in the new world of factory outlets and mail order. The discounts apply to bridal registry items also.

Junk-Tique

313 Main St., Frisco, (970) 668-3040.

9 a.m. to 6 p.m. daily.

This consignment and second-hand store has antiques, Western memorabilia, pottery, stained glass—a little of everything other than clothes.

Kitchen Collection

Castle Rock, 660-9396.

See Factory Outlet Malls for address, hours and directions.

This store carries an assortment of items such as gadgets and small electric appliances. The primary brands available are Anchor Hocking, Proctor Silex and Hamilton Beach. Don't rely on that, though, because this is not a "brand" outlet like Corning Revere. It's actually more of an odd-lot store, where what's on sale is what the wholesaler can buy inexpensively. Look for discounts between 10% to 50%, depending on the item.

Lenox

Loveland, (970) 663-0879.

See Factory Outlet Malls for address, hours and directions.

Lenox china, dinnerware, gifts, crystal stemware, table linens, pewter and brassware, candlesticks, stainless and silver flatware are all sold here at discounts ranging from 40% to 60%.

MacFrugal's Bargains and Close-outs

10 W. First Ave., Denver, 722-7667; 8125 Sheridan Blvd., Arvada, 429-7844; 15351 E. Hampden Ave., Aurora, 680-0310; 779 Peoria St., Aurora, 344-5322; 1951 S. Federal Blvd., Denver, 936-2799; 10575 W. Colfax, Lakewood, 202-1140; 5085 N. Academy Blvd., Colorado Springs, (719) 598-5554; 1990 S. Academy Blvd., Colorado Springs, (719) 591-7494. For information on other locations, call (800) 800-9992. (Be ready with the ZIP code for the area you need.)

9 a.m. to 9 p.m. Monday through Saturday; 11 a.m. to 7 p.m. Sunday.

MacFrugal's looks like a small department store with a little of everything. You can find some clothing here (check the pantyhose), but the real bargains are in the seasonal items (Halloween costumes, Christmas ornaments), housewares, office products, small toys and personal care products. It's a great place to buy baskets.

Mikasa

Castle Rock, 688-1109; Silverthorne, (970) 262-0715.

See Factory Outlet Malls for address, hours and directions.

Mikasa makes primarily crystal, china, flatware and giftware. The prices at the factory outlet stores are typically 20% to 70% off retail, depending on the item. You can also order Mikasa patterns not on display in the store at a discount.

99¢ Mart

3915 Federal Blvd., Denver, 477-6887.

10 a.m. to 7:30 p.m. Monday through Friday; 10 a.m. to 7 p.m. Saturday; noon to 6 p.m. Sunday.

Lovers of low-rent browsing adore this store. It has perhaps 1,000 items that sell for 99¢ or less, including shampoo, trash bags, makeup, razors, candy, light bulbs, soda pop, toothbrushes, school supplies, brooms, stationery, toys, cleaning supplies, cookware, kitchen tools, phone accessories, housewares, keychains, air freshener, jewelry, wallets, address books, hardware and hair accessories. It also gets a few more pricey items; these have included telephones for $14 to $20, Polaroid film for $1.99 and frames for $1.49 to $2.99.

Oneida Factory Store

Silverthorne, (970) 262-0731.

See Factory Outlet Malls for address, hours and directions.

This is the only Oneida store in Colorado, although one is on the agenda for Castle Rock. It carries baby sets that make nice baby gifts, as well as crystal and china. Good bets are the Oneida edge-plus cutlery and the silver holloware, including candlesticks, trays and other giftware. Look for discounts of 30% to 60%.

Pacific Mercantile

1925 Lawrence St. (Sakura Square), Denver, 295-0293.

8 a.m. to 6 p.m. Monday through Saturday; 9 a.m. to 2 p.m. Sunday.

If you are looking for bowls and other housewares with an Asian theme, Pacific Mercantile is the place. They have giftware, bowls, woks, ladles, steamers, and the food to cook and serve in them. The store is a Denver classic and well worth the visit.

Pfaltzgraff

Castle Rock, 660-9246; Silverthorne, (970) 468-9694.

See Factory Outlet Malls for address, hours and directions.

Look here for Pfaltzgraff stoneware, serving pieces, glassware and accompanying housewares. First-quality pieces are sold at retail, but seconds with some cosmetic problems are discounted.

Royal Doulton

Castle Rock, 660-1601.

See Factory Outlet Malls for address, hours and directions.

This is the only Royal Doulton outlet in Colorado, and the stock comes directly from the factory in England. All china patterns carried in the store are 40% to 60% less than retail; other patterns may be ordered at 20% less than retail. In addition to table china, look here for figurines, character jugs, teapots and bone china florals and animals. If you're a Beatrix Potter fan (or the parent, grandparent, uncle or aunt of one), here's a place to collect delicate porcelain miniatures of Potter's animal characters at a reduced price.

Sassafras

Silverthorne, (970) 468-2355.

See Factory Outlet Malls for address, hours and directions.

The primary products sold in this store are various housewares, gadgets, pizza stones and bread mixes. But the store has much more, including beach balls, inner tubes, seasonal knickknacks and other interesting goods. This *is* a factory outlet store. It's just that the factory is very eclectic.

79¢ Plus Mart

781 S. Federal Blvd., Denver, 937-3941.

9 a.m. to 6 p.m. Monday through Saturday; 10 a.m. to 5 p.m. Sunday.

This little odd-lot store chiefly serves Denver's community of Vietnamese and Thai immigrants. You never know what you might find—hardware, toys, household goods, batteries. Prices start at 79¢ and range up to $10 or so for larger goods.

Tuesday Morning

8270 W. 80th Ave. (the Meadows Center), Arvada, 422-9994; 7400 E. Hampden Ave., Denver, 488-9940; 4301 E. Virginia Ave., Glendale, 333-8156; 15372 E. Alameda Parkway, Aurora, 695-4357; 12790 W. Alameda Parkway, Lakewood, 989-2792; 7562 S. University Blvd. (Southglenn Square), Littleton, 779-0328; 8996 W. Bowles Ave. (Bowles Avenue Marketplace), Littleton, 972-2155; 4800 Baseline, Boulder, 494-1535; 3520 N. Academy Blvd., Colorado Springs, (719) 596-1043; 222 Walnut St., Fort Collins, (970) 224-3432.

See Direct and Seasonal Sales for hours and dates.

You'd have to shop well to find stainless steel flatware for $30 a place setting in a department store—that's $360 for a setting for 12, without serving pieces. But at Tuesday Morning we've seen a set for 12, with serving pieces, for $89. There's one important difference: there's only one pattern. Tuesday Morning is a great place to shop for wedding gifts. The crystal you see here is usually around half the price of what you'd pay at a department store. Of course, you have to guess what the couple would like. (You might go to the store where they're registered and look at the items to get a sense of their taste.) Here, in particular, it's important to be aware of values before you shop, because Tuesday Morning's "suggested retail" bears no relationship to reality. Also, we recently saw the same gift tin of popcorn for $5.99 at Tuesday Morning and $4.99 at Price Club.

Villeroy & Boch

Castle Rock, 688-1101.

See Factory Outlet Malls for address, hours and directions.

This factory-direct store sells Villeroy & Boch fine bone china, porcelain and crystal, which is manufactured in Luxembourg and Germany and other sites in Europe. Discounts range from 40% to 70% off suggested retail. Also, because this store is hooked up directly with the European factories, it offers a full range of services for Villeroy & Boch owners.

Walter Drake & Son Inc.

4510 Edison Ave., Colorado Springs, (719) 596-5769 or (719) 596-1882.

9 a.m. to 5 p.m. Monday through Saturday.

This well-known national mail-order company, which can help customers find matches for missing pieces of china and silverware sets, is headquartered in Colorado Springs. As readers of Dave Barry know, it also offers such oddities as a device that firms your chin while you sleep (Chin Firmer, $4.99, #N3168). Whether you need something specific or you're in the mood for an interesting browsing experience, stop in.

Home Accessories

You've got the house, the furniture, the appliances and the carpet—the basics. Now it's time to spruce up. You need things to make it *your* home, a home that could not possibly belong to anyone else. Your choices in pictures, decorative fabrics, flowers, linens, hobbies and window coverings give your house personality. Here are some places to look for good deals in decorating. This is a sort of catch-all category, and it's frankly just a little too subtle to be clear-cut. Where do we put a store that sells throw pillows (home accessories) and china (housewares)? Here, probably. But if you don't see a store you expect to find here, check the section on Housewares, Gifts, and General Merchandise; and the section on Home Improvement.

ABC Books and Posters

2550 S. Colorado Blvd., Denver, 759-0250.

9:30 a.m. to 9 p.m. Monday through Friday; 9:30 a.m. to 6 p.m., Saturday; noon to 5 p.m. Sunday.

ABC specializes in framing, especially fine art prints. And if you're a teacher or you work as volunteer with children (as a scout leader, for example), the shop will give you 10% discount on framing.

Acme-Western Upholstery Supply

1812 Wazee St., Denver, (800) 678-9330.

This wholesale supplier sells only to the trade. If your decorator has a retail-tax license, you will be able to gain access to the deals here. (For more on this, read the introduction to Home Improvement.)

Associated Wholesale Florist

2100 W. Mississippi Ave., Denver, 937-1222.

8 a.m. to 6 p.m. Monday through Friday; 8 a.m. to 5 p.m. Saturday.

This is the warehouse for Lehrer's. It offers floral and decorating supplies, including baskets, vases, ribbon and candles. It has flowers and plants, too.

Bed, Bath and Beyond

2500 E. First Ave., Denver, 321-0742.

9:30 a.m. to 9 p.m. Monday through Saturday; 9:30 a.m. to 6 p.m. Sunday.

This 75,000-square-foot store carries all kinds of items for the home, including small appliances, baby accessories, closet organizers, window coverings, lamps, cookware, rugs, baskets, tablecloths, storage systems and (of course) linens. Prices generally are 20% to 40% less than suggested retail.

Caboose Hobbies

500 S. Broadway, Denver, 777-6766.

9:30 a.m. to 6 p.m. Monday through Friday; 9 a.m. to 5:30 p.m. Saturday; noon to 5 p.m. Sunday.

Caboose claims to be the largest model-train store in the world, and even if they can't prove that claim, it's a great place to visit. Here you'll find trains and models of every size (that would be every *gauge* to those in the know) and variety, some of which are set up on tracks so the kids have something to watch while you browse. When he lived in the Denver metro area, actor Gary Coleman used to be a clerk here, just because it's a fun place to hang out and talk trains.

Calico Corners

6625 Leetsdale Drive, Denver, 320-5338.

9:30 a.m. to 5:30 p.m. Monday through Saturday; noon to 5 p.m. Sunday.

Check here for home-decorating fabrics to make slipcovers, pillows and window coverings. Even a beginner can save a bundle; it's pretty simple to make cushions and bedspreads. Calico Corners also makes up samples of these items, which they sometimes sell. It's worth a phone call.

Carol's Better Homes and Bargains

6490 W. 44th Ave., Denver, 424-0866.

10 a.m. to 5 p.m. Monday through Friday; 10 a.m. to 4 p.m. Saturday.

Owner Carol Ambrosio and her husband have operated the Ambrosio Company at the Denver Merchandise Mart for 12 years. Ambrosio opened Carol's Better Homes and Bargains as an outlet for samples, duplicates and discontinued items from the 30 manufacturers she represents at the Mart. Among the items you're apt to find on hand: crystal, candles, throw pillows, framed art, decorative coat racks, dried floral arrangements, baskets and bird houses. Prices are near wholesale.

Colorel Blinds

1690 S. Abilene St., Aurora, 337-6667; 5924 S. Kipling St., Littleton, 979-1999; 6000 W. 92nd Ave., Westminister, 428-6999; 2412 Arapahoe Ave., Boulder, 938-1150; 8200 Park Meadows Drive, Littleton, 799-3555; 5112 S. College, Unit B, Fort Collins, (970) 229-9990. Other areas of the state, call (800) 877-4800.

9 a.m. to 7 p.m. Monday through Friday; 9 a.m. to 6 p.m. Saturday; noon to 5 pm. Sunday.

Colorel Blinds is a genuine factory outlet. The firm has been manufacturing in Denver for 12 years and recently started offering cellular shades on a one-day turnaround and at factory-direct prices.

Colorful Images

Silverthorne, (970) 468-6375.

See Factory Outlet Malls for address, hours and directions.

This is an outlet for slow sellers from the Colorful Images catalog; everything in the store is half the catalog price. The store is small but offers nice touches for the home such as novelty doormats, windsocks, lamps and throws. There are also housewares such as teakettles, cookie jars and seasonal items, such as Christmas ornaments.

Cost Plus World Market

13940 E. Mississippi Ave., Aurora, 745-0311; 8601 W. Cross Drive, Littleton, 933-9515 260 S. Academy Blvd., Colorado Springs, (719) 570-4700.

9 a.m. to 9 p.m. Monday through Friday; 9 a.m. to 7 p.m. Saturday; 10 a.m. to 7 p.m. Sunday.

Try Cost Plus for inexpensive baskets, furniture throws, sofa pillows, frames, chairs, tables, bookcases, rugs, gift items and much, much more.

Decorator Fabrics

5910 S. University Blvd., Littleton, 795-1200.

10 a.m. to 5 p.m. Monday through Saturday.

Fabrics for upholstery, bedspreads and window coverings are always discounted by 40% to 60%, and there are additional discounts when this store has one of its frequent sales.

Discount flowers

We've found a number of florists throughout the metro area where it's possible to buy flowers at a discount. During certain times of the year, you can find roses at some of these places at $10 for 100. As a rule, the way to save real money is to go to a florist and buy the flowers yourself, cash and carry. If you know how to arrange flowers, or if you know someone who does, you can save lots of money for, say, a wedding, by buying flowers loose at one of these places and arranging them in your own vases—borrow or rent some, if you must. Florists make their profit in arranging and delivery; it's sort of like the difference between buying your food at the supermarket or at a restaurant. Sometimes the flowers purchased at discounters are "designer" (some imperfect flowers) or "distressed" (not freshly picked). Sometimes they need to have some of the outer petals trimmed off. Ask before you buy. And before you buy, inspect the goods at more than one place; quality varies. Each of these spots has its loyal customers, but some also have detractors. Only you can find the one that suits *your* needs, standards, budget and taste.

Blue Moon Florists, 300 E. Sixth Ave., Denver, 778-7220.

Blumen, 5398 Sheridan Blvd., Arvada, 455-1793.

Cool N Fresh Flowers, 1194 S. Federal Blvd., Denver, 936-2273; 5889 E. Evans Ave., Denver, 758-0093; 5022 Kipling St., Wheat Ridge, 423-5175; 6586 S. Broadway, Littleton, 730-1072.

Country Club Flowers, 1706 E. Sixth Ave., Denver, 399-3838.

Great Western Weed, 2700 E. Sixth Ave., Denver, 333-7555.

Happy Happy Balloon and Flower, 1500 W. Alameda Ave., Denver, 733-8913; 8799 W. Colfax Ave., Lakewood, 233-1222.

Tennyson Street Flowers, 4370 Tennyson St., Denver, 458-3656.

Tumbleweed Floral, 77 W. Alameda Ave., Denver, 871-8788.

DJB Enterprises

1390 S. Potomac St., Suite 136, Aurora, 696-9225.

This is a mail-order company sells fabric for home seamstresses and offers occasional direct sales from its warehouse. During one of these sales, you can find a very broad selection of rayons, silks, wools and cottons at significant discounts. Call to be placed on the mailing list.

Emily Griffith Opportunity School

1250 Welton St., Denver, 572-8218.

Emily Griffith Opportunity School is the Denver Public School adult vocational center, offering 350 day and evening classes at 120 metro area locations. If you've got a chair to reupholster, check into its upholstery class, offered once a year from September to May. There's always a waiting list. Your chair is your project; you not only gain a reupholstered item; you gain a skill.

Factory Fabric Outlet

1435 Wazee St., Denver, 623-2312.

8:30 a.m. to 5 p.m. Monday through Friday.

This outlet has been a source of inexpensive fabrics and notions for nearly 30 years. The selection can be sparse, but dress patterns are always 20% off of list price, some remnants are priced as low as 49¢ a yard, and you get free buttons (store's selection) with any purchase. It's also a great place to trawl for discounted upholstery and drapery fabric.

Fantasy Fabrics

6864 S. University Blvd., Littleton, 689-0302.

10 a.m. to 6 p.m. Monday through Saturday.

There's usually a sale here on home-decorating fabrics for window coverings, upholstery and bedspreads. They also do custom work.

Fieldcrest Cannon Factory Store

10590 Melody Drive, (Northglenn Mall), Northglenn, 280-2619.

10 a.m. to 9 p.m. Monday through Friday; 10 a.m. to 6 p.m. Saturday; 11 a.m. to 6 p.m. Sunday.

Irregular and discontinued towels, sheets, comforters, blankets, bath rugs and more are sold at this clearance center for the Fieldcrest Cannon warehouse in Eden, N.C., at 10% to 50% off retail prices.

Frame-It-Yourself

7301 W. Alameda Ave., Lakewood, 238-2769; 2504 E. Arapahoe Road, Littleton, 694-3229; 6787 S. Clinton, Englewood, 799-4755; 2370 S. Colorado Blvd., Denver, 757-5037; 560 S. Holly St., Denver, 320-1988; 1325 S. Inca St., Denver, 744-1401; 2625 S. Parker Road, Aurora, 337-2447; 4335 Wadsworth Blvd., Wheat Ridge, 423-9430.

10 a.m. to 8 p.m. Monday through Thursday; 10 a.m. to 5 p.m. Friday and Saturday; noon to 5 p.m. Sunday.

This Denver-based picture-framing company has offered a 20% discount for orders placed on Wednesday for 16½ of the 17 years they've been in business. They started the Wednesday discount because Wednesday was a slow day. That hasn't been true for more than a decade.

Heritage Fabrics

5550 E. Evans, Denver, 758-0566.

9 a.m. to 6 p.m. Monday through Friday; 9 a.m. to 5 p.m. Saturday; 11:30 a.m. to 4 p.m. Sunday.

Hundreds of bolts of upholstery, drapery and window-covering fabric are sold here at discounts of 20% to 50%.

Hobby Lobby

550 E. Thornton Parkway, Thornton, 450-2017; 441 Sable Blvd., Aurora, 360-9269; 5810 W. Alameda Ave., Lakewood, 922-1467; 7815 Wadsworth Blvd., Arvada, 425-7363; 920 S. Monaco Parkway, Denver, 321-3699; 139 W. Hampden Ave., Englewood, 762-8835; 6950 N. Academy Blvd., Colorado Springs, (719) 260-6920; 1830 W. Uintah, Colorado Springs, (719) 630-1977.

9 a.m. to 8 p.m. Monday through Friday; 9 a.m. to 6 p.m. Saturday; 11 a.m. to 5 p.m. Sunday.

Crafters can find anything from needlework kits to dried flowers, and those less crafty can find framed pictures. Hobby Lobby also has a large fabric department. If you're looking for an artificial Christmas tree, word has it that this is a good place to go. A reader called to say that she and her friends shopped all over town and found great deals and a great selection here, and she wound up buying a 9-foot Manhattan pine for $127.

Home Express

9289 Sheridan Blvd., Westminster, 657-3211.

9 a.m. to 9 p.m. Monday through Saturday; 10 a.m. to 7 p.m. Sunday.

Here's another superstore just entering the Denver market. Like its main national competitors—Bed, Bath and Beyond and Linens 'n' Things who also are just coming into Colorado with an eye to expansion—Home Express can offer substantial savings because of high-volume buying. Merchandise includes small appliances, linens and occasional furniture, such as folding chairs.

Keyston Bros.

222 Bryant St., Denver, (800) 258-2777.

This wholesaler offers fabric and upholstery supplies for the trade. If you want access, it will have to be through someone with a retail-tax license.

Lakewood Crafts

7777 W. Jewell Ave., Lakewood, 989-9616.

9 a.m. to 8 p.m. Monday through Friday; 9 a.m. to 6 p.m. Saturday; 11 a.m. to 5 p.m. Sunday.

This independent craft store has a wide selection of yarns, as well as other craft products, fabrics for home-decorating and a framing department.

LeGrue's

476 S. Broadway, Denver, 744-6275.

9:30 a.m. to 5 p.m. Monday through Friday; 10 a.m. to 4 p.m. Saturday.

LeGrue's has specialized in silk and dried flowers, vases, baskets, ribbons and other such room brighteners in Denver for decades. It's not a discounter, but it *is* an institution.

Linens 'n' Things

8527 E. Arapahoe Road, Greenwood Village, 689-9690; 5264 S. Wadsworth Blvd., Littleton, 904-0404.

9:30 a.m. to 9 p.m. Monday through Saturday; 11 a.m. to 6 p.m. Sunday.

Linens 'n' Things offers moderate discounts on a huge variety of household items—kitchen accessories, cookware, small appliances, clocks, frames, storage gear, toys and baby equipment. Oh, and linens.

Meininger's

499 Broadway, Denver, 698-3838.

9 a.m. to 6 p.m. Monday through Friday; 9 a.m. to 5 p.m. Saturday.

Meininger's is a venerable locally owned supplier of artist-quality supplies, such as oil paints, water colors, brushes and books about the visual arts. It's also a surprisingly good source of stuff for children, including good markers and modeling clay that goes beyond what's available in toy stores. The pre-cut frames here are an inexpensive option to custom framing. And look for the annual lobby sale each summer. We've found some amazing deals here, such as art books for 10¢ on the dollar.

Michael's Arts and Crafts

2580 S. Colorado Blvd., Denver, 756-2003; 7669 W. 88th Ave., Arvada, 431-7986; 14005 E. Exposition Ave., Aurora, 344-8902; 4800 Baseline Road, Boulder, 494-2008; 5066 S. Wadsworth Blvd., Littleton, 971-0745; 2200 E. Arapahoe Rd., Littleton, 730-1163; 1565 Quail St., Lakewood, 233-9273; 4438 Austin Bluffs Pkwy., Colorado Springs, (719) 599-4445. For other locations, call (800) 642-4235.

8 a.m. to 10 p.m. Monday through Saturday; 9 a.m. to 7 p.m. Sunday.

This is a great source for any sort of craft enterprise for the home, including needlework and appliqué. If you're looking for inexpensive framed pictures, check here. Michael's also has good deals on framing. It's also a good place to buy any seasonal merchandise because clearances often start *before* the holiday. We've done particularly well on calendars.

Mill End Drapery

600 S. Holly St., No. 10, Denver, 331-0801.

9:30 a.m. to 6 p.m. Monday through Friday; 9:30 a.m. to 5 p.m. Saturday.

At this shop you can buy fabric and have it custom made into window coverings, comforters or slipcovers. At a recent Mill End sale, tables of decorator fabric were $1.98, $4.98 and $6.98 a yard.

Nomad Design

1813 Pearl St., Boulder, 786-9746.

10 a.m. to 7 p.m. Monday through Friday; noon to 5 p.m. Sunday.

Nomad features an eclectic selection of rugs and beads, and prices are low enough that the store often supplies designers, jewelry-makers and other tradespeople. This store has the largest selection and best prices on Czech beads in Boulder.

Oops Window Covering Clearance Center

455 W. 115th Ave., Northglenn, 280-0021.

10 a.m. to 6 p.m. Monday through Friday; 10 a.m. to 5 p.m Saturday; noon to 3 p.m. Sunday.

Oops specializes in custom-ordered window coverings that have been returned to the manufacturer for a variety of reasons—size, small flaws, wrong fabric, etc. Manufacturers represented include Hunter-Douglas and Graeber. Make sure to bring your window measurements to get a good fit. If you can't find what you want, you can look again later. They get fresh stock often. Prices are 50% under retail or better.

Pacific Linen

265 Detroit St., Denver, 320-7880; 10051 E. Iliff Ave., Aurora, 369-0070; 8100 S. Quebec St., Englewood, 771-3826; 8055 W. Bowles Ave., Littleton, 972-8759; 9170 Wadsworth Parkway, Westminster, 456-8681; 3650 Austin Bluffs Pkwy., Colorado Springs, (719) 528-8985.

10 a.m. to 9 p.m. Monday through Friday; 10 a.m. to 6 p.m. Saturday; noon to 5 p.m. Sunday.

Pacific Linen limits itself to linens (unlike Linens 'n' Things; Bed, Bath and Beyond; and Home Express). It isn't a deep discounter, but neither, for that matter, are its major competitors. It always has a good selection of merchandise, and prices beat suggested retail. Pacific Linen also has a bridal registry.

Pier I Imports

7111 W. Alameda Ave., Lakewood, 233-5418; 8501 E. Arapahoe Road, Englewood, 220-9445; Arapahoe Village Shopping Center, Boulder, 447-0093; 6901 S. Broadway, Littleton, 797-9077; 1201 E. Colfax Ave., Denver, 831-7821; 4401 E. Evans Ave., 753-1923; 14100 E. Exposition Ave., Aurora, 337-7505; 5230 Wadsworth Blvd., Arvada, 425-4626; 7270 W. 88th Ave., Arvada, 422-0306; 1835 Dublin Blvd., Colorado Springs, (719) 528-1474; 1893 S. Nevada Ave., Colorado Springs, (719) 633-3973.

10 a.m. to 9 p.m. Monday through Saturday; 11 a.m. to 6 p.m. Sunday.

Many former college students remember Pier I as the place to get cheap wicker furniture and Indian bedspreads. Think again. It would not have flourished this long if that's all it sold. Pier I is a great place to look for sofa pillows, frames, framed pictures and all sorts of other items for the home including crockery, glassware and kitchen gadgets. While you're there, check out the clothing and personal gifts, such as imported soaps.

Quilts in the Attic

1025 S. Gaylord St., Denver, 744-8796.

9:30 a.m. to 5:30 p.m. Monday through Friday; 9:30 a.m. to 4:30 p.m. Saturday.

This cozy little store offers all sorts of support and supplies for quilters, including books, patterns, fabrics and notions, an array of classes, and, of course, knowledgeable people who will cheer you on in your efforts.

Ribbon Outlet

Castle Rock, 660-3591.

See Factory Outlet Malls for address, hours and directions.

This store offers more than 3,000 kinds of ribbons and trims, as well as silk flowers and other general craft supplies. Most merchandise is discounted by at least 10%.

Springmaid/Wamsutta

Castle Rock, 660-2070; Loveland, (970) 679-4600.

See Factory Outlet Malls for address, hours and directions.

These outlets sell sheets, towels, comforters, bedspreads and tablecloths from Springmaid, Wamsutta and other labels that are manufactured in the same plant. Some of the best deals are on discontinued patterns, particularly comforters. We saw a $140 comforter marked down to $40.

Swiss Miss Shop

8455 W. U.S. Hwy. 24, Cascade, (719) 684-9679.

9:30 a.m. to 5 p.m. Monday through Saturday; 1:30 p.m. to 5 p.m. Sunday.

This charming shop has been in business for 37 years and carries all the major collectibles, including figurines, music boxes and dolls. It's not a discounter, but if you're looking for bargains, check the basement for discontinued or flawed items that have had their prices reduced.

Welcome Home

Castle Rock, 688-6689; Silverthorne, (970) 468-2128; Durango, (970) 259-2827.

See Factory Outlet Malls for address, hours and directions.

These outlets sell afghans, doilies, pictures, wooden crafts, seasonal items and more from Cape Craft and other manufacturers at discounts of 10% to 50%.

Ye Olde Family Name

Silverthorne, (970) 468-2128.

See Factory Outlet Malls for address, hours and directions.

This store is an anomaly among the factory outlets—it's locally owned and it's not a discounter. It is, however, a nice place to browse for imported gift items and collectibles, including ships in bottles and porcelain figurines.

Home Improvement

Before you undertake a remodeling project, get out the *Yellow Pages* and look under such headings as Building Materials, Counter Tops, Hardware, Lumber, Plumbing Fixtures, Parts and Supplies, Kitchen Cabinets and Equipment, Kitchen Remodeling, and Tile. There are both wholesale and retail listings; check both. You can also learn what's available by cruising a nearby warehouse district. Many places have showrooms; go inside and browse. Don't be intimidated, even if the signs say the place is not open to the public. Tell the showroom that you're redoing a room and that your contractor told you to come in and look around. Then, when you know what you want, get on the phone and make oranges-and-oranges comparisons. A little research and personal involvement at this stage can save you a lot of money later.

If you're doing all this without a contractor, you'll need to find a friend in the trade in order to buy from a trade-only place. Interior designers are among those who may have retail-tax licenses that enable them to buy from wholesale sources. You may want to hire one; they do offer expertise and certain advantages, and some people argue that working with an interior designer is less expensive than working without one (see the Interior Designer entry in this section).

If you don't have a contractor but want someone with a retail-tax license to buy for you, the person may charge for the service—10% or 15% of the purchase is standard. Remember, even without a contact in the trade, you can look at trade-only places. You just can't buy. Someone in the home-improvement field will have to help you with that part of it.

Another way to remodel reasonably is to go to the big hardware centers—Hugh M. Woods, HomeBase, Builder's Square. If, for instance, you're planning to remodel your kitchen, arrange to talk to the people in the kitchen design center. Watch the newspapers and make the appointment when there's a sale on kitchen cabinets. If you decide to use one of these places to do the job, you'll be obligated to use their cabinets. But even if, eventually, you decide not to use them, you'll benefit. Most will send a designer to your home to do a plan for you at no charge.

Here's what to avoid if you're trying to save money. Don't go with any design company that reeks of "prestige." If you feel that a designer or contractor thinks your job is too small or that you're not willing to spring sufficient cash for it, find someone with an attitude closer to your expectations.

Also, get an idea of what's a realistic time frame for the job by talking with several remodelers. For instance, for a kitchen remodel it's a tipoff if the estimator says the job will take six weeks or more to complete. Unless someone doesn't know how to schedule, or you're moving walls, or there's a serious hangup, gutting a normal-size kitchen and replacing floors, cabinets, fixtures and counter tops shouldn't take a full month of actual construction. But some of the pricier companies know that if they're going to charge big, they have to look busy and important. So they have to be there, disrupting your life, for a long time.

American Olean Ceramic Tile Showroom

815 S. Jason St., Denver, 698-1400.

7:30 a.m. to 4:30 p.m. Monday through Friday.

The showroom here is open to the public, but if you want to buy wholesale through this outlet, you'll have to go through someone who has an account here.

Andrews Tools

72 E. Second Ave., Longmont, (303) 442-1619.

8 a.m. to 5:30 Monday through Friday; 8 a.m. to 3 p.m. Saturday.

All types of used tools are sold here, usually for about a third of the new retail price, depending on the condition.

Barry's Paint and Wallpaper

3305 S. Broadway, Englewood, 761-8743.

7:30 a.m. to 5:30 p.m. Monday through Friday; til 8 p.m. Thursday; 8:30 to 5 p.m. Saturday; 10 a.m. to 3 p.m. Sunday.

Whenever your fancy turns to home improvement, consider Barry's Paint and Wallpaper. The paint may not be the cheapest, but, given a day or two, they can come up with any color you can show them. Wallpaper (the choice is huge) is always discounted by 25% or more, and there's a good selection of borders. And check out the wallpaper bargain corner, where remnants are priced to clear.

Builder's Square

9050 Wadsworth Parkway, Westminster, 456-0021; 880 S. Abilene St., Aurora, 745-7090; 1725 Sheridan Blvd., Edgewater, 232-0237; 4887 S. Wadsworth Blvd., Littleton, 933-4466.

7 a.m. to 10 p.m. Monday through Saturday; 8 a.m. to 7 p.m. Sunday.

Builder's Square, which has immense stores filled to overflowing with every conceivable bit of building supplies and hardware, has at least one slight edge over the competition. It's open later. It's nice to know that, at 9:30 p.m. when Tab A won't match up with Slot A, someone's out there for you.

Capco Tiles remnant room

5101 E. Evans Ave., Denver, 759-1919.

7:30 a.m. to 4:30 p.m. Monday through Friday; 10 a.m. to 2 p.m. Saturday.

Denver-based Capco Tiles imports tile from Italy and South America and sells its products in four stores, one of which serves Aspen's elite. You can get first-quality remnant ceramic and natural stone tiles reduced by at least 30% from the original price at Capco's remnant room. Capco also carries hand-painted and other custom items that have been returned by decorators.

Ceramic Tile Outlet

940 Jason St., Denver, 744-3394.

8 a.m. to 4:30 p.m. Monday through Friday; 9 a.m. to 1 p.m. Saturday.

This outlet specializes in discontinued styles, liquidations and closeouts, so you can get some real deals.

Charlie's Second Hand Store

2227 Larimer St., Denver, 295-1781.

8 a.m. to 4:45 p.m. Monday through Friday; 8 a.m. to 3:45 p.m. Saturday.

Charlie's has been selling used tools for more than 45 years at half the price or less of what they sell for new. An electric circular saw, for example, can be had here for about $60.

Denver Brick Company

4225 Elati St., Denver, 433-8221; 402 Santa Fe Rd., Castle Rock, 688-6951.

Denver: 7:30 a.m. to 5 p.m. Monday through Friday; 8 a.m. to 1 p.m. Saturday. Castle Rock: 7:30 a.m. to 5 p.m. Monday through Friday; 8 a.m. to noon Saturday.

The Denver Brick Company has been part of Colorado since 1889. Its two brickyards are open to the public, and they occasionally have clearances, so watch the newspapers.

Discount Cabinets and Appliances

5969 Broadway, Denver, 292-9830.

8 a.m. to 5 p.m. Monday through Friday; 9 a.m. to 4 p.m. Saturday.

Forget buying appliances here unless you have access to a retail-tax license. All the cabinetry is available to the public, though. Lines include MasterCraft, Embassy, Midcontinent, Kraftmade and others, and discounts from "suggested retail" are generally in the 40 to 50% range.

Flooring Design Associates

3770 Paris St., Denver, 371-2929.

See Direct and Seasonal Sales.

At Flooring Design Associates they usually don't have retail sales, but in May there's a warehouse sale of remnant inventory. Merchandise includes carpet, ceramic tile, marble, Formica, vinyl floor coverings and cabinets. Supplies are limited. Call to get on the mailing list.

Front Range Lumber

1741 S. Wadsworth Blvd., Lakewood, 988-5980.

7:30 a.m. to 6 p.m. Monday through Friday; 8 a.m. to 5 p.m. Saturday; 10 a.m. to 3 p.m. Sunday.

Home improvers can save themselves the price of a power saw, to say nothing of the risk of bloodshed and the need for skill and effort, if they buy their lumber from a lumberyard like Front Range that will do custom cutting. Not all lumberyards have saws anymore; some of them can't even cut 2×4s so they'll fit into the station wagon. Front Range and a number of other lumberyards (check the *Yellow Pages*) will precut major projects for a fee. Front Range also offers free delivery, even for small orders.

HomeBase

1050 W. Hampden Ave., Englewood, 781-3600; 14000 E. Jewell Ave., Aurora, 750-1803; 5258 S. Wadsworth Blvd., Littleton, 973-6161; 7350 W. 52nd Ave., Arvada, 467-0111; 2855 S. Academy Blvd., Colorado Springs, (719) 390-3000.

7 a.m. to 9 p.m. Monday through Friday; 7 a.m. to 8 p.m. Saturday; 8 a.m. to 7 p.m. Sunday.

There seem to be acres of home-improvement items here. If you're a beginner, be sure to go at a slow time (not, for example, on Saturday morning) so that you can flag down some help. HomeBase can help with designing a project, and it offers installation services.

Home Clearance Center

2088 S. Huron, Denver, 777-1404.

9 a.m. to 6 p.m. Monday through Saturday.

Home Clearance Center offers new and used kitchen and bathroom cupboards from Republic, Aristocraft, Diamond and DeWills. Used cabinets sell at used prices, and new ones, except for Republic, sell at various discounts. If you don't buy through a contractor, there's a 5% surcharge.

Hugh M. Woods

13700 E. Colfax Ave., Aurora, 364-9353; 2150 S. Abilene St., Aurora, 751-8987; 6333 Lookout Road, Boulder, 530-4256; 9500 E. 104th Ave., Henderson, 287-3293; 6337 Federal Blvd., Denver, 426-0452; 2085 S. Sheridan Blvd., 988-3475; 1417 S. Holly St., Denver, 758-4024; 9700 E. Arapahoe Road, Englewood, 799-9600; 1420 Oak St., Lakewood, 238-8591; 4950 S. Kipling Blvd., Littleton, 972-4042; 4995 S. Santa Fe Drive, Littleton, 798-2463; 2390 W. 104th Ave., Thornton, 469-1776; 94000 Wadsworth Parkway, Broomfield, 425-8939; 12154 N. Dumont Way, Littleton, 791-3144; 5855 N. Academy Blvd., Colorado Springs, (719) 599-5400; 2425 E. Platte Pl., Colorado Springs, (719) 635-8974; 625 N. Murray Blvd., Colorado Springs, (719) 591-6700.

7 a.m. to 8 p.m. Monday through Friday; 7 a.m. to 6 p.m. Saturday; 9 a.m. to 5 p.m. Sunday.

There are more Hugh M. Woods stores than other hardware centers, so they're in more neighborhoods and they're smaller than the stores of the other hardware giants, Builder's Square and HomeBase. That means less selection but perhaps less anxiety, too. Hugh M. Woods has a great service for those who are considering a kitchen redo. They'll send out a designer, free, and the designer will produce a free, full-fledged computer drawing of what your new kitchen would look like. The service is free because they know people will feel obligated after having used so much of the designer's time and effort. You don't *have* to use them, though, and the drawing can help you solidify your ideas. We should note that we used Hugh M. Woods for a recent kitchen redo, and we were satisfied with the results.

Impo Glaztile

860 S. Jason St., Denver, 722-4627.

7:30 a.m. to 4:30 Monday through Friday; 9 a.m. to 1 p.m. Saturday.

Impo distributes Esquire, Graniti, Impo and Cerum, among others. The showroom is open to the public, but to buy you have to go through one of their dealers. But they'll rent tools and sell tile-setting necessities to anybody.

Interior designers

I recently heard from an interior designer who swears that consumers can do better buying through her than buying directly. The designer, Judy Shoppman Magara of MS Interiors in Aurora (750-5353), says she "recently redid a skylight shade for a client for under $200—(an outlet) had bid it at over $500." Says Magara, "With a high volume of sales, I can offer competitive prices and a quick production date (on window coverings). My product knowledge gives me the edge over most salespeople working in stores."

I've never used an interior designer, but Magara makes some good points. It seems logical that a well-selected interior designer, like a good travel agent, would know the industry and where the deals are. Before you spruce up your home, you may want to check the *Yellow Pages* under Interior Decorators and Designers. Do it after you've gotten some bids from companies that provide direct service, so you know the value of what you're shopping for. When you call, tell the designer that you're price shopping and listen for the reaction. Some designers, obviously, are more conscientious about saving money for their clients than others.

Another obvious advantage is that, through a designer with a retail-tax license, you gain access to many wholesale warehouses that are open only to the trade.

McMillan Sales Corp.

4801 E. 46th Ave., Denver, 399-8500.

7:30 a.m. to 5 p.m. Monday through Friday; 8 a.m. to 4 p.m. Saturday.

Before you buy sinks, faucets, toilets, bathtubs or similar necessities, check here. McMillan has a very good selection and good prices, and anyone can buy here.

Robinson Brick Company

1845 W. Dartmouth Ave., Denver, (800) 477-9002.

7 a.m. to 5 p.m. Monday through Friday.

Robinson, a family business in Colorado since 1880, works with all the big guys but also has a complete line of masonry tools and supplies and will offer counsel to the do-it-yourselfer. If you're planning a project that involves brick, give them a call. And here's a bit of Colorado trivia. Robinson Park in Denver's Hilltop neighborhood was once the site of Robinson Brick Co. When the company moved, the family donated the land to the city, which made it into a park and named the park for them.

Tile for Less

7450 W. 52nd Ave., Unit E, Denver, 431-0502; 1640 S. Abilene St., Aurora, 368-1963.

10 a.m. to 6 p.m. Monday through Friday; 10 a.m. to 5 p.m. Saturday; 11 a.m. to 4 p.m. Sunday.

A friend who redid her kitchen by herself swears by Tiles for Less. The store offers discounts on manufacturers' closeouts, discontinued styles, liquidations and overruns.

Wallpaper Warehouse

8223 S. Quebec St., Englewood, 796-9080.

9 a.m. to 8 p.m. Monday through Friday; 9 a.m. to 6 p.m. Saturday; 11 a.m. to 5 p.m. Sunday.

This is a national chain, begun in 1976, that is currently in the process of moving into Denver, where it eventually plans to have five stores. It specializes in discounted window coverings, wallpaper and borders.

Food

We can't tell you everything about saving money on groceries—that's another book or two. But here are some things we've learned:

•Buying in bulk can save money, particularly if you buy bulk for items that are expensive and on your grocery bill weekly, such as laundry detergent and disposable diapers. If you can keep a supply of such staples, you'll eventually notice the savings. But that doesn't mean that bulk is always the best way to buy. If we assume that items purchased in bulk are cheaper than items purchased in conventional sizes (and that's not always true), the issue becomes whether the savings outweigh the inconvenience, the possibility that the item's date will expire and the use of storage space.

I buy three basic categories of items in bulk: cleaning supplies, non-perishable meal builders and personal care items. The first category includes laundry supplies like detergent, refills for spray cleaners, toilet cleaner and trash bags. Non-perishable meal builders include items like rice, pasta, olive oil, tomato sauce, barbecue sauce, potato flakes and cooking oil. Personal care items include products like shampoo, toothpaste, toilet paper and soap.

There are some things that don't work well in bulk: anything that you don't use regularly; anything that you rotate for the sake of variety, such as cereal; anything that spoils, gets stale or needs to be refrigerated. And, unless it's on closeout, don't buy more of something before you've used it almost down to the last bit. Stockpiling is wasteful. And do you really want to leave your heirs 20 bottles of shampoo?

•Unit pricing isn't consistent within a store, much less between them. I don't know how many times I've given up on trying to compare prices when one item was unit priced by the ounce and the other by the pound. (My time is worth something, too.) Larger packages generally mean a lower cost per unit, with one notably consistent exception—tuna. Tuna comes in two size cans: 6 ounce and 9 ounce. Next time you're in the supermarket, do a unit-price comparison. The smaller can is invariably cheaper per ounce than the larger can.

•You're planning a big event—a wedding, an anniversary party, a holiday bash, a bar mitzvah. If you can do it at home or at another place where you can supply your own food and beverages, you can save lots of money over catering by buying everything yourself and hiring people to serve. Buy frozen hors d'oeuvres at Sam's Club or Price Club. Think about what you can buy wholesale or in cases. Check the *Yellow Pages* under wholesale food distributors. If you're buying big quantities, these places will probably be happy to oblige, although, as with other wholesale outlets, you may need to find someone with a retail-tax license to make the actual purchase.

Many liquor stores offer discounts of as much as 10% on cases. A case is only 12 bottles, and some places discount cases that contain bottles of different wines or that have liquor and wine together in the same case. Some stores also offer free counseling on how much and what to buy for the event you're planning, so do some phone shopping.

•Buy fresh salmon whole and ask the seafood clerk to filet it for you. You buy the whole fish, and they weigh it and charge you for everything, including head, tail and bones. You ask them to filet it. They discard the aforementioned parts, which, on a large salmon, amount to something more than a pound. Still, it's just a little cheaper than buying the filets, and much less trouble than fileting it yourself. I bought a whole salmon that was 6.5 lbs. The filets were 4.77 lbs. The whole fish was on sale for $2.99 per pound; steaks were $3.99; filets were $4.99. I got 4.77 lbs. of filets this way for $19.55. If I'd bought them straight out as filets, 4.77 lbs. would have been more than $22.

•Slim Fast powder (not Ultra Slim Fast) is essentially the same thing as Carnation Instant Breakfast, but at an average of 35¢ a serving for Slim Fast as opposed to 50¢ a packet for Instant Breakfast. Both are basically maltodextrin, a protein powder, plus sugar and flavorings. Slim Fast also has a bit more protein, vitamins and fiber than Instant Breakfast.

Enough philosophy. Here are a few places to find deals, particularly on food items that make good gifts, such as coffee, nuts and candy.

Boyer's Coffee Emporiums

747 S. Colorado Blvd., Denver; 7295 Washington St., Denver; 6820 S. University Blvd., Littleton; 289-3345 for all three.

7 a.m. to 5:30 Monday through Friday; 8 a.m. to 2 p.m. Saturday. Washington Street closes at 2 p.m. Saturday.

The best way we've found to buy premium coffee is in cases of ten 1-pound bags of Boyer's. That way, it's considerably cheaper than comparable brands would be in the stores, and each time you open a 1-pound bag, it's fresh. Boyer's also has spices at near-bulk prices and quantities (for example, a 14-oz. jar of seasoning salt for $3). And whenever you're in, check the area next to the cash register for 1-pound bags of ground coffee. If anything's there, it's less than half price.

Celestial Seasonings

4600 Sleepytime Drive, Boulder, 581-1202.

9 a.m. to 6 p.m. Monday through Friday; 9 a.m. to 5 p.m. Saturday.

Colorado-based Celestial Seasonings has a lovely factory store at its Boulder factory. Fresh boxes of its famous herb teas (24 bags) are $1.70; black and specialty teas are somewhat more. Check out the bin where factory overruns and crunched boxes are only $1 a box (limit six to a customer). There are also t-shirts, mugs, baskets and other gift items.

Colorado Nut Company

730 S. Jason St., Denver, 733-7311.

8 a.m. to 4:30 p.m. Monday through Friday.

This wholesaler sells cashews, pecans, walnuts, almonds and other nuts directly out of the roaster, as well as dried fruits and candies. Some prices are lower than retail, and others are not, but the product is always fresh.

Community Supported Agriculture

Blacksmith Ridge Farm, 5093 Nelson Road, Longmont, 80503, (303) 678-0399.

If you want to buy organic food directly from the farmer, call. Families buy a share, which consist of 10 lbs. of assorted produce a week, or a half share, 5 to 6 lbs. In the summer of 1994, a full share was $450 for 10 to 12 lbs. a week, a half share $250. The farm produces lettuce, spinach, radishes, peas, turnips, beets, carrots, beans, sweet corn, squash, pumpkins, strawberries, potatoes, garlic, herbs, cucumbers, tomatoes, peppers, eggplants, cabbage, cauliflower, broccoli, celery, brussel sprouts, brown eggs, peaches and cherries.

Dawn Food Products Service Center

11400 E. 51st Ave., Denver, 371-5100.

8 a.m. to noon and 1 p.m. to 3 p.m. Monday through Friday.

Dawn primarily serves the bakery and food service industry. They stock every baking need—sugar, vanilla, flour, etc.—but in huge bulk quantities. The smallest bag of flour is 50 lbs., and the smallest size of vanilla is a gallon! They also carry restaurant-quality frozen products such as pizza crust, cookies and croissants. A complete product guide is available at the store. Call ahead for prices.

Dietrich Chocolates and Espresso

1734 E. Evans Ave., Denver, 777-3358.

10 a.m. to 6:30 p.m. Monday through Saturday; noon to 6:30 p.m. Sunday.

The usual retail price for a 10-lb. block of chocolate for candymaking is $50. If you make your own candy, buy the chocolate here for $30.

Entenmann's/Oroweat Thrift Stores

5050 E. Evans Ave., Denver, 691-6342; 9192 W. 44th Ave., Wheat Ridge, 424-1432; 4715 Flintridge Dr., Colorado Springs (719) 528-8070.

Denver: 8:30 a.m. to 6 p.m. Monday through Friday; 9 a.m. to 5 p.m. Saturday and Sunday. Wheat Ridge: 9 a.m. to 5 p.m. except Wednesday, til 6 p.m., and Sunday, til 4 p.m.

You'll always save on bread and Entenmann's cakes here, and we've found it's the cheapest place in town to buy Boboli bread shells. Keep these stores in mind whenever you need bread or cake in quantity, because you get free merchandise with every $5 you spend. Sundays and Wednesdays feature additional discounts.

Farmers' markets

Farmers' markets offer fresh produce and an opportunity to chat with the people who grow it. They're tucked away in every corner of town, and they come and go, so finding one near you with hours that accommodate your needs can be a challenge. For a free list of more than 30 farmers' markets, send a request and a stamped, self-addressed envelope to Markets Division, Colorado Department of Agriculture, 700 Kipling St., Suite 4000, Lakewood 80215.

Gourmet Foods Warehouse

8223 S. Quebec St., Englewood, 796-7969.

9 a.m. to 9 p.m. Monday through Saturday; 10 a.m. to 7 p.m. Sunday.

There are some 6,000 square feet of hard-to-find non-perishable goodies in this locally owned operation. Since the emphasis is on items that are pricey to begin with, you probably won't be bowled over by the bargains. But the store claims to offer the best prices on the gourmet items it stocks, and there's a 10% discount on case purchases. Special orders are encouraged.

Great Harvest Bread Co.

8031 Wadsworth Blvd., Arvada, 420-0500; 765 S. Colorado Blvd., Denver, 778-8877; 5910 S. University Blvd., Littleton, 347-8767; 6924 N. Academy Blvd., Colorado Springs, (719) 528-6443; 3650 Austin Bluffs Pkwy., Colorado Springs, (719) 260-6960; 101 N. Tejon St., Colorado Springs, (719) 635-7379.

6 a.m. to 7 p.m. Monday through Friday; 6 a.m. to 6 p.m. Saturday.

Besides the kind of bread that seems like it really could be the staff of life, these places are sources of fresh-milled flour. Fresh-ground whole-wheat flour at the store in Arvada was $1.89 for five pounds last time we checked. Each of these stores is individually managed, so products, hours and prices vary somewhat.

Hammond Candy

2550 W. 29th Ave., Denver, 455-2320.

8 a.m. to 5:30 p.m. Monday through Friday; 10 a.m. to 3 p.m. Saturday.

The Hammond Candy Company, founded in 1920, is Denver's oldest candy manufacturer. The boxed and first-quality candy sold at this factory store is retail price. But you can buy premium chocolates here at $3.75 per 1-lb. bag if you're willing to buy seconds (imperfect shapes or sizes).

Harry & David

Castle Rock, 660-6651; Loveland, (970) 663-2990.

See Factory Outlet Malls for address, hours and directions.

Those Harry & David gift baskets containing fruit, meats, cheeses, cakes and more sell at these factory outlets for less than you'd pay through the catalog.

Jerry's Nut House

2101 Humboldt St., Denver, 861-2262.

8 a.m. to 5 p.m. Monday through Friday; 8 a.m. to 1 p.m. Saturday.

Jerry's Nut House packs the generic popcorn, cheese corn and caramel corn for Denver's major supermarkets and supplies nuts and other snacks for vending machines. All their products are produced fresh at this plant, and you can buy them at wholesale prices if you come down.

Membership warehouses

Price Club and Sam's Club.

See Discount Department Stores and Membership Warehouses for hours and locations.

People from Price Club and Sam's Club visit each other often to make sure their prices aren't too far apart. So you can be fairly sure that if you buy something at one place, it won't be much more at the other. When we surveyed the prices of 10 identical items (a book, paper towels, milk, cooking sauce, olive oil, sugar, broccoli, orange juice, sorbet and soda pop) bills of nearly $60 rang up within 25¢. You could save the cost of membership just by buying milk at a membership club weekly; it's a dollar less per gallon at Sam's or Price Club than it is in the supermarket. And if you're entertaining, check these places for frozen hors d'oeuvres.

Nutorama Little Nut Hut

7174 Washington St., Denver, 289-2820.

9 a.m. to 5:30 p.m. Monday through Friday.

Nutorama is a wholesale supplier of candies, nuts (roasted on these premises), dried fruit and trail mixes. The prices are not that low, but the product is fresh, and you can choose here from among 25 different kinds of trail mix. They also sell gift baskets.

Quiche Factory

7275 W. 88th Ave., Westminster, 431-4773.

8:30 a.m. to 6:30 p.m. Monday through Friday.

The Quiche Factory makes 14 varieties of deep-dish quiches, using only three eggs per quiche and 2% milk instead of cream. They're a good choice when entertaining.

Rocky Mountain Chocolate Factory

Castle Rock, 660-1320; Durango, (970) 259-1408; Silverthorne, (970) 468-9168.

See Factory Outlet Malls for address, hours and directions.

The chocolate and other candy sold here is made fresh on the premises. The prices are not significantly lower than they would be at any of the Rocky Mountain Chocolate Factories that dot Colorado's tourist towns.

Share Colorado

Sites all along the Front Range. Call 428-0400 or (800) 933-7427 to find one near you.

Would you work for food? Share Colorado, a project of Catholic Charities and Community Services, offers an opportunity to do just that. Members pay $13 and do two hours of community-service work (any kind—formal or informal) for each "share." Shares are distributed in the second half of each month. Anyone can join; there are no income restrictions. One month's share, for example, consisted of a 4-lb. package of chicken-leg quarters, 1 lb. of beef patties, 1 lb. of ground turkey, 1 lb. of chopped ham, 5 lbs. of potatoes, 2 lbs. onions, 1 head of lettuce, 4 tomatoes, 2 avocadoes, 2 zucchinis, 1 bunch of celery, 1 lb. of carrots, 3 lbs. of apples, 6 oranges, 5 nectarines, 1 cantaloupe, 8 peaches and an 18-ounce bottle of barbecue sauce.

Stephany's Chocolates

4969 Colorado Blvd., Denver, 355-1522.

8:30 a.m. to 5 p.m. Monday through Friday.

The Stephany's Chocolates factory outlet sells bagged "seconds" (in imperfect shapes or sizes) at half price. The store also sells boxed candy but at the same price you'd pay at a mall.

Sysco Food Stores

1440 W. 52nd Ave., Denver, 458-5005; 2191 S. Broadway, Denver, 733-2424; 10061 E. Colfax Ave., Aurora, 341-0456; 2325 E. Boulder, Colorado Springs, (719) 578-5939.

8 a.m. to 6 p.m. Monday through Friday; 8 a.m. to 5 p.m. Saturday; 10 a.m. to 4 p.m. Sunday.

Sysco has many deals as good as those at Sam's Club or Price Club, and you don't have to be a member; it's open to the public. The three Sysco Food Stores in the metro area are outlets for Nobel-Sysco Food Service, a food distributor for restaurants, institutions and grocery stores. The selection is limited to food and food-service related items (e.g., paper plates), but the stores don't just have huge cans labeled "Soup Base—Beef." They carry a variety of brands, fresh meat, some retail-size packages, dairy products, frozen prepared food, paper goods and produce. And if you call ahead, they'll get your order ready for you—no charge.

The Vintage Club

P.O. Box 151261, Lakewood, 80215-1261, 989-3338.

This group is dedicated to the proposition that even people who aren't wine snobs are better off if they know what tastes good. Membership ($25 annually for individuals, $35 for couples), includes a monthly 20-page newsletter that offers notice of events, recommendations on some 15 vintages and 10% discounts at selected liquor stores. If it keeps you from buying two bottles of undrinkable wine, the membership will pay for itself. To request one free newsletter, call the number above.

Vollmer's Cheesecake factory outlet

4850 E. 39th Ave. Denver, 388-8393.

9 a.m. to 5 p.m. Monday through Friday.

The wonderful cheesecake sold here is baked using European-style cream cheeses. Vollmer's makes at least 18 types of cheesecake— everything from plain (New York style) to chocolate, raspberry, cookies and cream, Gran Marnier and strawberry. Prices are good, too. A 10-inch 16-slice cheesecake is $12; a 6-inch unsliced cheesecake (serves six to eight) is $5; or you can get a six-slice sampler for $6. No credit cards; come with cash. The store has occasional specials and is always willing to let you sample the wares.

Women's Bean Project

2347 Curtis St., Denver, 292-1919.

8 a.m. to 5 p.m. Monday through Friday; 9 a.m. to 1 p.m. Saturday.

The prices at this outlet are the same as they are wherever soup packets from the Women's Bean Project are found. It is true that you could do better buying and mixing your own beans, but when you buy beans from the Women's Bean Project, you help impoverished and homeless women learn employable skills and get back on their feet.

Wonder-Hostess Thrift Shops

6680 Wadsworth, Arvada, 420-0998; 1695 Peoria, Aurora, 360-7998; 80 E. 62nd Ave., Denver, 428-7431; 11805 W. Colfax, Lakewood, 238-6102; 5002 N. Academy Blvd., Colorado Springs, (719) 598-5645; 1507 Dustry Dr., Colorado Springs, (719) 576-9259.

9 a.m. to 6 p.m. Monday through Saturday.

The stores have Wonder and Hostess products at about half of what they sell for in supermarkets, plus a variety of crackers, cookies, chips, candy and gift foods, some of which sell for reduced prices.

Books
and Paper

New Books

If you've got your eye on a current book but can't bring yourself to pay $35 for it, you don't need to resign yourself to being 249th on the waiting list at the library. There are stores that discount all bestsellers (Media Play, Barnes & Noble); stores that discount selected books (Capitol Hill Books, Park Hill Cooperative); stores that discount every book they sell (the Bookies, Sunnybooks for Kids); and stores that have lots and lots of remaindered (discontinued) and publishers' overrun titles (The Tattered Cover, Chinook). What's your pleasure? All of them combined mean that Colorado has lots of wonderful places for bargain-hunting booklovers to browse and buy. Don't forget King Soopers, Price Club and Sam's Club. They sell books at discount, too.

ABC Books and Posters

2550 S. Colorado Blvd., Denver, 759-0250.

9:30 a.m. to 9 p.m. Monday through Friday; 9:30 a.m. to 6 p.m. Saturday; noon to 5 p.m. Sunday.

If the parents in your child's class are collecting money for a teacher gift, consider purchasing a gift certificate at ABC Books and Posters. That memorable educator will get more bang for the buck at this independent bookstore, which gives teachers a 20% discount on books and a 10% discount on framing. ABC also has a good selection of discounted books.

Barnes & Noble

14015 E. Exposition Ave., Aurora, 366-8928; 1741 28th St., Boulder, 444-2501; 960 S. Colorado Blvd., Glendale, 691-2998; 8555 E. Arapahoe Road, Greenwood Village, 796-8851; 5392 S. Wadsworth Blvd., Littleton, 972-1468; 6925 W. 88th Ave., Westminster, 424-2493.

Greenwood Village and Denver: 9 a.m. to 11 p.m. daily. Aurora: 9 a.m. to 9 p.m. daily. All other stores: 9 a.m. to 11 p.m. Monday through Saturday; 9 a.m. to 9 p.m. Sunday.

Barnes & Noble is a discount outlet. Paperbacks are list price, but all hard-bound books are reduced by at least 20%. Hard-cover bestsellers are 30% off; paperback bestsellers are 20% off. There's a large selection of discount, remaindered and overstocked titles, and books on a changing staff-recommended list go at 30% off.

The Bookies

4315 E. Mississippi Ave., Glendale, 759-1117.

10 a.m. to 6 p.m., Monday through Saturday; noon to 5 p.m. Sunday.

Everything at this store sells at 15% off the suggested retail price. The bookstore is geared for children, with a particularly comprehensive selection of primers for those kids who are just on the verge of reading. There's also a decent-size adult selection, and they'll special order books at the same 15% off. We like to buy gift certificates here because, with the discount, the recipient gets more for the money. There are also toys. And, to meet the challenge of nearby Barnes & Noble, there's a 30% discount on bestsellers.

Book Warehouse

Castle Rock, 688-8085.

See Factory Outlet Malls for address, hours and directions.

Major publishers with overruns and remaindered copies ship their books, software, calendars and such to the Book Warehouse. The discounts are 10% to 90%—but any items reduced by 90% aren't selling at retail anywhere anymore. The best deal we found was on calendars. The one we bought was about the half the price that Sam's Club had it for.

Capitol Hill Books

300 E. Colfax Ave., Denver, 837-0700.

10 a.m. to 6 p.m. daily.

Capitol Hill Books is chiefly a used bookstore, but it orders new books as a service to its customers. That service blossomed, and now the store sends in its orders every Tuesday, and it usually gets the books back within five days. The staff will order anything but textbooks, and all new books are discounted by 20%. There's also a hand-picked selection of new books in the store, which are also 20% off.

Chinook Bookshop

210 N. Tejon, Colorado Springs, (719) 635-1195; (800) 999-1195.

9 a.m. to 7 p.m. Monday through Friday; 9 a.m. to 6 p.m. Saturday; noon to 4 p.m. Sunday.

Unfortunately, I can't tell you about every neat, cozy bookstore in every corner of Colorado, but I grew up in Colorado Springs, and I misspent the best part of my youth in this store. You'll like it, too. Chinook is service-oriented, and there's a good selection of remaindered titles. Their specialty is Western Americana, and they have a fine selection of maps and globes.

Colorado Historical Society

1300 Broadway, Denver, 866-4993.

10 a.m. to 4:30 p.m. Monday through Saturday; noon to 4:30 p.m. Sunday.

This store has a wonderful selection of books on Colorado history and other Western subjects, and members of the State Historical Society get a 10% discount.

Consumer Information Center

Post Office Box 100, Pueblo, 81002.

This U.S. government office in Pueblo has a huge array of free or very inexpensive consumer information publications. A great free resource is the *Consumer's Resource Handbook*, which has information on such topics as avoiding fraud, complaining effectively, car repair, telemarketing, 900 calls and home financing. The handbook also includes a consumer assistance directory with lists of 800 numbers for many national corporations, consumer organizations and regulatory agencies. To get a copy, just request one by writing to: Handbook, Consumer Information Center, Pueblo 81009.

Hatch's Bookstore

2700 S. Colorado Blvd. (University Hills Mall), Denver, 757-1028.

9:30 a.m. to 9 p.m. Monday through Friday; 9:30 to 6 p.m. Saturday; noon to 5 p.m. Sunday.

Hatch's has a good selection of value-priced and remaindered books, and the valued-reader program offers a $10 gift certificate for every $100 of books purchased. There's also a heck of a sale just before the holidays.

McKinzey-White

8005 N. Academy Blvd., Colorado Springs (719) 590-1700.

9:30 a.m. to 9 p.m. Monday through Friday; 9:30 a.m. to 9 p.m. Saturday; 11 a.m. to 6 p.m. Sunday.

McKinzey-White, which claims to have the largest selection of books in El Paso County, is also a discounter. All hard-covers are 10% off every day; all hard-cover bestsellers are 20% off; and all paperback bestsellers are 10% off. The store also has a large selection of sale books and publishers' overstocks.

Media Play

13600 E. Mississippi Ave., Aurora, 338-1970; 702 16th St., Denver, 893-1977; 9150 Wadsworth Parkway, Westminster, 456-1991; 8055 W. Bowles Ave., Littleton, 933-7510; 651 N. Academy Blvd., Colorado Springs, (719) 573-1977.

Downtown: 9 a.m. to 7 p.m. Monday through Saturday; noon to 5 p.m. Sunday. Others: 10 a.m. to 10 p.m. Monday through Saturday; 11 a.m. to 6 p.m. Sunday.

All *New York Times* bestsellers are 40% off; paperbacks are 10% off every day; and hard-cover books are 15% off every day. There's a well-stocked newsstand, and magazines are reduced by 10%. Media Play also carries hurt books, remaindered books, recycled library books and other bargain books. The stores also have music, videotape and computer software at similar discounts. Media Play is part of the immense Minneapolis-based

Musicland Corp., parent company for Musicland, Sam Goody, SunCoast and On Cue.

Open Door Bookstore

1032 S. Gaylord St., Denver, 744-6930.

10 a.m. to 7 p.m. Monday through Friday; 10 a.m. to 6 p.m. Saturday; 10 a.m. to 4 p.m. Sunday.

The focus of this store is on personal growth, self-help and spiritual issues. There's always a decent selection of discounted books, too.

Park Hill Cooperative Bookstore

4620 E. 23rd Ave., Denver, 355-8508

10 a.m. to 6 p.m. Tuesday through Friday; 10 a.m. to 5 p.m. Saturday

Membership is $15 annually; $7.50 for seniors or students. Members participate in special deals and get advance notice of sales. Non-members also can shop at the store, which usually features a selection of bargain titles.

Poor Richard's Bookstore

320 N. Tejon St., Colorado Springs, (719) 578-0012.

10 a.m. to 8 p.m. daily.

This discount-oriented store offers up to 65% off on list prices and also buys and sells used books. The top 10 on the *New York Times* list are 35% off; all new books, including paperbacks, in the store are reduced by at least 10%. They also show movies and have a restaurant.

Publishers Outlet

Silverthorne, (970) 468-8417.

See Factory Outlet Malls for address, hours and directions.

Most of the books sold at Publishers Outlet come from the parent company, Advance Marketing Services Inc., which also provides books to such discounters as Price Club and Sam's Club. When titles go off cycle at those outlets, they're sent here and marked down by 30% to 75%. The outlet also picks up discount books ordered directly from publishing houses, and these titles may be new on the market. Videos a couple of years old sell here for $2.99 to $7.99.

Publishers Warehouse

Loveland, (970) 593-0620.

See Factory Outlet Malls for address, hours and directions.

Books, software and book-related gifts are sold here at 20% to 90% less than suggested retail. The deeply discounted items are publishers' overruns or remaindered books. Publishers Warehouse will special order a book, then sell it to you at 10% off. *New York Times* bestsellers are discounted by 10%.

Sunnybooks for Kids

4233 S. Buckley Road, Aurora, 690-9590.

10 a.m. to 8 p.m. Monday through Friday; 10 a.m. to 6 p.m. Saturday; noon to 5 p.m. Sunday.

Rebecca of Sunnybooks always sells her books at a 10% discount, and prices go down further when she has a sale. There are books for every age category, from board books for babies up to young-adult paperback novels. There's also a frequent-buyer incentive card for the store's selection of stuffed animals, posters, gifts and toys. The birthday club offers birthday children a dollar off a purchase of $5 or more.

The Tattered Cover

2955 E. First Ave. (Cherry Creek North), Denver, 322-7727; 1628 16th St. (downtown), Denver, 436-1070.

Cherry Creek North: 9:30 a.m. to 11 p.m. Monday through Saturday; 10 a.m. to 6 p.m. Sunday. Downtown: 9 a.m. to 9 p.m. Monday through Thursday; 9:30 p.m. to 11 p.m. Friday and Saturday; 10 a.m. to 6 p.m. Sunday.

The Tattered Cover's knowledgeable staff, overstuffed chairs and reading lamps invite readers, and that's how the store manages to continue as the Rocky Mountain West's largest and favorite bookstore amid onslaughts from discounters. But if discount is what you're looking for, there are lots of remaindered and publishers' overstock titles at both stores. The huge selection at the main store is on the second floor.

U.S. Government Bookstore

1961 Stout St., Denver, 844-3964.

8:30 a.m. to 4:30 p.m. Monday through Friday.

You're always hearing about U.S. government studies, maps and publications. Here, in a little store on the ground level of a federal office building, you can find them on display and buy them. You can also get a free copy of the U.S. Government Information catalog.

University of Denver Bookstore

2050 E. Evans Ave., Denver, 871-3251.

8:30 a.m. to 6 p.m. Monday through Thursday; 8:30 a.m. to 5 p.m. Friday; 10 to 3 p.m. Saturday.

Software manufacturers want college students to use their software, so they offer very inexpensive student versions and sell them at college bookstores. If you're shopping for software, check here or at any college bookstore near you. Other good bets include college bookstores at Auraria, Boulder, Fort Collins and Greeley.

Used Books

Bookstores, particularly the ones that sell used books, come and go more quickly than practically anything but restaurants. This is a very volatile business, so a listing, by nature, may be outdated almost as soon as it's printed.

Used bookstores sometimes congregate. For example, there are several nifty places on South Broadway at about Bayaud, and not all of them are listed. Unfortunately, there's no space to list every cozy book nook in Colorado. The effort would be somewhat pointless, too, because you just can't shop well for used books unless you're a self-starter who's willing to devote time for leisurely personal exploration. We can provide a little direction, though. First, check the phone book under Books–Used, for shops near your house. Keep your eyes open for other sources in your neighborhood, too. Cheap, readable used books are easy to find. Among the best places to troll for goodies are thrift stores, garage sales, estate sales and church or school sales. People occasionally discard some treasures when they decide to clean off their shelves—and even if a book isn't worth much monetarily, if it's something you want to read, it's a treasure to you.

Libraries are also a good source of what rare-book sellers call "reading copies," which means they'll never be valuable, but they've got all their pages. In these tight times, many libraries around town get additional support from the sale of used books. When you walk into a library, look around to see if there's a rack of used books that have been either discarded from the collection or donated by readers. Most branches of the Denver Public Library have a few books on sale most of the time. (We especially like the deals at the University Hills branch, where a "Bag o' Horror" goes for a dollar.) The Englewood Public Library, 3400 S. Elati St., usually has some books for sale. And be sure to look for the Denver Public Library's used book sale in midsummer (usually July).

It's possible to make a few bucks by taking your finds to the places that buy used books outright. Don't plan on getting rich this way. If you want to learn about the strange (at least when it's fictionalized) world of Denver book scouting, read *Booked to Die* by Denver book lover and sometimes store owner

John Dunning. It's a *roman à clef*. See if you can guess which of the stores listed below are fictionalized in it.

Aberdeen Bookstore

1360-H W. Littleton Blvd., Littleton, 795-1890.

11 a.m. to 5 p.m. Monday through Saturday; noon to 4 p.m. Sunday.

There's a large general stock on such topics as history, the military, philosophy, Americana and literature. The store will buy books outright, and a representative will come to your home to do it. The store carries new books, mostly on World War II topics, and it discounts them by 10% to 20%.

Abracadabra Book Search and Bookshop

3827 W. 32nd Ave., Denver, 455-0317.

8 a.m. to 7 p.m. Monday through Friday; 9 a.m. to 4 p.m. Saturday.

If you're looking for an obscure, out-of-print book, Abracadabra can probably find it for you. The search is free. Once the first book that you're seeking is found, you have to pay a $10 deposit. That $10 will go toward the purchase price. And if you use Abracadabra again, you don't have to pay a deposit.

Aion Bookshop

1235 Pennsylvania Ave., Boulder, 443-5763.

10 a.m. to 7 p.m. Monday through Saturday; noon to 6 p.m. Sunday.

This store specializes in scholarly and academic topics; it also carries books on general topics such as travel, history and science, as well as some collectibles. There are about 30,000 volumes.

Books-Books-Books (Books Unlimited)

2070 S. University Blvd., Denver, 744-7180.

10 a.m. to 6 p.m. Monday through Saturday; noon to 5 p.m. Sunday.

Perhaps because it's practically on the campus of the University of Denver, this store specializes in academic books and literature. It has perhaps 70,000 volumes. Management will buy books outright or take them in trade.

Books Etc.

878 E. 88th Ave., Thornton, 288-2499.

10 a.m. to 6 p.m. Tuesday through Saturday.

You can find just about anything in this little shop—self-help, romances, literature, cookbooks, history, true crime—in both paperback and hard-bound. Paperbacks are traded at 25% of the face value and sold at half the face value.

The Book Forum

709 E. Sixth Ave., Denver, 837-9069.

Noon to 5 p.m. Monday through Saturday.

The Book Forum has been at the same location for 16 years offering chiefly scholarly books: history, fiction, philosophy, art, theater. Although the books are sorted by category, it helps to have an appetite for rummaging. A friend in the know says this is a great place to go treasure hunting.

The Book Outlet

14573 E. Alameda Ave., Aurora, 366-2434.

10 a.m. to 1 p.m. Wednesday; 10 a.m. to 4 p.m. Saturday.

This used bookstore is operated by the Friends of the Aurora Public Library. The collection is composed of discards from the library and donations from individuals. Paperbacks are 50¢ or three for a $1; hardbacks are $1; a few more valuable items are individually priced. There's also a selection of "oddball" books for a nickel. The store is staffed by volunteers, and profits fund library programs.

Book World

2223 S. Peoria St., Aurora, 695-1235.

10 a.m. to 6 p.m. Monday through Saturday.

This family-oriented bookstore has thousands of volumes with a little bit of everything, including cookbooks, children's books, self-help, philosophy, history, fiction, military history, art, true crime and mysteries, plus lots of first editions.

Capitol Hill Books

300 E. Colfax Ave., Denver, 837-0700.

10 a.m. to 6 p.m. daily.

This used bookstore right across the street from the Capitol building has a wonderful selection in a broad range of categories, and it will buy fiction and non-fiction titles outright. You can get twice as much for the books, though, if you'll take the value in trade for other used books. (Please, no textbooks, magazines or romances.)

Collegiate Book Basement

1400 Market St., Denver, 446-2665.

9 a.m. to 5 p.m. Monday through Friday.

This store specializes in textbooks for the Auraria campus and has used texts. It also carries new general-interest books and some computer software.

Colorado Pioneer Books

4755 S. Broadway, Englewood, 789-0379.

10 a.m. to 5 p.m. Tuesday through Friday; 10 a.m. to 4 p.m. Saturday.

This store specializes in rare and out-of-print books, especially Western history. It's been at the same Englewood location for 12 years.

Denver Book Mall

1232 E. Colfax Ave., Denver, 832-6163.

10 a.m. to 6 p.m. Monday through Saturday; 11 a.m. to 4 p.m. Sunday.

The Denver Book Mall is a co-op for more than 20 vendors, many of whom specialize in collectible books. There's a computer catalog to aid in title and author searches.

Four Corners Bookshop

119 E. Bijou St., Colorado Springs, (719) 635-4514.

9:30 a.m. to 7 p.m. daily.

In addition to a large selection of used books on diverse topics, this store handles new discounted books, including remainders and publishers' overstocks.

Gibson's Bookstore

1404 Larimer St. in Larimer Square, Denver, 620-0034.

10 a.m. to 7 p.m. Monday through Friday; 10 a.m. to 6 p.m. Saturday; noon to 5 p.m. Sunday.

The basement of Gibson's is devoted to textbooks, including used, and this store's selection is guaranteed to be lowest-priced among the stores serving the Auraria campus. The upstairs is a general-interest bookstore that includes bestsellers, stationery and greeting cards.

Half Price Books

16 E. Girard Ave., Englewood, 761-6474.

10 a.m. to 6 p.m. Tuesday through Friday; 10 a.m. to 5 p.m. Saturday and Sunday.

Unlike most used bookstores, Half Price Books does not offer trade-ins. If they like the books you have to sell, they buy them outright. They also handle some new computer books.

Hooked on Books

3918 Maizeland Road, Colorado Springs, (719) 596-1621.

10 a.m. to 6 p.m. Monday through Saturday; til 9 p.m. Friday.

This Colorado Springs shop claims it has one of the largest selections of used books in Colorado with almost half a million volumes, including bestsellers, collectibles, classics, children's books, science fiction, mysteries and Westerns.

Ichabod's Books

2 S. Broadway, Denver, 778-7579

10 a.m. to 7 p.m. Monday through Friday; 10 a.m. to 6 p.m. Saturday; 11 to 5 p.m. Sunday.

This is a pleasant place to browse for literature or academic titles. There's a surprisingly large Judaica collection and an extensive selection of art books. This is also one of the few places in town where you can still buy long-playing records, and they're only $1. Ichabod's will pay cash for used books. When you're done shopping, sit down and have a cup of cappuchino at Mrs. Crane's, which is part of the store.

Linda Lebsack Books

1228 E. Colfax Ave., Denver, 832-7190.

11 a.m. to 5 p.m. weekdays; 11 a.m. to 2 p.m. Saturday and by appointment; closed Wednesday and Sunday.

When Denver book and art legend Fred Rosenstock died, Linda Lebsack, who worked with Rosenstock during the last decade of his life, bought his store. She prints several catalogs of books on special topics, including railroads, American art and Western history, especially focusing on Colorado. Lebsack is a leader in the Colorado Antiquarian Booksellers Association. You may write to her (the ZIP is 80218), or call for a complete list of member bookstores.

Mad Dog & the Pilgrim Bookshop

5926 and 5920 E. Colfax Ave., Denver, 329-8011.

11 a.m. to 5 p.m. Tuesday through Saturday.

This bookshop is oriented to collectors, but just plain readers will also find a welcoming atmosphere, complete with hot coffee.

National Book Exchange and Abbey Road Bookstore

1813 Pearl St., Boulder, 465-5282, 939-8537, (800) 713-8539.

10 a.m. to 7 p.m. Monday through Saturday; noon to 5 p.m. Sunday.

The National Book Exchange buys and sells used and new textbooks for kindergarten through graduate school. Abbey Road specializes in scholarly books, collectibles and quality CDs.

Park Hill Cooperative Bookstore

4620 E. 23rd Ave., Denver, 355-8508.

10 a.m. to 6 p.m. Tuesday through Friday; 10 a.m. to 5 p.m. Saturday.

A $15 annual membership in this cooperative entitles members to trade used books two-for-one at no cost, to get an additional discount on new and used books, and to participate in the store's sales, which can be very good. Non-members also can shop at this non-profit community store, which usually features a selection of remaindered and new titles. Membership is half price for seniors and students with a valid ID.

Red Letter Second Hand Books

1737 Pearl St., Boulder, 938-1778.

10 a.m. to 9 p.m. Monday through Saturday; noon to 5 p.m. Sunday.

This general used bookstore carries an eclectic collection including children's books, technical books, fiction, Eastern religion and psychology.

Stage House Books and Prints

1039 Pearl St., Boulder, 447-1433.

10 a.m. to 9:30 p.m. Sunday through Thursday; 10 a.m. to 11 p.m. Friday and Saturday.

Stage House is a collector's place, specializing in out-of-print and rare books, but there are plenty of reading copies, too. There's also a huge inventory of art and collectibles.

Trails West

1032 S. Boulder Road, Louisville, 666-7107.

10 a.m. to 6 p.m. Monday through Friday; 10 a.m. to 4 p.m. Saturday.

Trails West specializes in books about the West, it has a catalog, and it has been around for 15 years. The store is not a discounter, but any book on the American West may be available here, even if it's new.

Willow Creek Books

8100 S. Akron St., Suite 310, Englewood, 790-7530.

11:30 a.m. to 6 p.m. Monday through Friday; 10 a.m. to 6 p.m. Saturday.

Almost all the books are hard-bound, and about 85% of them are used, rare, out of print or collectible. There are also some new books, particularly fiction, mystery, poetry and illustrated children's books. The store also offers appraisals and special orders.

Paperback Trading Stores

These stores are great places for readers whose thirst for books is unquenchable. Generally, they take paperbacks in for a credit and then sell or trade them at a higher price. Pricing policies vary, but these places are second only to the public library for feeding a reading habit cheaply. We actually find them cheaper, particularly for children's books, because kids have a knack for losing their library books—and replacing them or paying fines can get into real money. Many stores also have racks of books that are too dog-eared to resell. At the Book Rack, for example, these go for a quarter—and they read just fine.

Book Exchange

7800 W. Jewell Ave., Unit I, Lakewood, 989-2338.

10 a.m. to 7 p.m. Monday; 10 a.m. to 5 p.m. Tuesday through Saturday.

Bring in one used paperback and pay an additional 50¢ to get another one in exchange, or buy outright at half the cover price. There are also sale racks of books at four for a dollar or ten for a dollar.

The Booklovers

145 S. Sheridan Blvd., Lakewood, 274-7557.

10 a.m. to 8 p.m. Monday through Saturday; noon to 5 p.m. Sunday.

The Booklovers specializes in romances and carries the series romances all the way back to the first ones. It also has thrillers, Westerns, science fiction, horror, mystery and true crime. Books are $1.50, and people who bring books in can either get money for them or buy books for 50¢.

Book Nook

1886 W. 92nd Ave., Federal Heights, 650-8379.

10 a.m. to 5 p.m. Monday through Saturday.

The store offers a credit of 25% of the cover price, and books cost 50% of the cover price; there's also a 25¢ rack, and grab-bag books are as little as 5¢. There are some 10,000 books here, with an emphasis on romances, but mysteries, Westerns, adventures, historic novels, horror and science fiction are also well-represented.

Book Rack

4329 S. Buckley Road, Aurora, 690-5311; 1930 S. Havana Ave., Aurora, 752-4499; 4335 N. Academy Blvd., Colorado Springs, (719) 593-9463; 2710 S. Academy Blvd., Colorado Springs (719) 390-7657; 2382 S. Colorado Blvd., Denver, 756-9891; 2020 S. College Ave., Fort Collins, (970) 484-7898; 1229 Eighth Ave., Greeley, (970) 356-8961; 1535 S. Kipling Parkway, Lakewood, 988-0040; 138 E. 29th St., Loveland (970) 667-0118.

Lakewood and Denver: 10 a.m. to 6 p.m. Monday through Saturday. Call other stores for hours; they vary.

The stores in this nationally franchised operation offer credit for one-quarter of the book's face value and sell or trade at half the cover price. Children's books can be purchased only for credits from trading in children's books, and romance credits can be used only for more romances.

Book Scene of Parker

10441 S. Parker Road, Parker, 840-8056.

11 a.m. to 6 p.m. Monday through Friday; 10 a.m. to 4 p.m. Saturday.

The store offers some 10,000 titles, including hard-bound books, children's books and a corner stocked with books on crafts. Paperbacks sell for half the cover price, and tradable books get you a 25%-of-cover-price credit.

Book Swap

1201 16th St., Denver (Tabor Center), 893-2116; 5801 W. 44th Ave., Denver (Lakeside Mall), 477-6742; 8501 Bowles Ave., Littleton (Southwest Plaza), 933-6105; 10590 Melody Drive, Northglenn (Northglenn Mall), 252-1449.

Mall hours for each mall. Lakeside Mall, for example: 10 a.m. to 8 p.m. Monday through Friday; 10 a.m. to 6 p.m. Saturday; 11 a.m. to 6 p.m. Sunday.

Each store in this chain offers some 15,000 titles. The emphasis is on reading pleasure, not collectibles.

Denver Book Fair

44 S. Broadway, 777-9946.

10 a.m. to 7 p.m. Monday through Friday; 10 a.m. to 6 p.m. Saturday; noon to 5 p.m. Sunday.

This crowded spot is perfect for the reader who likes to get lost in the stacks. Anyone who might count could possibly find as many as a million books. People who bring in paperback books get credit for about a quarter of the price, and the books sell for about half the cover price. The store also carries hard-bound books and vintage magazines.

The Paperback

1500 W. Littleton Blvd., Littleton, 797-2243.

10 a.m. to 5:30 p.m. Monday through Saturday.

This is one of the few used-paperback stores that offers a book-search service. The store specializes in paperback collectibles and stocks around 45,000 volumes. The basic trading structure is two for one.

The Paperback Shack

3100 S. Sheridan Blvd., Denver, 922-7831.

10 a.m. to 8 p.m. Monday through Friday; 10 to 5 p.m. Saturday; noon to 5 p.m. Sunday.

This store trades and sells new and used hardback and paperback books and has thousands of titles. Used books are taken only in trade; credits are 25% of face value. The credits go into a credit ledger and are good on used books or audiotapes. New paperbacks are 10% off cover price. Hardback bestsellers are always 25% off the cover price.

Science Fiction Plus

210 S. Broadway, Denver, 871-9293.

11 a.m. to 7 p.m. Monday through Friday; 10 a.m. to 6 p.m. Saturday; 1 to 6 p.m. Sunday

This tiny store (700 square feet) carries new and used paperback and hard-bound books, as well as magazines, including a lot of collector-quality pulp magazines dating back as far back as the '30s. The emphasis is on science fiction, fantasy, horror and pulp.

Party, Holiday, Office and School Supplies

Smart shoppers shop for holiday cards and wrapping paper the day after the holidays and get everything at half price. The nice thing about Christmas, Hanukkah, Valentine's Day and Mother's Day is that they just keep coming around. Only one caution: keep everything in one reasonably accessible place so you know where to find it from one year to the next. And don't be too much of a tightwad; don't give old Christmas candy on Valentine's Day.

Since people buy school supplies only once a year, they don't know what they should cost. As a public service last fall, we ran around town and surveyed "apples-to-apples" prices on a six-item list at some familiar stores. Surprisingly, Target came out the clear winner, beating Kmart, Office Depot, Office Max and Walgreen Drugs (in fairness, Target was having a sale that week). Target isn't included in this section, but don't forget it's out there.

We're hoping that the following are a few places you may not know as well. Have fun comparing prices.

Current Factory Outlets

1250 S. Abilene, Aurora, 745-0525; 3550 S. Inca St., Englewood, 762-9803; 98 Wadsworth Blvd., Lakewood, 274-0718; 5654 W. 88th Ave., Westminster, 427-2616; 514 S. College Ave., Fort Collins, (970) 221-1176; 3106 N. Stone Ave., Colorado Springs, (719) 630-7446; 1005 Woodmen Road, Colorado Springs, (719) 548-9487.

9:30 a.m. to 7 p.m. Monday through Friday; 9:30 a.m. to 6 p.m. Saturday; 11 a.m. to 5 p.m. Sunday.

Current is a company based in Colorado Springs that sells its greeting cards, small gift items and wrapping paper nationwide through catalogs. It has factory outlets along the Front Range where, on a good day, you can find perfectly good birthday cards for 20¢. This is also a good place to find inexpensive gifts for teachers. Be sure to watch the newspapers for Current's ads. They have lots of sales on holiday items *before* the holiday. By the way, the factory outlet that's actually at the factory is the one on North Stone Avenue in Colorado Springs.

147

Dixon Paper Stores

106 S. Santa Fe Drive, 777-6688; 1985 S. Havana St., Aurora, 368-4545; 5290 Vance St., Arvada, 940-6167; 1960 32nd St., Boulder, 786-8703; 2441 N. Union Blvd., Colorado Springs, (719) 577-4260.

7:30 a.m. to 5:30 p.m., Monday through Friday; 9 a.m. to 1 p.m. Saturday.

Ever had a really big package to wrap? It's a pain to tape together a large enough piece of gift-wrapping paper out of those sheets they sell in card shops, and a 2-foot roll doesn't cover much territory, either. You can find rolls of gift wrap 50 feet long at Dixon Paper Stores, and they're only $8 to $15 each.

Kogle Cards

1498 S. Lipan St., Denver, 698-9007.

8 a.m. to 5 p.m. Monday through Friday.

This local manufacturer caters mostly to businesses that order imprinted cards for clients, but the showroom is open to the public and you can buy one card there, if that's your pleasure. The price depends on how many you order. A hundred birthday cards, for example, are about $65; less if you order more.

Leanin' Tree Inc.

6055 Longbow Drive, Boulder, 530-1442.

8 a.m. to 4:30 p.m. Monday through Friday; 10 a.m. to 4 p.m. Saturday.

Leanin' Tree makes cards that feature original Western art, and the originals of those artworks are housed at this private museum. The shop for the museum sells cards. The selection is complete, but the cost is retail: $1.50 each.

Office Depot

7330 W. 52nd Ave., Arvada, 423-0411; 1905 28th St., Boulder, 938-1800; 1045 N. Academy Blvd., Colorado Springs, (719) 673-5221; 615 N. Chelton Road, Colorado Springs, (719) 380-1200; 600 E. Colfax Ave., Denver, 832-2582; 8930 E. Hampden Ave., Denver, 741-0091; 1350 16th St., Denver, 571-0730; 1090 W. Hampden Ave., Englewood; 770 S. Colorado Blvd., Glendale, 782-9400; 8525 E. Arapahoe Rd., Englewood (Denver Tech), 741-0091; 650 S. Wadsworth Blvd., Lakewood, 727-8808; 142 Kennedy Drive, Northglenn, 252-9005. For information on other locations, call (800) 685-8800.

8 a.m. to 9 p.m. Monday through Friday; 9 a.m. to 9 p.m. Saturday; 11 a.m. to 6 p.m. Sunday; some variations.

Although Office Depot usually focuses on business supplies, in August it stocks up on such unbusinesslike items as wide-lined notepaper, washable markers and pocket folders featuring pictures of Barbie. There's a low-price guarantee. Office Depot will refund any difference between what they charge and any lower price you can prove exists out there. Always check the clearance tables at the front of the store for slow movers; we've found good deals on software, mugs, candy and personal organizers.

Office Max

2880 S. Colorado Blvd., Denver, 758-3767; 6791 W. Colfax Ave., Lakewood, 232-5101; 14030 E. Mississippi Ave., Aurora, 752-0040; 8657 Sheridan Blvd., Westminster, 650-2449; 343 S. Broadway, Denver, 722-1411; 823 N. Academy Blvd., Colorado Springs, (719) 380-1300. For information on other locations, call (800) 688-6278.

8 a.m. to 9 p.m. Monday through Friday; 9 a.m. to 9 p.m. Saturday; 11 a.m. to 6 p.m. Sunday.

Office Max compares to Office Depot in most ways. These two giant chains try to keep tabs on one another's prices, so it's not likely that something is going to be significantly more expensive at one than at the other. Selections vary, of course. Office Max is good place to shop for inexpensive office furniture, like a cheap bookcase for a child's room.

Oriental Trading Co.

(800) 228-2269.

This Omaha-based mail-order company is a great source of inexpensive favors for children's birthday parties—like soccer-ball erasers for $1.80 a dozen or tiny candy-filled "Our Earth" design yo-yos for $1.50 a dozen. Just call to request a catalog. Remember not to give any small toys to children under the age of 3. And beware of shipping costs. They do add to the final price.

Paper Outlet

Castle Rock, 688-8150; Loveland, (970) 593-0784.

See Factory Outlet Malls for address, hours and directions.

This shop offers as much as a 60% discount on party supplies. Boxed Christmas cards are reduced by 60% or more, and Gibson, Cleo and Gallant greeting cards are always half price.

Paper Warehouse

16821 E. Iliff Ave., Aurora, 369-6961; 8545 E. Arapahoe Rd., Greenwood Village, 741-5649; 8555 W. Belleview Ave., Littleton, 972-3349; 8591 Harlan St., Westminster, 426-6075; 3316 Youngfield Rd., Wheat Ridge, 232-4939.

Greenwood Village and Littleton stores: 9 a.m. to 9 p.m. Monday through Friday; 9 a.m. to 5:30 p.m. Saturday; 11 a.m. to 4 p.m. Sunday. Slightly different hours at other stores.

Paper Warehouse stores carry a vast array of stuff for various holidays, as well as food (well, snacks), home and office supplies. Gallant greeting cards are always 50% off.

Party America

13686 E. Alameda Ave., Aurora, 343-0042; 545 S. Broadway, Denver, 871-0880; 98 Wadsworth Blvd., Lakewood, 231-9844; 883 N. Academy Blvd., Colorado Springs, (719) 596-5406; 4360 S. College Ave., Fort Collins, (970) 223-1736.

9:30 a.m. to 9 p.m. Monday through Friday; 9:30 to 6 p.m. Saturday; 11 a.m. to 5 p.m. Sunday.

The Paramount line of greeting cards is always half the marked price. And check Party America for holiday supplies and for after-holiday clearances.

Party City

2350 S. Parker Road, Aurora, 696-6677.

9:30 a.m. to 9 p.m. Monday through Friday; 9:30 a.m. to 7 p.m. Saturday; 11 a.m. to 5 p.m. Sunday.

All greeting cards are always 40% off the marked price, and all patterned paper plates, napkins and tablecloths are always half the suggested price.

Phar-Mor

6795 W. 88th Ave., Westminster, 431-1383; 401 W. Girard Ave., Englewood, 762-0629.

8 a.m. to 10 p.m. Monday through Saturday; 9 a.m. to 7 p.m. Sunday.

Phar-Mor always sells its Gibson greeting cards at discounts of 10% to 50%.

UNICEF Shop

3300 E. 14th Ave., Denver, 355-9393.

10 a.m. to 4 p.m. Monday through Thursday. Staffed by volunteers, so call first to make sure someone is there.

You can buy toys, games, children's books, cards and wrapping paper benefitting UNICEF year-round in this little shop in the basement of the Eastside Christian Church. Proceeds help children in developing nations.

Section 4

Clothing

Sportswear for Men and Women

Some of the clothing sold at stores in this category is athletic wear, but most of it consists of the jeans, khaki slacks, knit shirts and cotton sweaters that used to be called preppie. In the informal, washable '90s, it's the clothing that many of us roll out of bed and put on each morning.

Many of these stores sell clothing that can be worn interchangeably by men and women (t-shirts, sweatshirts, sweaters) and some sell clothing that comes in similar styles for men and women but is cut differently (Levi's, Bugle Boy). Most sell both, and many of them have children's clothing, too. Sportswear can mean sweats, à la Champion Hanes or Russell, but it also means khakis and plaid shirts, à la Boston Traders or Woolrich. This category also includes shops for business clothing, such as Brooks Brothers, if they serve both men and women. It even includes Donna Karan, because her stores sell clothing for both sexes, although not much of it is designed for jogging.

American Eagle Outfitters

Castle Rock, 660-8390.

See Factory Outlet Malls for address, hours and directions.

Casual clothing for men and women, including jeans, shorts, skirts, polo shirts, rugby shirts, flannel shirts, sweaters, jackets, vests, stirrup pants, cotton shirts, t-shirts, slacks and sweatshirts. This is an outlet for the many American Eagle mall stores found throughout Colorado. It sells discontinued items, special buys, past-season merchandise, seconds and stuff that hasn't moved at the malls. Discounts are 50% to 75% less than mall-store prices.

Australian Outback Collection Inc.

Showbarn Plaza, 27905 Meadow Drive, Evergreen, 670-3933.

9:30 a.m. to 5:30 p.m. Monday through Saturday; 11 a.m. to 5 p.m. Sunday.

If you want to look like Paul Hogan, this place is for you. It's the only outlet store in the world for this wholesaler, whose corporate headquarters and main warehouse are in Colorado. The main line is oilskin coats, bushman and plainsman shirts, jackets and hats. These goods are usually sold in department stores and through catalogs, and this outlet is the only place where you can get a discount. That discount is generally around 30% off retail, but it can be deeper for samples or discontinued items, which compose the majority of the merchandise.

Balizoo

Durango, (970) 247-1119.

See Factory Outlet Malls for address, hours and directions.

Sporty all-cotton clothing for children and adults is sold here at discounts of 30% to 50%. The store also carries Bird Legs (girls' 2T to 10) and Boogie Bird (boys' 2T to 7) sportswear, made in Denver.

Bass

Castle Rock, 688-3676; Loveland, (970) 679-4606; Silverthorne, (970) 262-2077.

See Factory Outlet Malls for address, hours and directions.

Bass makes more than Weejuns. It has expanded into a sportswear line for men and women, and this clothing is sold in the outlet malls at discounts of 20% to 40% for discontinued or clearance items. The clothing is sold in the same store with shoes at Castle Rock and Loveland, and in a separate Bass clothing store in Silverthorne. The Bass store in Durango sells only shoes.

Benetton Factory Outlet

532 Main Ave., Durango (970) 259-4431.

See Factory Outlet Malls for address, hours and directions.

The Benetton outlet in Durango offers casual and dressy clothes for men, women and children (infants to size 12). The discounts depend on whether the merchandise is first quality or seconds, and on how current it is. Look sharp, know your values, and you'll do well. Recently a size 9-10 women's linen coat, seen in New York for $196, sold in Durango for $69. Great deal, but there was only one, and you had to be there. That's what factory outlet shopping is about. Generally, prices at this store start at around $15 for t-shirts and top out at around $120 for blazers.

Big Dog Sportswear

Castle Rock, 688-1831; Loveland, (970) 593-0313.

See Factory Outlet Malls for address, hours and directions.

This outlet sells shorts, fleece, t-shirts, outerwear, caps, watches, bags and accessories bearing the Big Dog label at discounts of 20% to 40%.

Boston Traders

Castle Rock, 660-0393; Loveland (970) 667-3150.

See Factory Outlet Malls for address, hours and directions.

Men's and women's sportswear, outerwear and accessories bearing the Boston Traders label are sold here at discounts of 10% to 60%.

Boulder Apparel Corporation

2108 55th St., Boulder, 444-3390.

See Direct and Seasonal Sales for possible sale dates.

This company manufactures logo sweatshirts, t-shirts and other sportswear for resorts, colleges and sports teams throughout the country. They have warehouse sales every two months at which t-shirts will go for as little as $1 and sweatshirts for $5. Call to find out when the next one is scheduled.

Brands

Silverthorne, (970) 262-0312.

See Factory Outlet Malls for address, hours and directions.

Brands? What brands? Well, there's Perry Ellis, Le Coq Sportif, Leon Levin, Paul Alexander, Buck and Sebago shoes, all at 30% to 70% less than suggested retail.

Britches Great Outdoors

Castle Rock, 688-4596.

See Factory Outlet Malls for address, hours and directions.

This factory outlet is the only place in the middle of the United States where you can find Britches Great Outdoors clothing, a line that a company spokesman describes as less boring than L.L. Bean and less trendy than The Gap. The merchandise here consists of rugby shirts, turtlenecks, t-shirts, sweaters, technical clothing and so on that is past its cycle at the company's mall stores back East. Prices are 30% to 50% less than original retail.

Brooks Brothers

Castle Rock, 688-8894; Loveland, (970) 663-5460.

See Factory Outlet Malls for address, hours and directions.

Brooks Brothers carries suits and sport coats for men and boys, dresses for women and sportswear for everyone. All merchandise bears the Brooks Brothers label, and discounts average about a third.

Bugle Boy factory stores

1316 Main Ave., Durango, (970) 259-1727; 167 Meraly Way, Dillon, (970) 468-0143; Loveland, (970) 663-2213.

Dillon: 10 a.m. to 8 p.m. Monday through Saturday; 10 a.m. to 6 p.m. Sunday. See Factory Outlet Malls for address, hours and directions for Durango and Loveland.

The discounts aren't as deep here as they are at the clearance centers, but there are still good deals. The base discount is less than 30%—a $17.99 kids' polo shirt was $14.99, for example. But something's always on sale.

Bula Factory Outlet Store

145 E. Sixth St., Durango, (970) 259-1727.

10 a.m. to 9 p.m. Monday through Saturday; noon to 6 p.m. Sunday.

There really is a Bula factory in Durango, and this is the outlet store for the funky wild-print clothing and accessories produced here by three local guys who started the business when they were still college age. The merchandise got a big boost during the 1994 Winter Olympics because members of the U.S. ski team wore hats from Bula that showed its logo to the world.

B.U.M. Equipment

Castle Rock, 688-5050; Loveland, (970) 593-0123.

See Factory Outlet Malls for address, hours and directions.

There's clothing at this outlet for men, women and children—even infants—and it's not all fleecewear and tees. The store also carries slacks, blouses, button-down shirts, socks, skirts, shorts, shoes, hats, sunglasses and watches. There's no direct comparison to suggested retail, but prices are moderate. A women's hooded sweatshirt, for example, was $22 the day we checked.

Cape Isle Knitters

Castle Rock, 688-2281; Durango, (970) 259-6604; Loveland, (970) 679-4608; Silverthorne, (970) 468-5338.

See Factory Outlet Malls for address, hours and directions.

Many of the intricate sweaters sold here portray scenes or geometric designs. Discounts are 25% to 50% less than retail.

Champion Hanes

Castle Rock, 688-6159; Loveland, (970) 667-5336; Silverthorne, (970) 468-9462

See Factory Outlet Malls for address, hours and directions.

Although sportswear is a category that involves a lot more than jogging outfits, jogging clothes are 90% of what's sold here. Discounts are 10% to 50%.

Dockers

Castle Rock, 688-3717.

See Factory Outlet Malls for address, hours and directions.

Men's and women's slacks, shirts, sweaters, wallets and other basics in the thirty-something uniform are sold here at very decent discounts. A pair of wrinkle-free men's Dockers that goes for $47 at a department store is $28 here.

Donna Karan

765 Anemone Trail, Dillon, (970) 262-2151.

Ski season hours: 10 a.m. to 8 p.m. Monday through Saturday; 10 to 6 Sunday. Off season: 10 a.m. to 6 p.m. every day.

The upstairs is devoted to a fairly complete men's line, and downstairs is for women. How good are the deals? Depends on how much you're used to spending. A t-shirt was the cheapest thing we found—$20, marked down from $35. The sweatshirts designed to sell for $65 are $40 here, and they do say DKNY. You may find them to be slightly less in the men's section. The day we visited, a $395 women's blazer was $235; another was marked down from $675 to $375.

Duck Head

Castle Rock, 660-9669.

See Factory Outlet Malls for address, hours and directions.

Duck Head's traditional casual clothing is sold here for 20% to 60% off retail. Sizes serve men, women and children.

Durango Threadworks

809 Main Ave., Durango, (970) 259-3783.

9 a.m. to 9 p.m. Monday through Saturday; 11 a.m. to 9 p.m. Sunday.

This is an outlet for a Durango factory that makes sweatshirts, backpacks and wallets and that screen prints, appliqués and embroiders those items with touristy designs, logos or sayings. Seconds are sold at discount.

DV8 Sportswear

528 S. Broadway, Denver, 777-9275.

10 a.m. to 6 p.m. Tuesday through Saturday.

This Denver manufacturer works mostly in Polar Fleece, flannel and very heavy cotton knits, and its sweatshirts, t-shirts, polos and pullover jackets are sold at this factory outlet at modest discounts. For example, a hooded Polar Fleece pullover jacket that would retail for $100 at some Vail boutique is $65 here. There's usually a rack of seconds at more significant discounts.

Eddie Bauer Factory Store

750 16th St., Denver, 825-0495.

9:30 a.m. to 7 p.m. Monday through Friday; 9:30 to 6 p.m. Saturday; 11 a.m. to 5 p.m. Sunday.

The normal discount for this downtown factory outlet is 40% to 70% off the original price for items that are new but aren't current in the retail Eddie Bauer stores. This is a great place to shop for cotton-knit dresses, walking shorts, backpacks, twill slacks, duffel bags, sweaters and denim shirts.

Fashion Bug

7380 W. 52nd Ave., Arvada, 422-3634; 859 N. Academy Blvd., Colorado Springs, (719) 596-7431 or 596-5423; 407 S. Broadway, Denver, 422-3634; 4336 College Ave., Fort Collins, (970) 225-9495.

10 a.m. to 9 p.m. Monday through Saturday; 10 a.m. to 6 p.m. Sunday.

Fashion Bug is actually a fairly complete mini-department store. It has men's clothing; women's shoes; a good selection of clothing for adolescent girls that goes up to size 16; and womenswear including sizes up to 32. We were not terribly impressed with the prices, though.

Fila

Castle Rock, 688-2208; Silverthorne, (970) 468-0232.

See Factory Outlet Malls for address, hours and directions.

The clothing and shoes you need for tennis, skiing, golf, jogging and swimming are all here at 40% to 50% off suggested retail.

Galt Sand

Castle Rock, 660-0699; Loveland, (970) 593-0504; Silverthorne, (970) 468-0568.

See Factory Outlet Malls for address, hours and directions.

If it's fleece, it's here, including sweatshirts, sweatpants, t-shirts, hoods and shorts in men's and women's sizes and at discounts of up to 50%.

The Gap

14200 E. Alameda Ave. (Aurora Mall), Aurora, 364-7408; 1400 S. Havana Ave., (Buckingham Square), Aurora, 695-8895; 1700 28th (Crossroads Mall), Boulder, 447-8082; 833 16th St. (downtown), Denver, 629-5020; 6911 S. University Blvd. (Southglenn Mall), Littleton, 797-2677; 8501 W. Bowles Ave. (Southwest Plaza), Littleton, 973-0063; 7777 E. Hampden Ave. (Tamarac Square), Denver, 368-8576; 7200 W. Alameda Ave. (Villa Italia), Lakewood, 934-4701; 5461 W. 88th Ave. (Westminster Mall), Westminster, 427-1927; 3000 E. First Ave., Denver (Cherry Creek Mall), 388-0393; 750 Citadel Drive East, Colorado Springs, (719) 597-3719.

10 a.m. to 9 p.m. Monday through Friday; 11 a.m. to 8 p.m. Saturday; 11 a.m. to 6 p.m. Sunday.

The Gap isn't a discounter, but it has frequent clearances. If you hit the store on the right day, you can find good prices on stuff everyone wears, including polo shirts, jeans, socks, turtlenecks, shorts and khakis. Watch for The Gap to open all-discount outlets.

Gart Sports Final Markdown

2875 S. Santa Fe Drive, Englewood, 761-3043.

10 a.m. to 8 p.m. Monday through Friday; 10 a.m. to 6 p.m. Saturday; 11 a.m. to 5 p.m. Sunday. See also Direct and Seasonal Sales for Gart's once-a-year Sniagrab.

This is a clearance center, so you never know what you'll find when you walk through the door, but if your path ever takes you down South Santa Fe, plan a half hour or so to stop in and paw through the bins. There can be great deals on such items as thermal underwear, soccer cleats and an assortment of sporting goods.

Guess?

Castle Rock, 688-6588; Silverthorne, (970) 262-9093.

See Factory Outlet Malls for address, hours and directions.

Men's and women's clothing and accessories—including jeans, sweatshirts, t-shirts, bags, caps and sunglasses—usually sell here for half of suggested retail. The dressier Guess? Collection features such items as blazers and sport coats. Children's clothing has been cleared out of the factory outlets, and children's sizes now will be found only at Baby Guess? stores, which we don't seem to have yet in Colorado.

Izod/Gant

Castle Rock, 688-2393; Silverthorne, (970) 262-0667; Durango, (970) 247-1119.

See Factory Outlet Malls for address, hours and directions.

Izod and Gant both make sportswear for men and women, but Izod tends toward knitwear for golf and tennis, and Gant tends more toward shirts, jackets and slacks. This outlet starts its discount at half of the original price.

J. Crew Factory Store

Silverthorne, (970) 262-1612.

See Factory Outlet Malls for address, hours and directions.

J. Crew's women's and men's apparel and accessories sell here at discounts of about a third.

Jockey

Castle Rock, 660-0880; Loveland, (970) 669-7002; Silverthorne, (970) 262-1643.

See Factory Outlet Malls for address, hours and directions.

Jockey carries sportswear—including polo shirts, t-shirts and tank tops—and underwear for men and women. Prices are generally 25% to 30% below those at standard retailers.

J-Rat Performance

1630 N. 63rd., #1, Boulder, 444-2779.

9 a.m. to 4 p.m. Monday through Friday.

This local manufacturer sells seconds and overruns of fleece, jackets, canvas pants and shorts, t-shirts and more at good discounts.

Just a Second

521 and 534 Main Ave., Durango, (970) 259-2970.

See Factory Outlet Malls for address, hours and directions.

This outlet features Basic Threads 100% cotton fleece activewear, priced wholesale. There are men's and women's tank tops, shorts, coverups, and sweats and children's playwear.

Levi's outlets

Castle Rock, 688-6711; 1316 Main Ave., Durango, (970) 247-2945; Loveland, (970) 635-9333; Silverthorne, (970) 262-0133.

See Factory Outlet Malls for address, hours and directions.

These outlets carry Levi's brand jeans, jean jackets, Dockers for men and women, shirts, sweaters, belts, kids' jeans and shirts, shoes and socks at a moderate discount. Adult-size jeans are about $25-$30; silver-tab loose-fit jeans, which sell for $40 to $50 elsewhere, are $30 here.

Liz Claiborne

Silverthorne, (970) 468-2484.

See Factory Outlet Malls for address, hours and directions.

Every woman alive seems to own something from Liz Claiborne, but did you know Claiborne makes men's clothing, too? The men's line includes ties, dress shirts, twill pants and sport coats. As with the women's line, discounts range from 35% to 50%.

London Fog Factory Outlets

Durango, (970) 385-7546; Loveland, (970) 593-9851; Silverthorne, (970) 468-5295.

See Factory Outlet Malls for address, hours and directions.

In addition to all those trench coats, London Fog makes a full range of clothing for men, women and children, including, slacks, shirts, fleecewear, blouses and sweaters. Discounts range from 35% to 50%.

Mountain Fashions

28005 Highway 74, Evergreen, 674-6220.

9:30 a.m. to 5:30 p.m. Monday through Saturday; noon to 4 p.m. Sunday.

This independent outlet gets returned merchandise from I. Magnin, Nordstrom's, Brooks Brothers and Victoria's Secret, as well as cosmetics from Estée Lauder, Borghese and Clinique. Most of the returned merchandise is reduced by 70%. Check the $4.98 and $2.98 racks for stuff that looks like it's been worn.

Nike

Silverthorne, (970) 468-6040.

See Factory Outlet Malls for address, hours and directions.

Athletic footwear, apparel and accessories for men, women and children, at bargains that run from amazing to ho-hum.

Outlet Marketplace

Castle Rock, 688-7490.

See Factory Outlet Malls for address, hours and directions.

Vanity Fair, Lee, Health Tex, Wrangler and Jantzen are among the brands represented in men's, women's and children's clothing. There are also a few accessories, including Jansport backpacks.

Polo Ralph Lauren

110 E. Fifth St., Durango, (970) 259-2241; Colby, Kansas, (913) 462-3364; Jackson, Wyoming, (307) 733-8333.

See Factory Outlet Malls for address, hours and directions.

The Polo Ralph Lauren outlets carry pretty much everything Ralph makes, including knit polo shirts for men and women, women's classic rough wear, children's clothing in sizes 4 to 20, men's clothing from t-shirts to sports jackets in natural fabrics, home accessories such as table linens and bedclothes, shoes and furnishings. Discounts range from a third to a half, and there are also additional markdowns and sales, particularly on factory seconds. But you don't need to travel to find Ralph Lauren at a discount. Try T&C Men's Center and the off-price department stores such as Ross, T.J. Maxx and Marshall's; his things also sometimes show up at Sam's Club and Price Club.

Russell

Castle Rock, 660-1161.

See Factory Outlet Malls for address, hours and directions.

This outlet sells sportswear with an emphasis on fleece for men, women and children at a third to a half off retail.

SBX

Castle Rock, 660-1100.

See Factory Outlet Malls for address, hours and directions.

Dress Barn is the parent company for the outlet stores of Westport and SBX. Prices and merchandise are identical among the three stores; only the names are different. SBX is the casual side of this line. SBX unisex tops and pants are 35% to 50% off retail here.

Sequel Outdoor Clothing

108 E. Fifth St., Durango, (970) 385-4421.

See Factory Outlet Malls for address, hours and directions.

Sequel Outdoor Clothing is a North Face–like line manufactured in Durango and shipped worldwide. This outlet carries clothing for every season and for every rugged outdoor sport. Visit here before you climb Everest. Outlet prices are lower than retail, and there are additional discounts, too. The standard discount on a Gore-tex jacket, for example, is 15%.

Sergio Tacchini Factory Store

528 Main Ave., Durango, (970) 385-4945.

See Factory Outlet Malls for address, hours and directions.

A large selection of warmups, golf and tennis clothing from Sergio Tacchini, a gigantic multi-national corporation based in Italy, is sold here at discounts starting at 30%. The presence of other labels depends on what the parent firm buys. A recent check revealed some items from Bronson, Misty Harbor and Anchor Blue.

Ski Country Outlet

3065 S. Broadway, Englewood, 762-1720.

10 a.m. to 6 p.m. Monday through Friday; 10 a.m. to 5 p.m. Saturday.

This store is an outlet for an Englewood factory that embroiders the names of resorts on t-shirts, hats and sweatshirts. It has classy embroidered t-shirts and lots of hats, including warm fleece baseball-style caps that are great for kids because they'll wear them. There's always a special, and prices go very low.

Southern Cross

Silverthorne, (970) 262-1180.

See Factory Outlet Malls for address, hours and directions.

Imports from South America include sweaters and shirts for men and women, as well as weavings, jewelry and other ethnic items, all sold here at a modest discount.

U-Trau Factory

1170 E. 49th Ave., Denver (just north of I-70 at the southeast corner of East 49th Avenue and Nome St.), 375-9620.

8 a.m. to 5 p.m. Monday through Friday.

The U-Trau Factory outlet sells more than boxer shorts. There are also t-shirts, jam shorts, pants and other items that can be worn on the street by people older than 20. This outlet may not be open as often as the hours listed here; call first.

Van Heusen

Castle Rock, 688-3477; Silverthorne, (970) 468-0793.

See Factory Outlet Malls for address, hours and directions.

Both of these stores carry clothing for men and women, although there's a larger selection of women's clothing in the Van Heusen for Her store at Castle Rock. Shirts, pants, dress shirts and other casual clothes, all with the Van Heusen label, are sold at a standard discount of around 30%.

Woolrich Factory Outlet

Castle Rock, 660-9580; 6900 W. 117th Ave., Broomfield, 469-5257.

Broomfield: 9:30 to 5:30 Monday through Saturday; also 10 a.m. to 5 p.m. Sundays, November and December only. Castle Rock: see Factory Outlet Malls for address, hours and directions.

The very first factory outlet we ever discovered was the one attached to the Woolrich factory in Broomfield, and we've gotten some great deals there over the years. Sure, we get misty when we recall the sound of the sewing machines, ka-chunging as we balanced in the changing room. But, frankly, the outlet in Castle Rock is much more easily accessible from the southern half of the metro area, and if the deals are any different, we couldn't tell.

Outerwear

Coats can be very expensive, particularly for children, who outgrow them or even (gasp) lose them. Put the child's name and phone number inside each coat and jacket. That way, if a coat is found by a well-meaning individual, the person has a way to contact you and return it. If you've got the kind of kid who loses coats (there was one in my Girl Scout troop who lost three by mid-November), don't buy them new. Get them from a consignment or thrift store. Yes, I realize that the problem is with the children, not the coats. But while you're teaching them responsibility, preserve your sanity and dignity. You won't get as upset about something you didn't pay $150 for.

One more tip. It's probably better not to launder coats with poplin exteriors; nylon and other synthetics seem to do better in the washing machine. We've had some bad experiences, for example, with a couple of London Fog jackets that had labels indicating they could be washed. They came out looking faded and shabby. A Columbia jacket that said it could be laundered, on the other hand, came out of the wash just fine. And we've never had a bad experience washing a nylon jacket filled with down. Before laundering, just be sure to check for any place on the jacket where the down might leak out; feathers in your washing machine will destroy it. And when you dry the jacket, put a sneaker in the dryer with it to fluff the down.

Australian Outback Collection Inc.

Showbarn Plaza, 27905 Meadow Drive, Evergreen, 670-3933.

9:30 a.m. to 5:30 p.m. Monday through Saturday; 11 a.m. to 5 p.m. Sunday.

Oilskin coats are available here from a factory outlet that's actually in the same building as the manufacturer's corporate headquarters. The discount is generally 30% off retail, and on many items it's deeper.

Burlington Coat Factory

12455 E. Mississippi Ave., Aurora, 367-0111; 3100 S. Sheridan Blvd., Denver, 937-1119; 400 E. 84th Ave., Thornton, 287-0071;

7325 W. 88th Ave., Westminster, 431-9696; 545 N. Academy, Colorado Springs, (719) 597-8505.

10 a.m. to 9:30 p.m. Monday through Saturday; 11 a.m. to 6 p.m. Sunday.

Burlington Coat Factory doesn't have a factory. It buys in volume from established manufacturers, and, as they say in the commercials, passes the savings on to you. We get mixed reviews on Burlington. On one hand, selection and prices are good. On the other, return policies are very restrictive. Examine anything you buy here very carefully, and don't buy gifts unless you're absolutely sure they won't need to be returned.

Gart Sports Final Markdown

2875 S. Santa Fe Drive, 761-3043.

10 a.m. to 8 p.m. Monday through Friday; 10 a.m. to 6 p.m. Saturday; 11 a.m. to 5 p.m. Sunday. Also see Direct and Seasonal Sales for Gart's Sniagrab.

This is a clearance center, so there's no predicting what you'll find. But we know people who have found high-ticket down jackets for $20. If you're looking for a ski parka, check. You may get lucky.

G III Outerwear

Castle Rock, 688-8189.

See Factory Outlet Malls for address, hours and directions.

G III, a manufacturer represented in such retail outlets as Joslins and The Limited, does intentional overruns to stock its factory outlets. We've seen children's pigskin varsity jackets sell here for $39 and a lambskin jacket marked nearly $400 in the mall go for half that. G III carries leather coats for men, women and children as well as other leather clothing (vests, skirts) and accessories.

Great Outdoor Clothing Co.

Silverthorne, (970) 262-0807.

See Factory Outlet Malls for address, hours and directions.

Great Outdoor offers several brands of ski parkas (Snowlum, Hi-Tec, Helly Hansen), many of which feature Gore-Tex or Thinsulate. They also have other outdoor clothing and some footwear. Discounts range from 10% to 50% less than retail. Most of the store is dedicated to sportswear for men or women, but there are a few items for children.

Leather Loft

Castle Rock, 688-5836; Loveland, (970) 593-0535; Silverthorne, (970) 262-0259.

See Factory Outlet Malls for address, hours and directions.

The regular discount for the jackets sold at these outlets is 20%. Be sure to check the clearance wall.

London Fog Factory Outlet

Silverthorne, (970) 468-5295; Durango, (970) 385-7546; Loveland, (970) 593-9851.

See Factory Outlet Malls for address, hours and directions.

Prices for London Fog merchandise—rainwear, topcoats and jackets for men, women and children, as well as men's sport clothes—are routinely 40% to 50% less than regular retail.

Santa Fe Re-creations

Mercantile at Ojo, New Mexico State Highway 414 (off Highway 285), Ojo Caliente, New Mexico, (505) 583-9131.

10 a.m. to 6 p.m. daily.

Some of the beautifully detailed jackets, coats and clothing sold at this outlet feature paintings on suede signed by artist Pam Pappas. The wearable art sold at this outlet is made in Denver, but Denver is too close to some of the resort boutiques that jealously guard their (high) prices. (For more information on Santa Fe Re-creations, you might call 777-6745 in Denver.)

Ojo Caliente is about 60 miles south of Antonito, on the road to Española, New Mexico. The outlet would be a worthwhile stop, particularly if you're planning a vacation in southern Colorado that includes a ride on the Cumbres and Toltec Scenic Railroad, which originates in Antonito.

Woolrich Factory Outlet

5050 Factory Shops Blvd., Castle Rock, 660-9580; 6900 W. 117th Ave., Broomfield, 469-5257.

Castle Rock: 9 a.m.to 9 p.m. Monday through Saturday; 11 a.m. to 6 p.m. Sunday.

The very first factory outlet I ever discovered was the one attached to the Woolrich factory in Broomfield, and I've gotten some great deals there over the years. Sure, I get misty when I recall the sound of the sewing machines, kachunging as I balanced on one foot in the changing room. But, frankly, the shop in Castle Rock is much more easily accessible, and if the deals are any different, I couldn't tell. Discounts aren't outrageous, but I seldom visit without finding something that's been marked down to the point of irresistibility.

Woolrich coats generally have poplin exteriors and blanket-like linings featuring Thinsulate, giving them the sportswear look that fits in with khaki pants and turtlenecks (which the outlets also sell). Woolrich also offers blankets, sweaters, gloves, hats, skirts, nightgowns, plaid button-down cotton-polyester shirts, hiking socks and almost anything else "Lands' End–ish."

Western Wear and Cowboy Boots

Yee-hah. Western wear has been a popular fashion statement since the mid-70s (remember *Urban Cowboy*?), and the trend shows no sign of slowing. In the '90s, though, we're not just talking about checkered shirts with pearl buttons and jeans with no holes. No-siree. Western wear has gone haute, with lots of brightly colored, hand-pieced, suede and fringed items that may be deservedly expensive. Here are some places, though, where a buckaroo can get a break.

Attitudes

77 S. Sheridan Blvd., Denver, 238-4738.

11 a.m. to 5 p.m. Monday through Saturday.

This consignment shop specializes in Western wear for women and also carries country crafts for home decorating. The store carries lots of new sample specialty t-shirts and sweatshirts and has standard women's consignment clothing, too. There's also a corner devoted to angels and angel-related merchandise.

Barb's Bargain Boutique

9585 Montview Ave., Aurora, 344-2909.

10 a.m. to 5:30 p.m. Monday through Saturday.

Consignment clothes for men and women, plus samples. Barb's tries to have a selection of Western wear, especially around the time of the Denver Stock Show and Cheyenne Frontier Days.

Colorado Gals Consignment

3105B W. Colorado Ave., Colorado Springs, (719) 475-1512.

10 a.m. to 5 p.m. Monday through Friday; 10 a.m. to 4 p.m. Saturday.

Women's and children's consignment square dance and Western wear are carried at this shop, which also carries more traditional consignment clothing for children and women.

Denver Boot Outlet

3795 Kipling St., Wheat Ridge, 425-6597.

9 a.m. to 8 p.m. Monday through Friday; 9 a.m. to 5 p.m. Saturday; noon to 4 p.m. Sunday.

This store has some 4,000 pairs of cowboy boots made by Olathe Boot Company, and this is the only factory outlet for that Kansas manufacturer in Colorado. The boots are sold at 30% to 50% less than retail. The emphasis is on boots for men and women, although there are a few boots in children's sizes. They also take special orders. Sizes range from 4 to 15 in widths from AAA to EEE. The outlet also carries hats, belts and other accessories for cowboys and cowgirls.

Miller Stockman Western Wear

Silverthorne, (970) 468-5133.

See Factory Outlet Malls for address, hours and directions.

Lots of Western clothing is made in Colorado, but this outlet for Denver-made Rocky Mountain Clothing is one of only a few factory outlets for local manufacturers. Rocky Mountain Clothing makes only women's shirts and jeans, but the outlet helps bridge the outlet gap by carrying seconds from other manufacturers, notably Wrangler. There are boots from Justin, Nocona, Abilene and Larry Mahan, among others, plus belts, bolos, men's shirts, hats, jackets, sweaters and a few items for children, including boots, hats, shirts and jeans. The big majority of merchandise is imperfect and sells for around half of retail.

Mountain Fashions

28005 Highway 74, Evergreen, 674-6220.

9:30 a.m. to 5:30 p.m. Monday through Saturday; noon to 4 p.m. Sunday.

In addition to merchandise returns from a number of traditional department stores, this independent outlet usually carries Western wear samples, including shirts, dusters, hats and boots. The selection varies widely, so if you're looking for something specific, call first to make sure it's there.

National Western Stock Show

4655 Humboldt St., Denver, 295-1660.

Once a year in January. See Direct and Seasonal Sales.

The Stock Show can be viewed as a gigantic, hucksterish country-and-western mall where it's fun to stroll and easy to compare prices. When we were shopping for children's cowboy boots, we found the best deals there. Many local retailers have booths at the Stock Show and run show specials, and they compete with out-of-town retailers who come only during the Stock Show. If there's a specific item you're looking for, phone shop around town first so you'll recognize a good deal. If you buy from an out-of-towner, get a business card and ask about return policies but be pretty sure you're getting something you intend to keep.

Santa Fe Re-Creations

Mercantile at Ojo, New Mexico State Highway 414 (off Highway 285), Ojo Caliente, New Mexico, (505) 583-9131.

10 a.m. to 6 p.m. daily.

If you ever spend much time at such as events as the WestFest at Copper Mountain, where women take their Western wear seriously, you've seen clothes made by Santa Fe Re-Creations. This Denver manufacturer sells the romance of the Southwest to boutiques all over the country. If you want to learn more about what's in the New Mexico outlet without making a long-distance call, talk to someone at the Denver factory, 777-6745. The New Mexico outlet, by the way, is just across the state line from Antonito.

Smelter's Coalroom

801½ Main Ave., Durango, (970) 259-3470.

See Factory Outlet Malls for address, hours and directions.

This outlet sells a line of women's Western clothing, Dineh, that is made in Durango and includes vests, skirts, shirts and other items both dressy and casual. There are also items from other Western lines, including Calamity Jeans.

Soda Creek Western Mercantile

335 Lincoln Ave., Steamboat Springs, (970) 879-3146; order desk: (800) 824-8426.

Store: 9 a.m. to 9 p.m. Monday through Saturday; 10 a.m. to 6 p.m. Sunday. Order desk: 8 a.m. to 5 p.m. Monday through Friday.

Soda Creek sets up a booth at the National Western Stock Show every year, and that's where we became acquainted with it. We've bought two years worth of cowboy boots for the kids at this booth. The prices are good (less than $50 a pair), and the boots are snazzy and sturdy. They have adult sizes, too, of course. Soda Creek takes phone orders on the toll-free 800 number. But if you're in Steamboat, check them out.

Menswear

In the course of doing the Shop Smart column for the *Rocky Mountain News*, we've learned that men are just as interested in bargains as women. At first we were surprised that such a large proportion of inquiries and comments concerning the column came from men. We'd always believed those demographic studies that said women do all the shopping. Then we realized that lots of men are single, and they either have to shop for themselves or go in rags. And most women are too busy to find time to resupply their own pantyhose, much less spend hours going through racks in a menswear store, trying to figure out whether their mates would prefer pinstripe to herringbone.

Fortunately for men, and for the women who do sometimes still shop for them, there's a whole new world of bargain menswear out there. Most of the stores in this listing are no more than three or four years old. Discount menswear stores are everywhere, and the bargains are significant enough that they should be explored.

But remember that service is worth something, too, especially for men, who don't always tend to regard shopping as recreation. The down side of the discount trend is that little family haberdasheries are quickly becoming a thing of the past. So if you need a personal relationship with the guy who fits your suit, you may want to throw some business to the more traditional retailer, if only so he'll still be there the next time you have an anxiety attack when faced with 14 racks of tweed. For example, Grassfield's, a menswear shop in Cherry Creek North, will open up early or late for a customer, go to his office or deliver to his home. Customer sizes are kept on a computer, so that relatives seeking gifts for a Grassfield's customer can get the information they need in the store. And Concord Clothiers, a competitor of Grassfield's in Cherry Creek, will go to offices or to the homes of customers it knows. Its custom department makes pants and suit jackets for men, and it will also do women's suits.

For information on jeans, t-shirts, shorts and fleecewear, *see* Sportswear for Men and Women. *Also see* Near-New for Men and Women.

Arrow Factory Store

167 Meraly Way, Silverthorne, (970) 262-1742.

10 a.m. to 8 p.m. Monday through Saturday; 10 a.m. to 6 p.m. Sunday.

With the closing of the Arrow factory store in Durango, this became Colorado's only Arrow factory outlet. The standard discount is about 30% throughout the store, but discounts are deep for the items that are on sale. There's a wide selection of dress shirts (Fairfield, Kent Classics, Brigade, Dover, Broadstreet, Yves St. Laurent) all at around $12 to $22. Ties, originally $15, were $8.99 the day we were there. This is also an outlet for Gold Toe socks and River Brand sports shirts.

Barry Manufacturing

700 S. Santa Fe Drive, Denver, 722-2230.

10 a.m. to 7 p.m. Monday through Friday; til 8 p.m. Thursday and Friday; 10 a.m. to 6 p.m. Saturday; noon to 5 p.m. Sunday.

Here you can find wool blend suits at $89.95; 100% wool suits at $129.95; and tuxedos for $99.95. These prices apply to sizes regular and long, 37 to 60; short, 37 to 54; and extra long, 40 to 56. Sizes 48 to 60 are slightly higher.

Colours by Alexander Julian

Castle Rock, 660-3810; Silverthorne, (970) 262-2476.

See Factory Outlet Malls for address, hours and directions.

Only clothing with the Alexander Julian label is sold here. It's first quality from mall and department stores that send their overstocks here instead of putting them on clearance. Discounts range from 10% to 70%. The merchandise turns over very quickly, so there's always something new. Goods include jackets, sweaters and shirts. The stores also carry boys' sizes.

Also see Discount Department Stores and Membership Warehouses

Menswear is a standard item at Sam's Club and Price Club, which (sporadically) carry everything from briefs to topcoats. But if you're going to succeed at a membership warehouse, discount department store or clearance center, you need to be a shopper. Selection depends completely on what comes to the loading dock. An item you're considering probably won't be there the next time you go. And forget about service. If you find a dressing room, consider yourself fortunate.

Geoffrey Beene

Castle Rock, 688-2993; Loveland, (970) 667-2317; Silverthorne, (970) 468-5727.

See Factory Outlet Malls for address, hours and directions.

This outlet features dress shirts, neckties and casual sportswear by Geoffrey Beene at as much as 50% less than suggested retail.

John Henry & Friends

Silverthorne, (970) 262-2494; Castle Rock, 660-3305.

See Factory Outlet Malls for address, hours and directions.

Men's sportswear, dress shirts, pants and furnishings are featured here, and labels include Perry Ellis, John Henry, Thomson, Nino Cerutti, World Wildlife Fund and Liberty of London.

Just Samples

8215 S. Holly St., Littleton, 843-0269.

Open periodically. See Direct and Seasonal Sales.

The annual golf sale is usually held in March, and a ski sale in August; both usually feature clothing and equipment for both men and women. Men's clothing sales are usually held a week or so before Father's Day. Merchandise from past sales has included samples from Geoffrey Beene, London Fog, Ixspa, Dockers, Oleg Cassini, Van Heusen, Gant and Haggar. A suit, for example, from Haggar would probably sell for around $65 to $75. Prices for these samples are always wholesale plus 10%. The size range may be limited to the middle of the spectrum. There is a second, smaller men's clothing sale in October for fall clothing.

Kuppenheimer Men's Clothiers

8500 W. Crestline Ave., Littleton, 933-0246; 14000 E. Mississippi Ave., Aurora, 750-5300; 5740 W. 88th Ave., Westminster, 429-3702.

10 a.m. to 9 p.m. Monday through Friday; noon to 6 p.m. Saturday; noon to 5 p.m. Sunday.

All clothes sold here bear the Kuppenheimer label and are made in factories in Ohio, Georgia, Florida and Alabama. Suits range from $195 to $295. Merchandise also includes shirts, ties, slacks and some sports clothes.

Lee's Men's Store

3463 S. Broadway, Englewood, 761-7302.

9:30 a.m. to 6 p.m. Monday through Thursday; 9:30 a.m. to 8 p.m. Friday; 9:30 a.m. to 5 p.m. Saturday.

Lee's has been in business 42 years, although it just recently moved to Englewood from downtown Denver. As both a traditional haberdashery and a discounter, it combines the best of both worlds. Everything in the store is reduced by 40% to 50%. There are good labels (Armani, Talia, Caveli, Manhattan, Cotton Club, Generra), and they also have sales.

Marc Jeffries

1636 Stout St. (downtown), Denver, 572-0918; 8200 S. Quebec St., Englewood, 689-0193.

Downtown: 10 a.m. to 5 p.m. Monday through Saturday. Englewood: 11 a.m. to 6 p.m. Tuesday through Saturday; 11 a.m. to 4 p.m. Sunday.

Marc Jeffries doesn't look like a discounter, but don't bypass this store just because it doesn't resemble Kmart. The early fall poplin suit sale, for example, usually offers suits designed to sell for $124 each at $99.95 each. That's close to what you'd pay at

Penney's or Sears, and the suits are better. Comparable bargains are offered throughout the year.

Men's Wearhouse

201 Fillmore St., Denver, 322-1535; 1113 S. Abilene St., Aurora, 750-1463; 2525 Arapahoe Road, Boulder, 440-3684; 2050 E. County Line Road, Highlands Ranch, 347-8533; 650 S. Wadsworth Blvd. (Villa Italia), Lakewood, 937-0400; 8501 W. Bowles (Southwest Plaza), Littleton, 973-1852; 8801 Harlan St., Unit C, Westminster, 650-1900; 693 N. Academy Blvd., Colorado Springs, (719) 637-1574. Opening in summer 1995 in Fort Collins.

10 a.m. to 9 p.m. Monday through Friday; 9:30 a.m. to 9 p.m. Saturday; 10 a.m. to 6 p.m. Sunday; or mall hours.

This rapidly expanding Texas- and California-based chain opened in Colorado only two years ago and now has nine stores throughout the state. Apparel lines include Botany, Halston (Burberry), Givenchy, Vito Ruffalo, Geoffrey Beene and Isamo. Suits generally are 20% to 40% off retail, ranging from $199 to $495. The stores also carry a wide selection of dress shirts, a somewhat more limited selection of sports shirts and Florsheim, Bostonian and Rockport shoes. Silk ties range from $14.99 to $39.99. Men's Wearhouse stages one annual clearance sale each December and January, so watch for the ads.

Nautica Factory Outlet

765 Anemone Trail, Dillon, 262-1615; Castle Rock, 660-6095.

Dillon, ski season: 10 a.m. to 8 p.m. Monday through Saturday; 10 a.m. to 6 p.m. Sunday. Dillon, off season: 10 a.m. to 6 p.m. every day. For Castle Rock, see Factory Outlet Malls.

Nautica outlets feature a base discount of around 30%, with additional markdowns for sale items of 25% to 50%. But even at that, don't plan to find anything for $10 or less. When we visited, robes originally priced at $115 were $79, rugby shirts originally priced $78 were $58, and cotton sweaters originally $123 to $178 were marked half price. The store offers a full range of men's clothing from dressy to casual, including dress shirts, ties, dress pants, sweaters, vests, rugby shirts, khakis and jeans.

Quality Apparel Outlet

1485 S. Colorado Blvd., Denver, 756-6102; 5117 S. Yosemite St., Englewood, 290-0366.

10 a.m. to 6 p.m. Monday through Friday; 10 a.m. to 5 p.m. Saturday; noon to 4 p.m. Sunday.

These stores are factory outlets for Hart, Schaffner & Marx, Austin Reed and Christian Dior men's clothes. Merchandise is all first quality, and suits, sport coats and topcoats go for 30% to 40% below the original retail price.

T&C Men's Center

7400 E. Hampden Ave. (Tiffany Plaza), Denver, 770-9700.

10 a.m. to 7 p.m. Friday and Saturday; noon to 6 p.m. Sunday.

Wool suits in a full range of sizes sell here for $100 to $150. Camel hair sportcoats are $110; long-sleeve designer sport shirts, $20; sweaters, $20; silk ties, $8; leather belts, $10; wool gabardine dress trousers, $40; suspenders, $10; and 100% cotton pinpoint Oxford dress shirts are $20. Most items sell here for about half of suggested retail, but the deepest discounts are on items with the Polo Ralph Lauren label. All Ralph's pants and shirts sell for $34.90 at T&C; since they're usually $60 to $90, that can be nearly two-thirds off.

Tommy Hilfiger

Castle Rock, 688-8877; Loveland, (970) 669-8877.

See Factory Outlet Malls for address, hours and directions.

Hilfiger's sportswear is a hot commodity in department-store boutiques, and the designer is frequently compared to Ralph Lauren. The clothes are classics with a twist: chambray shirts with collars lined in oxford cloth, for example. Men's and boys' sportswear is discounted at these factory outlets when it's past its cycle in the department stores.

Van Heusen

Castle Rock, 688-3477; Durango, (970) 385-5001; Loveland, (970) 669-6667; Silverthorne, (970) 468-0793.

See Factory Outlet Malls for address, hours and directions.

Dress shirts and neckties with the Van Heusen label sell here for 20% to 50% less than retail. These stores also carry women's clothing.

Wemco Factory Store

Silverthorne, (970) 262-1919.

See Factory Outlet Malls for address, hours and directions.

This outlet offers men's sportswear, including denim shirts, sweaters, turtlenecks, socks, pants and shorts, at about 40% to 85% less than suggested retail. The big emphasis, though, is on ties. Labels include Resilio, Wembley, Je Suis, Oscar de la Renta, Countess Mara, Allyn St. George and Tabasco, as well as Saia and Grace Newberry handpainted ties.

Windsor Shirt Company

Castle Rock, 688-2802; Silverthorne, (970) 262-0815.

See Factory Outlet Malls for address, hours and directions.

Windsor, a line of dressy, high-end menswear, sells here at 25% to 50% less than suggested retail. The outlet also carries women's clothing.

Women's Clothing

No book needs to tell you that clothes are important to women; dozens of fashion magazines exist on that premise. Clothes are important not only for how they make you feel, but for how they make you look as you present yourself professionally in the world. Women don't want cheap clothing. They want great well-made clothing; they just don't want to go into debt to get it.

The discount trend is so prevalent in the women's clothing trade that it's hard to imagine that any store selling only at "suggested retail" could survive. Every store from Neiman Marcus to Kmart has sales. A basic item like a solid-color cotton sweater might fetch anything from $200 to $5. So the question a woman needs to ask is, "What is this sweater worth to *me*?" Some women are untroubled by the prospect of a $200 sweater; finding what they want at the quality they seek is a higher priority than finding it on sale. If you're that kind of shopper, it would probably be wise to make frequent visits to the factory outlet malls, where you can find your favorite designer's clothing at a modest discount—although you may not find much from the couturier line or the current season's collection.

A more typical reader of this book probably has drawers full of cotton sweaters, but she'll buy the next one she sees on clearance for $5 even if the color isn't exactly what she wants, because it's such a good deal. Bargain hunters need to show restraint. Try to think in terms of the total volume of your clothing. If something comes in, something equal should go out, or you'll find yourself facing overstuffed hampers, laundry rooms, ironing baskets and closets, and you'll still have nothing to wear.

Here are some places where you can find clothing worth having at prices worth paying. How can you tell when something's a good deal? It has to feel like a good deal to *you*. Once you've got a general idea of what something usually sells for, there's no other objective standard. If I know I'll have regrets if I walk away, I buy.

Try not to use credit cards when you buy clothing. Credit is for the day your washer breaks down or your car's timing chain goes kaflooey. Before you shop for yourself, decide how much money you can spend, take that amount in cash, and quit when the money is gone. There are few deals in clothing that are worth going into debt over.

For jeans, shorts and fleece, and for stores such as Woolrich that sell clothing for both men and women, *see* Sportswear for Men and Women.

Adler and York

7180 W. 38th Ave., Wheat Ridge, 234-0314.

10 a.m. to 4 p.m. Monday through Friday.

This company manufactures and hand paints resort wear under the internationally distributed Ivor and The Blues labels. At this small factory outlet they sell sample t-shirts, dresses, skirts, pants, shorts and sweatshirts at a discount. They also offer classes in painting designs on silk.

Adolfo II

Castle Rock, 688-4130; Silverthorne, (970) 468-7552.

See Factory Outlet Malls for address, hours and directions.

Sportswear, knits, basically casual, directly from the factory, no seconds. Discounts are 20% to 70% off retail.

Aileen

Castle Rock, 688-9530; Loveland, (970) 663-2747.

See Factory Outlet Malls for address, hours and directions.

Aileen's 100% cotton knit casual dresses, pants and tops are sold only in factory outlet malls, which means there are no seconds. There are also no discounts, but the prices are kept low because there's no middle man. Nothing in the store sells for more than $50.

Ann Taylor

Castle Rock, 688-3335.

See Factory Outlet Malls for address, hours and directions.

Ann Taylor clothing focuses on career, casual and weekend wear. At this outlet sweaters, business suits, slacks, skirts and silk blouses for the sophisticated shopper are sold at discounts of around 33%.

Anne Klein

Silverthorne, (970) 262-1266.

See Factory Outlet Malls for address, hours and directions.

Previous-season merchandise is reduced by about a third here, which still doesn't make it inexpensive. In Anne Klein, the top label in the line, a blazer would be $800 at suggested retail. This outlet carries more from the more casual Anne Klein II line, which is found at such department stores as Neiman Marcus and Saks. An Anne Klein II blazer would retail at closer to $600. Figure your discount from there. And check the back of store for items that have been reduced more than once.

Bisou-Bisou

Loveland, (970) 667-1705.

See Factory Outlet Malls for address, hours and directions.

Loveland has the only factory outlet in Colorado for Bisou-Bisou, a trendy line of junior fashions that's featured in *Vogue* and sold on Rodeo Drive.

Boofers

2425 Canyon Blvd., Boulder, 388-9830; 2350 N. 95th St., Boulder, half a mile north of Arapahoe, 666-1883, 666-1884, 442-3334; The Total Look, 2120 S. Holly St., Denver, 758-6976.

Canyon Blvd.: 10 a.m. to 5 p.m. Monday through Friday; 11 a.m. to 4 p.m. Saturday. 95th St.: 10 a.m. to 6 p.m. Fridays; variable hours Monday, Wednesday and Saturday—call first. Total Look: 10 a.m. to 5 p.m. Monday through Friday; 11 a.m. to 4 p.m. Saturday. See Direct and Seasonal Sales.

This Boulder manufacturer of brightly colored all-cotton clothing offers a wide variety of dresses and separates. The company has recently expanded into washable sueded rayon and silk separates and into sweaters and accessories. Normal prices range around $33 to $85. They have sales, and if you want to learn about them, ask to get on the mailing list. This clothing comes in sizes from petites to 4 extra-large (about size 28), and there's also maternity, tennis and golf wear.

Carole Little

Silverthorne, (970) 262-1437.

See Factory Outlet Malls for address, hours and directions.

Carole Little lines sold at this outlet at discount include street wear, career wear, casual wear, petites and Carole Little II, for sizes 18 to 24.

Casual Corner

Castle Rock, 688-3818; Loveland, (970) 669-5332.

See Factory Outlet Malls for address, hours and directions.

In recent years, Casual Corner retail stores have put their focus completely on career wear. You'll find that, as well as more casual pieces such as jeans, fleecewear and sweaters, at the factory outlet stores. Most of the clothing sold here is made specifically for these stores and bears the "Casual Corner & Co." label. These stores also carry some mall-store returns and past-season items, as well some additional labels such as 62E and Capacity.

Casual Glamour

7562 S. University Blvd., Littleton, 771-6849.

10 a.m. to 6 p.m. Monday through Friday; 10 a.m. to 5 p.m. Saturday.

Owner Gail Winslow takes buying trips all over the country just so she can get lines that other stores don't carry. So if you don't want to see what you're wearing on five other women, you may want to check out this store. It has accessories, too.

Chico's

Castle Rock, 688-2950.

See Factory Outlet Malls for address, hours and directions.

The distinctive ethnic-looking clothing sold here is all 100% cotton. Pieces include separates, vests, sweaters, sweater vests, dresses and coats. Almost everything in the store is marked down by 50%, but it's all 60 to 90 days past retail-store season.

Danskin

Castle Rock, 660-9073.

See Factory Outlet Malls for address, hours and directions.

Women's and children's leotards, tights, aerobic wear at 40% to 70% less than suggested retail.

Designers 3

3000 E. Third Ave., Denver, 329-8228.

10 a.m. to 6 p.m. Monday through Saturday; 10 a.m. to 2 p.m. Sunday. Evenings by appointment.

This store offers haute couture women's clothing, and leading American and European designers such as Gispa, Louis Feraud, Carolina Herrera and Albert Nipon are among the labels that show up on the racks, all at 30% to 70% less than retail. A designer wool suit, once $450, might sell here for $199; a washable silk dress, originally $350, might be $179. These are special purchases, not samples, and most items are one of a kind. There's an emphasis on coordinating accessories and natural fabrics. There are more small sizes than large.

Also see Discount Department Stores and Membership Warehouses

Whether you're picking up some frozen chicken legs at Sam's Club, buying a wedding gift at Tuesday Morning or pawing through the baby clothes at T.J. Maxx, take an extra 10 minutes to see what's on sale in your size.

Donna Karan Company Store

765 Anemone Trail, Dillon, (970) 262-2151.

Ski season: 10 a.m. to 8 p.m. Monday through Saturday; 10 to 6 Sunday. Off season: 10 a.m. to 6 p.m. every day.

DKNY is within sight of the Silverthorne factory outlets, on Exit 205, the same exit from I-70 you would use for the factory outlets. Take a left from the interstate; it's directly behind City Market. You say you want deals? How about a mustard-colored leather and suede varsity jacket, made to sell for $1,995, for only $1,195? A savings of $800! To be fair, most of the prices aren't all that stratospheric, although you'd never mistake this outlet for Wal-Mart. The least expensive thing we found was a t-shirt for $20 (originally $35). The clothing all looks very nice, but the deal with Donna Karan is status. It has to say DKNY on it somewhere, or why else would you pay $65 for a sweatshirt? Those sweatshirts, by the way, are only $40 here, and they may be less in the men's section, which offers a full range of men's clothing, including jeans, t-shirts and sports jackets. Back in the women's section, which is the largest part of the store, the handbags are a pretty good deal at $125. A $395 blazer was $235; another was marked down from $675 to $375.

Dress Barn and Westport Ltd.

Dress Barn: 8031 Wadsworth Blvd., Arvada, 425-5886; 2520 Arapahoe Ave., Boulder (Arapahoe Village Shopping Center), 545-5745; 10705 W. Colfax Ave., (Westland Town Center), Lakewood, 462-0238.

10 a.m. to 9 p.m. Monday through Friday; 10 a.m. to 6 p.m. Saturday; noon to 5 p.m. Sunday.

Westport Ltd.: Castle Rock, 688-9281; Colby, Kansas, (913) 462-2221; Loveland, (970) 669-8903.

See Factory Outlet Malls for address, hours and directions.

Dress Barn is the parent company for the outlet stores of Westport and SBX. Price points and merchandise are identical among the three stores. Only the names are different. Westport Woman is the large-size line, and it's carried at both Dress Barn and Westport Ltd. SBX, an outlet at Castle Rock (660-1100), is the casual side of this line. The clothing sold at these stores is made for them, and the stores also carry other lines of women's dress, casual and career wear. The merchandise is basically mid-range. At these stores, a $120 lined wool suit would go on sale for $89.

Eagle's Eye

Castle Rock, 660-0477; Loveland, (970) 593-0736.

See Factory Outlet Malls for address, hours and directions.

Eagle's Eye is the place to go for a hand-knit sweater that's themed for a holiday—Halloween, Christmas, Valentine's Day—they've got it, and at $30 to $50 less than what you'd pay at a department store. They also carry cotton-knit stirrup pants, turtlenecks and other items that would complete an outfit with a fancy sweater at its center.

Esprit Direct

1200 Pearl St. (Pearl Street Mall), Boulder, 447-9488; Loveland, (970) 669-1324.

10 a.m. to 7 p.m. Monday through Saturday; noon to 5 p.m. Sunday.

This Esprit factory outlet usually gets Esprit clothing about eight to ten weeks after the department stores and starts with a 30% discount, then continues to mark down, sometimes reaching as much as 70% off. It's all women's clothing, in sizes ranging from 1-2 (which works for preadolescent girls) to 13-14. T-shirts and novelty tops are usually $12 to $20. The Esprit line also includes blouses, jumpers, jeans and sweaters. Dresses, originally made to sell for around $60, are usually about half that. These include rayon floral prints and cotton knits. The Esprit outlet also carries clothing by Susie Thompkins, a more conservative office-oriented line that includes blazers, skirts, blouses and sweaters, some in silk and linen. It, too, starts discounts at 30%.

Fashion Distributors Inc.

7641 W. 88th Ave., Westminster, 420-1797.

10 a.m. to 8 p.m. Monday through Friday; 10 a.m. to 6 p.m. Saturday; noon to 5 p.m. Sunday.

The decor of this store in the Mission Commons shopping center may be early warehouse, but it does indulge in the luxury of a partner who personally travels to New York to check out the deals in the Garment District. The store carries career wear in petite and plus sizes, in addition to your basic 4-16. Lines include Jessica Howard, Positive Attitudes, Jeffrey & Dara, Tess, Daniel B., Dani Max and All That Jazz.

Fashion Gal

2495 S. Havana Blvd., Aurora, 696-8617; 15241 E. Mississippi Ave., Aurora, 755-9937; 890 S. Monaco Blvd., Denver, 388-3629; 8011 Wadsworth Blvd., Arvada, 420-2834; 8555 W. Belleview Ave., Littleton, 973-5662; 747 N. Academy Blvd., Colorado Springs, (719) 591-9442.

9 a.m. to 9 p.m. Monday through Saturday; noon to 6 p.m. Sunday.

The emphasis at this chain is on juniors, although there is a full array of women's sizes. Leggings, tops, vests, shirts, tunics, sweaters, jeans, dresses and pant sets are sold at discounts that start at around 30% and can drop to more than 65% during clearances.

Geoffrey Beene Woman

Castle Rock, 660-1924; Silverthorne, (970) 262-2980.

See Factory Outlet Malls for address, hours and directions.

The Geoffrey Beene women's line broke off from this well-known men's line a couple of years ago. The emphasis is on career wear and more casual, yet sophisticated clothing. Discounts are 25% to 30%.

harve benard

Silverthorne (970) 468-1338.

See Factory Outlet Malls for address, hours and directions

The harve benard line of women's career wear is featured here for 20% to 50% less than retail. It includes such businesslike items as blazers, skirts, separates and coat dresses.

He-Ro Group Outlet

Silverthorne, (970) 262-1944.

See Factory Outlet Malls for address, hours and directions.

Although this store carries such casual items as blouses, cashmere sweaters and lined slacks, the emphasis is on glitz. The He-Ro Group manufactures evening wear with such labels as Black Tie and Bob Mackie. So if you're looking for a prom dress or something for the mother of the bride, this is probably a worthwhile stop. One dress spotted at a Cherry Creek Mall boutique for $400 was $150 here.

Hit or Miss

7721 Wadsworth Blvd., Arvada, 431-1240; 15081 E. Mississippi Ave., Aurora, 337-9724; 1645 Quail St., Lakewood, 232-1159; 8555 W. Belleview Ave., Littleton, 973-9598.

10 a.m. to 9 p.m. Monday through Friday; 10 a.m. to 6 p.m. Saturday; noon to 5 p.m. Sunday.

The emphasis is on career wear at this chain, which seems to go straight for the baby-boom market. A wool blazer sold in department stores or mall boutiques for $70 would be closer to $50 here. They also carry casual items such as jeans and shirts. Discounts range from 20% to 50%.

I.B. Diffusion

Silverthorne, (970) 468-2288.

See Factory Outlet Malls for address, hours and directions.

I.B. Diffusion is the only line sold at this outlet. The line features some resort and career wear, although it's most memorable for the glitzy sweaters. Discounts range from 30% to 80%.

JH Collectibles

Silverthorne (970) 468-9023.

See Factory Outlet Malls for address, hours and directions.

JH Collectibles clothing is on the preppy side, with lots of wool, corduroy, silk and cotton. The store carries only items from JH

Collectibles, which include slacks, skirts, blazers, coats, blouses and accessories, as well as casual wear. Discounts range from 20% to 60%.

Jonathan Logan

Castle Rock, 660-3848.

See Factory Outlet Malls for address, hours and directions.

The main line sold in this outlet is Jonathan Logan, but from time to time it gets other labels, including Requirements, Miss Erica and Sag Harbor.

Jones NY Factory Finale

Castle Rock, 660-2083; Loveland, (970) 669-8887; Silverthorne, (970) 468-2484.

See Factory Outlet Malls for address, hours and directions.

Women's career wear, sportswear, dresses—even lingerie at the Silverthorne outlet. Although the Jones New York line heavily dominates, you also may find occasional items from Evan Picone or Christian Dior. Discounts range from 25% to 50%

Just Samples

8215 S. Holly St., Littleton, 843-0269.

Open periodically.

See Direct and Seasonal Sales.

This store sells new sample clothing at wholesale prices, and the women's clothing sales are usually held in February, April, July, September and November. If you want to know exact dates, call and leave a message—they'll get back to you. Sizes are mostly 6-12 from a variety of lines, including Carol Anderson, Jansen and Lanz. Check the bargain racks for deals on the previous season's clothing. The annual golf sale is usually held in March, and a ski sale in August; both usually feature clothing and equipment for both men and women.

Koret

Castle Rock, 660-1740.

See Factory Outlet Malls for address, hours and directions.

Although most women think of Koret as a line for older women, with an emphasis on polyester, it has come into the '90s with wool, cotton and silk done up in sports and career wear. The base discount is 35% and goes deeper during frequent sales.

Leslie Fay

Castle Rock, 688-2861; Silverthorne, (970) 468-9311.

See Factory Outlet Malls for address, hours and directions.

In addition to those pretty Leslie Fay dresses, these outlets also carry the Alpert Nipon designer line and Theo Miles sportswear. Discounts range from 20% to 30%.

Liz Claiborne

Silverthorne (970) 468-2484.

See Factory Outlet Malls for address, hours and directions.

There may be one woman in Outer Mongolia who's never owned something made by Claiborne under one of the firm's plethora of labels (Liz & Co., Lizwear), but we doubt it. Claiborne's popularity makes this one of the busiest factory outlets in the state. Discounts range from 35% to 50%.

Loehmann's

7400 E. Hampden Ave., Denver, 779-6890.

10 a.m. to 6 p.m. Saturday and Monday; 10 a.m. to 9 p.m. Tuesday through Friday; noon to 6 p.m. Sunday

Loehmann's has always been a great place for the woman who considers bargain hunting her *raison d'être*. It's a great place for someone who's dedicated and has time to visit frequently and really look around. It's possible to stumble on terrific labels in an array of merchandise including women's shoes, lingerie, accessories and "dress-up" clothes.

Women's Clothing **197**

But don't ever buy here for another person, and be sure to try on anything you're considering, because the return policy is heavily weighted toward management. Items must be returned within seven days of purchase, the ticket must be attached and it must be accompanied by a receipt. Then you get a store credit, not cash.

It's a good idea to get on the mailing list so you can be notified of semi-annual half-off sales.

Marie Diamond

Castle Rock, 660-9121.

See Factory Outlet Malls for address, hours and directions.

Marie Diamond is a division of I.B. Diffusion, and lines sold here include those two plus Centuria, a third line from the same firm. The clothing is essentially dressy casual—lots of brightly patterned sweaters and stirrup pants—and discounts range from 30% to 70%.

Marika

Silverthorne, (970) 468-1515.

See Factory Outlet Malls for address, hours and directions.

Finally, an outlet where the merchandise really is inexpensive! About 90% of the dancewear, aerobics wear and casual clothing sold in this store ranges in price from $7.99 to $15.99. The most expensive thing in the store the day we were there was a silk jogging suit for $50.

Marisa Christina

Silverthorne, (970) 262-9322.

See Factory Outlet Malls for address, hours and directions.

The emphasis at Marisa Christina is on decorated sweaters and other dressy casual clothing, including slacks, shorts, vests and blouses. An $88 vest would sell here for $66. With the Silverthorne Preferred Client Card, which offers at discounts at several stores in the factory outlet mall, Marisa Christina offers an additional 10% discount.

NPR

7700 E. Iliff Ave., Suite B, Denver, 695-9596.

10 a.m. to 4 p.m. Monday through Saturday.

If you're a sample-size kind of gal—say size 8 to 10—you should know about NPR samples. The store stocks women's sample clothing from a variety of designers, and it's all marked just 8% over wholesale. Because this is sample clothing, it's usually a season or so ahead of what you'll find in the stores. The store is tucked away in an office park and is hard to find, so call for directions.

Robert Scott & David Brooks

Castle Rock, 688-3275.

See Factory Outlet Malls for address, hours and directions.

The parent company for Robert Scott & David Brooks makes the clothing sold by Talbot's through both mail-order and retail outlets. You can generally expect to pay 35% less here than suggested retail, and items may be identical, although the labels will be different. The company supplies other mail-order firms, too.

Sandy's Upscale Outlet

7220 W. 38th Ave., Wheat Ridge, 467-6979.

11 a.m. to 5 p.m. Tuesday through Saturday; til 7 p.m. Thursday.

This store is an outlet for new sample clothing, accessories and jewelry, with prices generally 30% to 50% less than the retail. Because the merchandise is samples, the clothing is current or slightly ahead of the department stores, and frequent sales bring prices even lower. Labels include Sandy Sandy, Pykette and Sabino. Former clients of Darlene's Sample Shop will be interested to know that Darlene Hedrick started working here shortly after her store closed.

Smelter's Coalroom

Durango, (970) 259-3470.

See Factory Outlet Malls for address, hours and directions.

This outlet offers a mixture of Western clothing, some of which is made in Durango, and discounted designer clothing bearing the Sarah Campbell label.

The Snob Shop

2804 E. Sixth Ave., Denver, 355-6939.

10 a.m. to 7 p.m. Monday through Friday; 10 a.m. to 6 p.m. Saturday.

Although people think of the Snob Shop as a consignment store, it also gets new clothes that the carriage trade stores in Cherry Creek North don't want to put on clearance. Sometimes you can find something wonderful that still has the original store tags. (A friend found a wedding dress with Auer's tags indicating that suggested retail was more than $1,000—and she got it at the Snob Shop for less than $200.)

A Step Ahead

8200 S. Quebec St., Englewood, 694-0404.

10 a.m. to 6 p.m. Monday through Saturday.

Owner Sandy Eames makes frequent buying trips to Los Angeles, and that's how she's able to offer up-to-the-minute women's fashions in labels not usually seen in Colorado for discounts of 20% to 60%.

Tanner

Castle Rock, 660-8769.

See Factory Outlet Malls for address, hours and directions.

Tanner is the parent company for Doncaster clothing, which is only sold direct to customers. When it's one year old, however, the Doncaster line shows up in factory outlets like this one at significant discounts. Doncaster is a very classic line; it doesn't change all that much from year to year, so the outlet offers a good opportunity to find such items as good wool blazers, linen dresses and raw-silk suits.

Turtle Lake Clothing Co.

835 Main Ave., #108, Durango, (970) 247-0151.

See Factory outlet malls for address, hours and directions.

This outlet carries women's sportswear and accessory closeouts from several manufacturers, including Jantzen, Duofold, Wigwam, Speedo, Wrangler, Leslie Fay and Woolrich.

Van Heusen for Her

Castle Rock, 660-0958.

See Factory Outlet Malls for address, hours and directions.

The label says Van Heusen, but the line isn't particularly tailored. Women's clothing in the Van Heusen line includes sweaters, skirts and dresses, and fabrics include silk, flannel and rayon, as well as cotton and wool. Discounts start at 25% and go deeper the longer items are in the store or when there's a sale.

Warehouse of Fashion. *See* Fashion Gal

1625 Quail St., Lakewood, 232-5436 and 238-8459.

9 a.m. to 9 p.m. Monday through Saturday; noon to 6 p.m. Sunday.

Westport Ltd. *See* Dress Barn

Castle Rock, 688-9281; Colby, Kansas, (913) 462-2221; Loveland, (970) 669-8903.

See Factory Outlet Malls for address, hours and directions.

Clothes for Large Women

Large women haven't always had much choice in clothing. Since the first Lane Bryant store opened at the turn of the century, the development of fashionable clothing lines for the ample woman has been a slow process. But in the mid-'90s we're almost there. Nearly a decade ago, someone with an eye for statistics and money noticed that most women don't wear a size 8. The result was a flourishing of fashion for large women, and the subsequent flourishing of stores that stock high-quality large-size clothing. Here are some places that specialize in either discount or consignment clothes for women who may have given up on dieting but haven't given up on looking great. Also check the store around the corner from your house. Chances are good that there's a rack dedicated to size 14 and up.

The Avenue

1306 S. Havana Ave. (Buckingham Square), Aurora, 751-4117.

10 a.m. to 9 p.m. Monday through Friday; 10 a.m. to 7 p.m. Saturday.

Although this place isn't technically a discount store, something is always on sale. It carries size 14 and up in good labels and styles.

Boofers

2425 Canyon Blvd., Boulder, 388-9830; 2350 N. 95th St., Boulder, half a mile north of Arapahoe, 666-1883, 666-1884, 442-3334; The Total Look, 2120 S. Holly St., Denver, 758-6976.

Canyon Blvd.: 10 a.m. to 5 p.m. Monday through Friday; 11 a.m. to 4 p.m. Saturday. 95th St.: 10 a.m. to 6 p.m. Fridays; variable hours Monday, Wednesday and Saturday—call first. Total Look: 10 a.m. to 5 p.m. Monday through Friday; 11 a.m. to 4 p.m. Saturday.

This Boulder manufacturer of brightly colored all-cotton clothing offers a wide variety of dresses and separates in sizes up to 4 extra large (about size 28). There are also does sueded rayons and silks. Normal prices range around $33 to $85. For information on how to get this clothing on sale, see the entry under Direct and Seasonal Sales.

Carole Little

Silverthorne, (970) 262-1437.

See Factory Outlet Malls for address, hours and directions.

Carole Little lines sold at this outlet at discount include Carole Little II for sizes 18 to 24.

Christine's Upscale Plus

3890 Kipling St., Wheat Ridge, 420-5423.

10 a.m. to 6 p.m. Tuesday through Saturday; open til 7 p.m. Thursdays.

Clothing at this new and resale shop starts at size 14 and goes to about 5x, with occasional larger sizes. The emphasis is on career wear, including suits, dresses, blouses, slacks, skirts and sweaters.

Also see Discount Department Stores and Membership Warehouses

The selection is spotty, but you can find large-size women's clothing at TJ Maxx and similar off-price outlets. When you do, the items are likely to be attractive and the prices more modest than they would be in some stores that specialize in large sizes.

Fashion Bug

7380 W. 52nd Ave., Arvada, 422-3634; 859 N. Academy Blvd., Colorado Springs, (719) 596-7431 or 596-5423; 407 S. Broadway, Denver, 422-3634; 4336 College Ave., Fort Collins, (970) 225-9495.

10 a.m. to 9 p.m. Monday through Saturday; 10 a.m. to 6 p.m. Sunday.

Fashion Bug is actually a fairly complete mini–department store. Included in the women's clothing are sizes up to 32.

Fashion Distributors Inc.

7641 W. 88th Ave., Westminster, 420-1797.

10 a.m. to 8 p.m. Monday through Friday; 10 a.m. to 6 p.m. Saturday; noon to 5 p.m. Sunday.

This store doesn't specialize in large sizes, but it carries plus sizes in a number of good labels and benefits from having a partner who personally travels to New York to check out the deals in the Garment District.

Full-Size Fashions

Loveland, (970) 593-0633.

See Factory Outlet Malls for address, hours and directions.

This store carries career and casual wear as well as lingerie for sizes 16 and up from a variety of manufacturers. Not everything is discounted, so know your values before you go.

Koret

Castle Rock, 660-1740.

See Factory Outlet Malls for address, hours and directions.

Although most women think of Koret as a line for older women, with an emphasis on polyester, it has come into the '90s with wool, cotton and silk done up in sports and career wear. Sizes go up to 4X or 28. The base discount over department store prices is 35% and goes deeper during frequent sales.

Plus Repeats

1677 Wadsworth Blvd., Lakewood, 238-8070.

10 a.m. to 6 p.m. Monday through Friday; 10 a.m. to 5 p.m. Saturday. Open til 7 p.m. Thursday and Friday.

Besides consignment clothing starting at size 16, both stores carry never-worn seconds from Lane Bryant, Roamans, Venezia, Sue Brett and Bon Jour. They also have new undergarments and accessories.

Repeat Boutique

7495 E. Iliff Ave., Denver, 755-9204.

10 a.m. to 7 p.m. Monday through Saturday; noon to 5 p.m. Sunday.

There's a rack or two of women's large sizes, making this an appropriate place to browse.

Second-Hand Rose Ann

3426 E. 12th Ave., Denver, 321-5530.

Noon to 6 p.m. Tuesday, Wednesday and Thursday; 10 a.m. to 5 p.m. Friday and Saturday.

Second-Hand Rose Ann carries size 12 and up, specializing in moderate to high-end casual and career wear, including good-label consignments. There are several lines of never-worn items, such as Kitavi's ethnic batik rayons, Cut Loose crinkled rayon separates, Liz & Jane silk-screened cottons and Steven B vests. The store also stocks shoes, jewelry, scarves and hats.

Westport Ltd. and Dress Barn

Westport Ltd.: Castle Rock, 688-9281; Colby, Kansas, (913) 462-2221; Loveland, (970) 669-8903.

See Factory Outlet Malls for address, hours and directions.

Dress Barn: 8031 Wadsworth Blvd., Arvada, 425-5886; 2520 Arapahoe Ave., Boulder (Arapahoe Village Shopping Center), 545-5745; 10705 W. Colfax Ave. (Westland Town Center), Lakewood, 462-0238.

10 a.m. to 9 p.m. Monday through Friday; 10 a.m. to 6 p.m. Saturday; noon to 5 p.m. Sunday.

Dress Barn is the parent company for the outlet stores of Westport, and prices and merchandise are identical. Westport Woman is the large-size line, and it's carried at both Dress Barn and Westport Ltd.

Maternity Clothes

If you're pregnant, you need maternity clothes. Particularly if you've got a career, an oversize sweater and an elastic-waist skirt will take you only so far. But all but the most avid clotheshorse is going to resent paying good money for maternity clothing that is worn only five or six months. The cost of maternity clothing can get really ridiculous if the pregnancy spans two seasons. For example, if you're in your third month in July and due in December, you're going to have to buy both a summer and a winter wardrobe. Things are tough enough; don't pay retail. Listed below you'll find a variety of money-saving options—leasing, consignment and discount.

Blessings

Denver, 791-7308.

By appointment only.

Owner Dana Berting operates this source for resale maternity clothing out of her home. She has career wear for $20 to $50 and a full range of other maternity clothing, including cocktail clothing, swimsuits and jeans. Berting is service oriented, and, if you need her to, she will come to you. She'll also pay cash for maternity clothes you don't want anymore.

Boofers

2425 Canyon Blvd., Boulder, 388-9830; 2350 N. 95th St., Boulder, half a mile north of Arapahoe, 666-1883, 666-1884, 442-3334; The Total Look, 2120 S. Holly St., Denver, 758-6976.

Canyon Blvd.: 10 a.m. to 5 p.m. Monday through Friday; 11 a.m. to 4 p.m. Saturday. 95th St.: 10 a.m. to 6 p.m. Fridays; variable hours Monday, Wednesday and Saturday—call first. Total Look: 10 a.m. to 5 p.m. Monday through Friday; 11 a.m. to 4 p.m. Saturday.

This Boulder manufacturer of brightly colored all-cotton clothing offers maternity clothing in dresses and separates and will take special orders. Normal prices range around $33 to $85. The manufacturer also offers sueded rayons and silks. For information on how to get this clothing on sale, see the entry under Direct and Seasonal Sales.

The Changing Shape

791-9007.

By appointment only.

Jody Peper, a former buyer for Joslins, has started a company called the Changing Shape that leases maternity career wear and party clothes. After a $20 deposit, refundable at the end of the pregnancy, career clothing goes by the month, at $20 per item; party clothes are available for a three-day period at $30 to $50. Peper operates out of her home.

Cotton Kids

10920 S. Parker Rd., B-10, Parker, 840-9901.

10 a.m. to 6 p.m. Monday through Saturday.

This store carries maternity wear as well as children's clothing. It also has baby equipment.

Dan Howard's Maternity Factory Outlet

2223 S. Monaco Parkway, Denver, 757-6070.

10 a.m. to 6 p.m. Monday through Wednesday and Saturday; 10 a.m. to 9 p.m. Thursday and Friday; noon to 5 p.m. Sunday.

Dan Howard's clothing is based in Chicago and, in Colorado, is sold only in this factory outlet. Dresses start at around $50; a pair of dressy slacks would be $34; tops start at $24.

Gumballs Kids Outlet

5524-A Prince St., Littleton, 795-6557.

10 a.m. to 5 p.m. Monday through Saturday.

Gumballs carries several racks of maternity clothing as well as baby and children's equipment and toys.

Just Kids Consignment Boutique

4450 Barnes Road, Colorado Springs, (719) 570-7122.

10 a.m. to 6 p.m. Monday through Friday; 9 a.m. to 5 p.m. Saturday.

Just Kids includes kids who are still in utero. The store usually has at least a full rack of slacks and dresses and a full rack of blouses for the expectant mother.

Kids Again

8253 S. Holly St., Littleton, 740-7333; 9116 W. Bowles Ave., Littleton, 973-9234.

Holly: 10 a.m. to 5 p.m. Monday through Saturday (open Thursday until 7 p.m.). Bowles: 10 a.m. to 6 p.m. Monday through Friday; 10 a.m to 5 p.m. Saturday.

If you can't find that special-occasion maternity dress on the racks, Kids Again will lease it to you.

The Kids' Collection

2200 S. Monaco Parkway, Denver, 757-2512.

10 a.m. to 5:30 p.m. Monday through Friday; 10 a.m. to 5 p.m. Saturday; noon to 4 p.m. Sunday.

This store has been in the area for 14 years carrying children's and maternity clothing. The clothes are bought outright, and the store claims a large clientele from mountain towns.

Lil Darlins

1050 S. Wadsworth Blvd., Lakewood, 935-7990.

10 a.m. to 6 p.m. Monday through Thursday; 10 a.m. to 4 p.m. Friday; 10 a.m. to 5 p.m. Saturday; noon to 4 p.m. Sunday.

Lil Darlins carries consignment maternity clothing in addition to baby equipment, new craft items, toys and children's clothing.

Lil Duds

6470 W. 120th Ave., Unit D-1, Broomfield, 465-1228.

9:30 a.m. to 5:30 p.m. Monday, Wednesday through Saturday.

This store is clean and large—2,500 square feet. The owner accepts only the best, stain-free maternity and children's clothing. There's also baby furniture.

Maternity Works

Castle Rock, 660-2030.

See Factory Outlet Malls for address, hours and directions.

Clothes from Mother's Work, Mimi, Maternity Works and a few other vendors are sold here. Not everything is discounted (so be sure to check), but most things are, and discounts range from 30% to 70%. Jeans are $39, skirts start at around $29, and dresses start at around $50.

Pockets

2862 Bluff, Boulder, 444-3554.

9:30 to 5:30 p.m. Tuesday through Friday; 10 a.m. to 5 p.m. Saturday.

The consignment maternity clothing here includes lots of dresses, pants, tops and two-piece outfits.

Teddy Bear's Trunk

967 N. Park St., Castle Rock, 660-2120.

10 a.m. to 6 p.m. Monday through Friday; 10 a.m. to 4 p.m. Saturday; 12:30 to 4 p.m. Sunday.

Douglas County has a high average per-capita income, which means that particularly nice things make it to Castle Rock's consignment stores. This consignment store sells children's and maternity items.

Twice Upon a Time

8166 S. Holly St., Littleton, 220-5075.

10 a.m. to 5 p.m. Monday through Saturday; til 6:30 p.m. Thursday.

Maternity clothing, baby equipment and children's furniture are taken on consignment.

Near-New for Men and Women

Don't think of this clothing as "used." Think of it as "gently worn," "classic," "vintage" or "near-new." Or, if you must be blunt, "second-hand." And don't think of it as cheap. Reasonable, perhaps. Your sources here are thrift stores and consignment shops. There is a difference.

A good consignment store won't take "gently used" clothing unless it's been dry-cleaned; is on hangers; is no more than a year or two old; and has no spots, pulled threads or other visible flaws. A thrift store differs from a consignment store in that it owns its merchandise outright, and no "cut" of the price goes back to the original owner. A couple of these thrift stores (Savers, the Thrifty Scotsman) are private, for-profit organizations. Most thrift stores listed here, however, are run by charitable organizations, and the merchandise has all been donated. In general, you'll find lower prices and a less carefully picked-over selection at charitable thrift stores that rely on donations than at consignment shops or for-profit thrift stores. The charitable stores have to sell whatever comes to them. But as anyone who has been contacted by one of the 85 Janes employed by Value Village can tell you, what they lack in selectivity is compensated for in raw persistence. Stores that phone everyone in town regularly get a lot of good stuff because they ask for it and they pick it up at your doorstep.

It's impractical to list all the stores in Colorado for the *really big* thrift store operations—Disabled American Veterans, Goodwill, Salvation Army, Value Village. So the only ones listed here are in the Denver metro area. All of them sell anything that might be donated—from broken lunch boxes to fur coats. You may be interested to know that most of these large operations are run by management companies; the profits are divided between the professional staff and the charity.

In smaller towns, these shops may be run directly by the charitable organization. And we urge you to check out the small-town versions. A source in the consignment business says she gets her best stuff at Goodwill and Salvation Army stores in small towns that don't have consignment shops. Her personal favorite is in Canon City.

If you're used to the prices at thrift stores, consignment stores may give you a bit of sticker shock. Consignment prices are not always low, but you don't have to plow through bins of odd shoes, either. Each consignment store has its own personality. If you don't feel comfortable in the first one you visit, try another. Consignment stores that have been in business for several years tailor their merchandise and prices to their clientele; they know what will sell in their store. What sells in Basalt may not be the same as what sells in Aurora.

Speaking of Basalt, armed with this guide, you can check out near-new shops whenever you visit the mountains. That cashmere sweater you buy in Aspen may not have actually belonged to Ivana Trump—but if it's more fun to wear because it's trimmed with fantasy as well as fur, dream on.

Most consignment stores use a color-tag system to keep track of how long something is in the store. Clothing that arrives in November, for example, gets a pink tag. In, say, February, all pink-tagged clothing is reduced for quick sale. Always ask about this when you go into a consignment store. Consignment and thrift stores have clearances at season transitions. In late summer and early fall, most of these places cut prices mercilessly on summer goods. That's when you find that perfect dress for $8. The same thing happens with winter clothing in the spring.

Near-new stores that carry only men's clothing are very rare, but all the stores in this listing have at least some men's clothing. The big majority also sell women's clothing, and some have children's things and household items, too.

Men who shop consignment need to be more careful than women. If fashion is important, examine the clothes carefully. To pass muster for women's consignment, clothes may be no more than a year or two old. In men's consignment, though, suits or sportcoats from the past four or five years are acceptable. Formal wear rental outlets offer an additional source of near-new men's clothing. Many of them sell the rental garments.

These are by no means the only good near-new stores around; sometimes it seems that there's one on every corner in every town in the state. For a complete list, check your *Yellow Pages* under Consignment, Second Hand Stores and Thrift Shops. These places generally are glad to field telephone queries.

In this volume, *see also* Women's Consignment; Clothes for Large Women; Children's Consignment; and Maternity Clothes.

Affordable Fashions

8103 E. Colfax Ave., Denver, 321-7170.

Noon to 5 p.m. Monday through Thursday; 10 a.m. to 7 p.m. Friday and Saturday.

Dan and Mary Pawletzki, owners of Repeat Boutique, recently opened Affordable Fashions and moved all the menswear there. This new store has racks of men's suits, sportcoats and trousers, and a good selection of women's career wear. There are no household items or children's clothing.

Annie's Attic

921 E. 19th Ave., Denver, 861-6161.

10 a.m. to 3 p.m. Tuesday through Thursday; 10 a.m. to noon Friday.

Annie's Attic helps support charitable programs for Denver's Children's Hospital. Donors tend to be generous. Try to be there on a day when everything a customer can stuff into a plastic grocery bag is $1.

Assistance League Thrift Mart

563 E. Colfax Ave., Denver, 861-2122.

10 a.m. to 3 p.m. Monday through Saturday.

The league carries clothing for men, women and children and a wide variety of other merchandise, including jewelry, books, toys, household goods and furniture. There's a standardized pricing system. Proceeds purchase new clothing for underprivileged schoolchildren.

Barb's Bargain Boutique

9585 Montview Ave., Aurora, 344-2909.

10 a.m. to 5:30 p.m. Monday through Saturday.

Consignment clothes for men and women, plus samples. Barb's tries to have a selection of Western wear, especially around the time of the Denver Stock Show and Cheyenne Frontier Days.

Boss Unlimited

301 E. 57th Ave. (at I-25), Denver, 296-2677.

10 a.m. to 6 p.m. Monday through Friday; 11 a.m to 5 p.m. Saturday.

The items in Boss may not be "near new." They may never have been used. What they are is old. Or vintage, if you prefer. The buyers for Boss are famous all over the West in towns that still have movie theaters with marquees. They visit frequently and buy up polyester-knit bellbottoms that have been collecting dust since 1971. So this is the place to shop if you want to look like Kramer on the *Seinfeld* show. Boss has men's, women's and children's vintage clothing, leather jackets, jewelry, hats, shoes, boots—even underwear.

Channel 6 Reruns

3270 S. Broadway, Englewood, 761-0666.

9:30 a.m. to 4:30 p.m. Tuesday through Saturday.

Items that don't sell at the Channel 6 auction sometimes wind up here. Besides clothing, Reruns carries housewares, toys, furniture, books, hardware and clothing. Proceeds help pay for programming on Channel 6.

The Consignment Store

2921 Galley Rd., Colorado Springs, (719) 591-1721.

10 a.m. to 6 p.m. Monday through Friday; 10 a.m. to 5 p.m. Saturday.

This Colorado Springs store features clothing for men, women and children, as well as household items and electronics.

Disabled American Veterans Thrift Stores

5505 W. Colfax Ave., Lakewood, 233-5349; 8755 Washington St., Thornton, 289-4849; 7400 Highway 2, Commerce City, 286-1781; 9701 Montview, Aurora, 341-7280. For pick up in Denver area, call 288-8387.

9 a.m. to 6 p.m. Monday through Saturday.

Some percentage of the money from these thrift stores supports rehabilitation and other programs that benefit Disabled American Veterans.

Discovery Shop

2200 S. Monaco Blvd., Unit G., Denver, 758-2030.

9:30 a.m. to 6 p.m. Monday through Saturday.

Proceeds from this upscale resale shop benefit the Colorado division of the American Cancer Society.

Dress for Less Clothiers

3041 S. Broadway, Denver, 761-0560.

10 a.m. to 6 p.m. Monday through Friday; 10 a.m. to 5 p.m. Saturday.

This is a consignment store for men only. It has sales twice a year; all suits and other items of fall and winter men's apparel go on sale around late February and early March. Summer and lighter-weight clothing go on sale in late summer and early fall.

Emily's Thrift Shoppe

1250 Welton St., Room 152, Denver, 575-4849.

10 a.m. to 2 p.m., Monday through Friday.

The sale of books, small appliances, clothing, housewares, lawn and garden items, sporting equipment and toys benefits the Emily Griffith Foundation, a non-profit organization that provides funds for student assistance and other school needs. Emily Griffith Opportunity School is the Denver Public School adult vocational center, offering 350 day and evening classes at 120 metro area locations.

First-Class Trash

3330 S. Glen Ave, Glenwood Springs, (970) 945-0533.

11 a.m. to 6 p.m. Monday through Saturday.

This store has a little of everything—clothes for the whole family and some household goods as well.

Goodwill Industries

3181 W. Alameda Ave., Denver, 934-4008; 4011 S. Broadway, Englewood, 781-8511; 10590 E. Colfax Ave., Aurora, 364-6385; 15509 E. Iliff Ave., Aurora, 745-4481; 6850 Federal Blvd., Westminster, 650-7724; 1450 S. Wadsworth Blvd., Lakewood, 987-3678; 149 N. Main, Brighton, 659-8416.

9 a.m. to 8 p.m. Friday; 9 a.m. to 6 p.m. Saturday; noon to 5:30 p.m. Sunday.

Goodwill does good work; the stores have helped fund programs for the disabled and disadvantaged of Denver since 1918.

Gracy's of Aspen

202 E. Main St., Aspen, (970) 925-5131.

10 a.m. to 6 p.m. Monday through Saturday; noon to 5 p.m. Sunday.

Gracy's is the best-known Aspen consignment store, featuring clothes, antiques, jewelry and collectibles. The biggest sellers are clothing and accessories for men, women and children. This store also usually has a good selection of used ski clothing, accessories and jackets.

Repeat Performance

829 N. Union St., Colorado Springs, (719) 633-1325.

11 a.m. to 5:30 p.m. Tuesday through Saturday.

Here you can buy or rent wedding or prom dresses, tuxedos and costumes.

Rich Rags

600 Downing St., Denver, 861-2130.

11 a.m. to 7 p.m. Monday through Friday; 10 a.m. to 6 pm. Saturday; noon to 5 p.m. Sunday.

Rich Rags has more than 600 evening gowns for rent or to buy and an additional 200 that are on consignment, which makes it a vital stop if you're hunting for, say, a prom dress. Rich Rags' strength, though, is in its selection of career wear. It also carries menswear, with several racks of suits, sport coats, shirts and trousers. This consignment store doesn't carry children's clothing.

Robert Wilson Formal Wear

1718 E. Sixth Ave., 321-2315; 6530 Wadsworth Ave., Arvada, 425-0360; 5910 S. University Blvd., Littleton, 794-7969.

9 a.m. to 6 p.m. Tuesday through Friday; 10 a.m. to 7 p.m. Saturday; 10 a.m. to 4 p.m. Sunday.

If you're looking for formal wear, check rental places, such as this one, off season. When their season is up, they clear away "gently worn" items, selling tuxedos that originally were nearly $500 for less than $200. "Off season" can be at any time, since these stores continually replenish stock to keep current with fashion.

Salvation Army

2205 E. Colfax Ave., Denver, 329-6490; 15575 E. Colfax Ave., Aurora, 344-8916; 421 S. Federal Blvd., Denver, 922-3024; 101 W. Floyd Ave., Englewood, 761-8087; 880 E. 88th Ave., Thornton, 289-5523; 9771 W. 58th Ave., Arvada, 423-6517; 3280 W. 28th, Boulder, 443-3806. For pick up in Denver area, call 294-0571.

9 a.m. to 5 p.m. Monday through Saturday.

A portion of the money from these stores supports drug and alcohol rehabilitation programs.

Savers Thrift Department Store

1977 Sheridan Blvd., Denver, 274-8452.

9 a.m to 9 p.m Monday through Saturday; noon to 7 p.m. Sunday.

This is something different—a thrift department store. Savers gets first crack at items collected by various charitable groups, pays a fair price, then sells the merchandise in this huge store. Savers claims to have some 100,000 items in every category, including clothing, housewares, books, furniture and toys.

Second Time Shop

351 W. Girard Ave., Englewood, 789-4055.

10 a.m. to 6 p.m. Monday through Saturday.

The Junior League runs this shop, and items are most likely to be donated by members, who tend to be comfortably fixed. Revenues of the shop finance a portion of the Junior League of Denver's good works in children's welfare and education.

The Snob Shop

2804 E. Sixth Ave., Denver, 355-6939.

10 a.m. to 7 p.m. Monday through Friday; 10 a.m to 6 p.m. Saturday.

The Snob Shop, an institution in Denver, stocks high-quality consignment clothing for men, women and children. It's the place to go first if you're looking for dressy children's clothing, such as a boy's suit.

Suit Smart

305 S. Kipling St., Lakewood, 980-6261.

10 a.m. to 6 p.m. Monday through Friday; 10 a.m. to 5 p.m. Saturday.

This consignment store for men carries suits, sportcoats and dress slacks in pristine condition.

Susie's Limited

623 E. Hopkins, Aspen, (970) 920-2376.

9:30 a.m. to 5:30 p.m. Monday through Saturday; noon to 5 p.m. Sunday.

Susie's has seasonal clothes, including ski clothes for men and women. The store has skis and poles available also, but no boots. And look here for antiques and gifts.

The Thrifty Scotsman

1500 W. Littleton Blvd., Littleton, 347-8827.

9:30 a.m. to 6 p.m. Monday through Friday; 9:30 to 5 p.m. Saturday.

The Thrifty Scotsman isn't a true consignment store, but a private thrift store. And it's the largest thrift store in Littleton, featuring two floors full of used furniture; antiques; books; men's, women's and children's clothing; and other unanticipated treasures.

Treasures and Trinkets

132 Midland Ave., Basalt, (970) 927-3078.

10 a.m. to 6 p.m. Monday through Saturday.

Fine consignments and antiques. (It has to be good!) The owner accepts only things that people are willing to pay for—not the things that would otherwise be given away. Her philosophy is that she wants to provide goods that the working woman can buy at a reasonable price.

Unique Thrift Store

2085 S. Federal Blvd., Denver, 984-3806; 7221 W. Colfax Ave., Lakewood, 233-6919.

9 a.m. to 7 p.m. Monday through Saturday.

Money from items sold in these two thrift stores benefits Good Shepherd Lutheran churches and homes, which provide shelters for the homeless.

Use It Again

465 N. Mill St., No. 9, Aspen, (970) 925-2483

10 a.m. to 6 p.m. Monday through Saturday.

Kids', junior and adult sporting equipment and clothing.

Value Village

3047 W. 74th Ave., Westminster, 428-1591; 255 Hooker St., Denver, 936-4371; 1515 S. Broadway, Denver, 777-3703; 10000 E. Colfax Ave., Aurora, 343-9843; 5151 W. Colfax Ave., Lakewood, 825-7033. To find other locations in Colorado, call (800) 275-1703.

9 a.m. to 9 p.m. Monday through Saturday; 10 a.m. to 6 p.m. Sunday.

This non-profit venture raises funds for distribution to programs in metro Denver that serve the developmentally disabled. The metro area's first Value Village opened in 1967, and ever since the stores have been good sources for inexpensive clothing, household items, furniture, working appliances, sporting goods, toys and books. Several Value Village stores also offer reconditioned mattresses. If you've got a store in your neighborhood, keep tabs on it. Value Village has frequent but unadvertised half-price sales.

Your Kind of Thrift

7150 Pecos St., Denver, 650-1122.

9 a.m. to 6 p.m. Monday through Saturday; 10 a.m. to 4 p.m. Sunday.

Men's, women's and children's clothing as well as household goods, jewelry and other items are sold here. Profits benefit the Mile High Down Association.

Women's Consignment

Because women buy new clothing so much more often than men, there are lots of consignment stores that sell only women's clothing. Consignment stores generally demand that any clothing they take in be in perfect condition, dry-cleaned and no more than a year old.

Almost all of these places promote their "designer labels." But "designer" is a term almost as meaningless as "suggested retail." Designer could be anything from a $5,000 gown from the Carolina Herrera trunk show to a $45 pair of Lizwear jeans from Joslins. You're more apt to find the jeans than the gowns, but the fun is in the search.

If you're a shopper, perhaps your closets are getting a little full. Remember that you frequently can earn a few extra bucks by shipping your clothes off to these places. A good relationship with one of the women who run these stores can be a warm, wonderful and profitable thing.

This is not a complete listing; it includes only stores we've become familiar with. Check the *Yellow Pages* for a store near you.

Act II Clothing

1226 W. Littleton Blvd., Littleton, 795-1122.

10 a.m. to 6 p.m. Monday through Saturday.

This consignment store has both new and used upscale women's clothing and household items.

Anna's New and Near New Boutique

1244 S. Sheridan Blvd., Denver, 934-3322.

Noon to 5 p.m. Monday; 10 a.m. to 6 p.m. Tuesday through Saturday.

There's consignment clothing here for women and children, including infants; porcelain dolls, jewelry and vintage clothing from the '60s and '70s.

Consigning Women

3504 S. Pennsylvania St., Denver, 761-3532.

11 a.m. to 5 p.m. Monday through Friday; 11 a.m. to 3 p.m. Saturday.

This small store is across from the Swedish Medical Center. It is jam-packed with dresses, jeans, shoes, purses, blouses, sweaters and accessories. The stock changes for the season, and the owner has a good knowledge of what she has in stock.

Designer Encore

12087 W. Alameda Parkway, Lakewood, 988-2803.

9:30 a.m. to 6 p.m., Monday, Wednesday, Friday and Saturday; noon to 8 p.m. Tuesday and Thursday.

Allow some time to browse through the carefully selected merchandise at this little shop. Anything that's been in the store for several months is reduced.

Dottie's New and Nice as New

5055 W. 72nd Ave., Westminster, 650-1955.

9:30 a.m. to 5:30 p.m., Monday through Saturday.

Dottie buys "gently worn" clothing outright, so technically this is not a consignment shop, and she's very picky. She also finds some good deals on new clothes, and her labels include Anne Klein and Liz Claiborne, among other stalwarts of the working woman. The store also carries accessories and children's clothing.

Encore Shop

3920 E. Exposition Ave., Denver, 744-2587.

10 a.m. to 5 p.m. Monday through Saturday.

Everything here is marked one-third of what it was when it was new. The owner says, "I'm in the business of selling things." For example, a Liz Claiborne dress that retailed for $150 new would probably first go on the rack for about $50; if it goes to the basement, it's $25. Check the basement often; you may find a designer jacket or a great sweater.

Fabulous Finds

328 N. Nevada Ave., Colorado Springs, (719) 634-8654.

10 a.m. to 5 p.m. Monday through Friday; 10 a.m. to 2 p.m. Sunday.

Word of mouth brings many Aurora brides to Fabulous Finds in downtown Colorado Springs. This little store has a fairly large selection of worn-once wedding gowns (some may have been worn more than once), as well as previously owned bridesmaid dresses, furs and formals.

Favorites Again

963 Park St., Castle Rock, 688-8383.

10 a.m. to 6 p.m. Monday through Friday; 10 a.m. to 4 p.m. Saturday.

Douglas County has a high average per-capita income, which means that particularly nice things make it to Castle Rock's consignment stores. Favorites Again is in the shopping center behind McDonald's. When the store is having a clearance, an alert shopper might find a silk blouse for $3.

Flo's Elite Repeat Boutique

2725 S. Colorado Blvd., Denver, 753-6003.

10 a.m. to 6 p.m. Monday through Saturday; noon to 5 p.m. Sunday.

Flo has lots of "worn-once" prom dresses at prices ranging from $25 to $99. There's a big selection of carefully selected clothing for children, some of which is new. Flo and her staff also offer dressing rooms, one-on-one, old fashioned service and honest opinions.

Irene's

2342 S. Colorado Blvd., Denver, 759-3010.

10 a.m to 5:30 p.m. Monday through Friday; 10 a.m. to 5 p.m. Saturday.

This store specializes in better and designer clothes. Irene says she's not snobbish, but she has nice quality current clothing. Look for "labels" at reasonable price. These clothes are not cheap, but prices are fair for well-cared-for, gently used clothing.

Modern Millie's

2223 S. Monaco Parkway, Denver, 759-4861.

10 a.m. to 6 p.m. Monday through Friday; 10 a.m. to 5 p.m. Saturday; Noon to 5 p.m. Sunday.

Millie's, which has been in business 25 years, calls itself a "recycle boutique." All items are consignment only and nothing is more than two years old. All types of clothes and accessories are available: dress, office, sport. Millie's offers 30-day layaway with half down.

My Sister's Secret

12543 N. Highway 83 (Parker Road), Parker, 840-0791.

10 a.m. to 6 p.m. Monday through Saturday.

During a sale, you could find a good wool suit for around $20 at this store, which carries lots of women's and some children's clothing. It's in the Pine Lane Center, about 12 miles south of Denver on Parker Road, just past the E-470 off-ramp.

Rags to Riches

610 Main St., Frisco, (970) 668-3775.

10 a.m. to 5:30 p.m. Monday through Saturday.

This store is a nice stop if you're up in the mountains. The focus is on designer goods, including furs and leathers.

Rags to Riches Consignments

310 S. Baldwin, Woodland Park, (719) 687-8518.

9 a.m. to 5 p.m. Tuesday to Saturday.

This store is in Woodland Park, a small mountain town about 18 miles west of Colorado Springs up Ute Pass on the way to Cripple Creek. It and the town are friendly, casual and clean; the store has been open for six years. The clothes are displayed well and include jeans and boots as well as women's and children's items.

Repeat Boutique

7495 E. Iliff Ave., Denver, 755-9204.

10 a.m. to 7 p.m. Monday through Saturday; noon to 5 p.m. Sunday.

The emphasis is on glitz at this crowded shop, which gets lots of dressy and party clothes. There are a couple of racks of clothing in large sizes, too.

Ritzy Recalls Ltd.

41131 U.S. Highway 6 & 24, Eagle-Vail, (970) 845-7646.

10 a.m. to 6 p.m. Monday through Friday; 10 a.m. to 4 p.m. Saturday.

Ritzy Recalls offers new and consignment goods with an emphasis on name brands. This store has velvet, velour, sweaters, new and used jewelry (silver as well as costume), boots and Western wear, blanket coats and lots of other interesting items.

Sara's Sequels

6657 W. Ottawa Ave., Suite E-4, Littleton, 973-5922.

10 a.m. to 6 p.m. Tuesday, Thursday and Friday; 10 a.m. to 7:30 p.m. Wednesday; 10 am. to 5 p.m. Saturday; Noon to 5 p.m. Sunday.

This friendly store carries merchandise appropriate for the season. Look for department store brands of clothes for working women.

Scene 2

4130 Austin Bluffs Parkway, Colorado Springs, (719) 593-0442.

10 a.m. to 6 p.m. Monday through Friday; 10 a.m. to 4 p.m. Saturday.

This women's consignment store has formal clothing and bridal wear as well as career and casual clothing.

Second Chance Boutique

2223 S. Monaco A-5, Denver, 757-7805.

11 a.m. to 6 p.m. Monday through Friday; 10 a.m. to 5 p.m. Saturday; noon to 5 p.m. Sunday.

This store specializes in upscale and designer clothes in sizes 4 through 16. The type of clothes here is less "office clothes" and more "going out" clothes.

Second Expressions

8050 W. Jewell Ave., Lakewood, 988-6715.

11 a.m. to 5 p.m. Monday through Friday; 10 a.m. to 5 p.m. Saturday.

Here's a women's consignment store that handles lots of top labels and is heavy into having sales, especially during the holiday season.

Second Look Ltd.

2328 E. Exposition Ave., Denver, 777-2473.

Noon to 5:30 p.m. Monday through Friday; 10 a.m. to 6 p.m. Saturday.

In business more than 14 years, this store accepts merchandise from fashionable women in Denver. Look for women's designer clothes no more than a year old. As in other stores, prices aren't cheap, but they're good for what you get. Check the trunk where clearance items are $2 a piece.

Sixth Avenue Fashion

1704 E. Sixth Ave., Denver, 377-4327.

11 a.m. to 6 p.m. Monday through Saturday.

This relatively new store has been getting good word-of-mouth for a well-chosen selection of new and consignment women's clothing. The merchandise is upscale, with lots of designer labels, and there's an additional 15% discount all the time. Dresses, for example, are in the $30-$50 range for good labels, and the discount is subtracted from that.

Twice As Nice

909 S. Oneida, Suite 3B, Denver, 331-0969.

11 a.m. to 6 p.m. Monday through Friday; 11 a.m. to 3 p.m. Saturday.

Anita and Carol have brought some nice things into the store; check it out when you're in the neighborhood.

Unique Boutique

2021 E. Colfax Ave, Denver, 320-0797.

10 a.m. to 6 p.m. Monday through Saturday.

When clearing away its off-season inventory, this store's items can be half of what they sold for when they came in. During a clearance, suits start at $30 to $40, dresses about $15 and most lined wool skirts around $10. The store has some cocktail dresses, and it carries new jewelry and accessories.

Yesterday's

120 Broadway, Eagle-Vail, (970) 328-2315.

9:30 a.m. to 5:30 p.m. Monday through Friday; 10 a.m. to 2 p.m. Saturday.

This store has a little of everything for the whole family but specializes in women's clothing.

Shoes

Shoes for Men, Women and Children

If there's a difference among the athletic shoes made for children, men and women, we can't figure out what it is. We were recently able to buy a brand-new pair of $60 Reebok cross-trainers for $15. Here's how. We started out at Gart Sports Final Markdown, which has low prices but a very unpredictable selection. There wasn't much available in a women's size 7, and what Gart's had was priced at between $30 and $60 a pair. So we asked the clerk what size we'd wear in a boys' shoe. She told us a size 5, and brought out a whole new selection. It would have been worth asking just to see a larger selection, but it turns out the prices were lower, also. The cheapest pair that fit were some Turntecs for $11, but we splurged on the $15 Reeboks because we liked them better. You can "cross dress" children, too. And this strategy can work for any man who's brave enough to ask to see what's available in women's shoes in his size. (To avoid unnecessary embarrassment, be sure to mention that you're interested in athletic shoes only—no pumps.)

It's not just athletic shoes. Try this when you're buying any kind of unisex shoe—penny loafers, deck shoes, Doc Martens, cowboy boots, tennies, river sandals, hiking boots, orthopedic walking shoes, snow boots.

Athlete's Foot

Castle Rock, 660-3820.

See Factory Outlet Malls for address, hours and directions.

This outlet carries Converse, Reebok, Nike and other brands of athletic shoes, as well as hiking boots. Each pair is marked down by $7 automatically, and some pairs may be reduced by as much as $15.

Banister Shoes

Silverthorne, (970) 468-8824.

See Factory Outlet Malls for address, hours and directions.

Perhaps you've never gone into this store because you don't know what "Banister Shoes" are. This is an outlet for U.S. Shoe, which makes many well-known brands, and the buyer also picks up good deals from other manufacturers. Women's brands include Easy Spirits, Reebok, Pappagallo, Capezio, Joyce, Gloria Vanderbilt, Eastland and more. Men's brands include Cole-Haan, Rockport, Sperry, H.H. Brown, Florsheim and more. Be sure to check the sale wall for clearances.

Bass

Castle Rock, 688-3676; Durango, (970) 259-6483; Loveland, (970) 679-4606; Silverthorne, (970) 468-2025.

See Factory Outlet Malls for address, hours and directions.

Shoes for men, women and children are discounted by 20% to 25% from suggested retail. Discontinued or clearance pairs may be marked down by as much as 40%. The outlets in Castle Rock and Loveland feature both clothing and shoes. In Silverthorne there are separate outlets for each, and in Durango, only shoes.

DSW Shoe Warehouse

8051 S. Broadway, Littleton, 347-2995.

10 a.m. to 9 p.m. Monday, Thursday, Friday and Saturday; noon to 6 p.m. Sunday.

Here you'll find more than 25,000 pairs and some 900 styles of men's and women's designer and brand-name shoes at discounts of 20% to 50%. The store is closed on Tuesdays and Wednesdays for restocking. There are no children's shoes.

Factory Brand Shoes

Castle Rock, 660-3620; Loveland, (970) 593-0831.

See Factory Outlet Malls for address, hours and directions.

Factory Brand Shoes is what Famous Footwear calls its stores when they're in factory outlet malls. The reductions are not necessarily any greater than they are at the Famous Footwear near you.

Famous Footwear

Throughout Colorado. Check the *Yellow Pages* under Shoes for the location near you.

9:30 a.m. to 9 p.m. Monday through Friday; 9:30 a.m. to 6 p.m. Saturday; 11 a.m. to 5 p.m. Sunday.

Famous Footwear advertises that it has name brands for less, and it does. We've found some good deals here, because Famous Footwear is a place where lots of clearance shoes are gathered under one roof. We must confess, though, that one policy irritates us. Famous Footwear won't take coupons (found in the Gold C book) on shoes that are already marked down. Bargain hunters live for double markdowns like that; when we don't get them, we feel stymied.

Gart Sports Final Markdown

2875 S. Santa Fe Drive, Englewood, 761-3043.

10 a.m. to 8 p.m. Monday through Friday; 10 a.m. to 6 p.m. Saturday; 11 a.m. to 5 p.m. Sunday.

Gart's Final Markdown is a clearance center, so you never know what you'll find when you walk through the door, but there can be great deals if you get lucky. The selection of children's shoes starts at size 13, but there's not much until you get up to size 4 or 5. This should be the first place you go (although, given the quirky selection, it probably won't be the last) when you're looking for something special, like basketball shoes or soccer cleats. Brands include Avia, Nike, Adidas, Turntec, Pima and Reebok.

Nike

Silverthorne, (970) 468-6040.

See Factory Outlet Malls for address, hours and directions.

This outlet sells clothing (sweats and tees mostly) as well as shoes, but the discounts are better on shoes. Sizes are completely unpredictable, and the best deals seem to be at the smaller end of the size range. The standard markdown is only around 30%, but when Nike wants to get rid of a certain style, discounts can go deep indeed—we've seen odd pairs for as little as $5. So check whenever you're in the neighborhood.

Payless Shoesource

Throughout Colorado. Check the *Yellow Pages* under Shoes for the location near you.

9 a.m. to 9 p.m. Monday through Saturday; 11 a.m. to 6 p.m. Sunday. Mall hours for mall stores.

There's no reason to pay prime prices for shoes that will be abused (like the sneakers going to camp with your child) or that will be worn only a few times (like the pumps that match that hideous bridesmaid dress). Payless is great for those occasions. Generally, the shoes are composed of manmade materials, not leather; they're not top quality. But they're inexpensive, and you don't always need the best.

Reebok

Loveland, (970) 669-1204.

See Factory Outlet Malls for address, hours and directions.

Discounted colors and styles for men, women and children are sold at discounts starting at 25%. The store also carries some apparel, but only in adult sizes.

Rockport

Loveland, (970) 669-1313.

See Factory Outlet Malls for address, hours and directions.

Rockport is known for walking shoes, but it also makes sandals, dress shoes, hikers and casual shoes for men and women (not children). Discounts at this outlet range from 25% to 30%, and the store also carries some athletic clothing.

SAS Shoes

Castle Rock, 660-3822; Loveland, (970) 635-9246.

See Factory Outlet Malls for address, hours and directions.

The discount at this factory store is only 10% off suggested retail on SAS "comfort" shoes for men and women. But everything is first quality, and there's a complete range of sizes and styles.

Women's Shoes

My closet is stuffed with shoes, and to quote Sheryl Crow, "I got a feeling I'm not the only one." If there's any place where the shopping habits of men and women differ, it's in buying shoes. Men wear shoes until they have holes, then throw them away and buy another pair just like the old ones. Women buy any pair of shoes that catches their eye, wear them once or twice, notice that they rub or that there's a nick, and decide that they need another pair. We then keep the "old" pair, because there's really nothing all *that* wrong with them. This is how Imelda Marcos put together her collection.

Smart shoppers can take advantage of this gender habit by making frequent checks at consignment shops, because some women *do* dump the shoes they no longer wear. And usually the reason they no longer wear them is not apparent to the person who's thinking of buying them used. I know the thought of used shoes makes some people squeamish. Get in touch with your squeamishness, buy a can of Lysol, and get over it.

But if you can't, here are a number of stores where you can feed your addiction at a discount. Check, too, the chapter entitled Shoes for men, women and children.

Capezio

Castle Rock, 660-0797; Silverthorne, 468-9556; Durango, (970) 259-3335.

See Factory Outlet Malls for address, hours and directions.

It's not just Capezio here. Other brands, all sold at discounts ranging from 10% up, include Pappagallo, Bandolino, Ann Marino, Caressa E, Easy Spirit, Eastland and Dexter. There's always something on sale, so check the clearance rack.

Etienne Aigner

Castle Rock, 688-9650; Silverthorne, (970) 468-6455.

See Factory outlet malls for address, hours and directions.

These stores carry Etienne Aigner women's leather goods, including shoes, handbags and wallets. There are also a few items

of apparel, such as jackets. The standard discount is about 30%.
A pair of shoes made to sell for $102 would be $69 here.

Naturalizer

Castle Rock, 660-9277; Silverthorne, (970) 262-5856.

See Factory Outlet Malls for address, hours and directions.

These outlets for the Brown Shoe Co. of St. Louis carry factory
closeouts and past-season shoes bearing the labels Naturalizer,
Connie, Lifestride, Basswood, Jordache and more. Discounts are
30% to 50%.

9 West

Castle Rock, 660-9177; Silverthorne, (970) 262-2460.

See Factory Outlet Malls for address, hours and directions.

Past season models of the shoes made by 9 West, which include
Enzo and Calico, are sold at discounts of 15% to 30%.

Republic Shoes

2482 S. Colorado Blvd., Denver, 756-9164.

9 a.m. to 6 p.m. Monday through Saturday.

This isn't a discounter. But some women need a pair of size 12
extra narrows. This is the place where you'll find them.

South Gaylord Shoe Company

1018 S. Gaylord St., Denver, 722-9578

*10 a.m. to 6 p.m. Monday through Friday; 10 a.m. to 5 p.m.
Saturday.*

This small but well-stocked store offers many of the top brands,
including Van Eli, Joan & David, Aigner, Bandolino, Paloma,
Margaret Jerold, Unisa, Evan-Picone, Anne Klein, Enzo and Ann
Taylor at 30% to 60% off retail prices. The emphasis is on dressy
flats or low heels.

Villa Rossi

3945 A Palmer Park Blvd., Colorado Springs, (719) 597-4334.

10 a.m. to 9 p.m. Monday-Friday; 10 a.m. to 6 p.m. Saturday; noon to 5 p.m. Sunday.

Nothing at this women's shoe store sells for more than $30, and most shoes are less than $20. Brands include Clarks, Penaljo, Calico, Joyce and Impos. Villa Rossi is in the Rustic Hills Shopping Mall next to Furr's Cafeteria. From Denver, take Interstate 25 south to the Academy Boulevard exit, then go south on Academy to Palmer Park Boulevard.

Men's Shoes

I worked with a guy on the copy desk of the *Rocky Mountain News* whose wife bought every pair of shoes he owned from the time they married. "How can she do that?" I asked naively. "I just always get the same pair at Florsheim, and when one pair wears out, she goes and gets another one just like it." None of the other guys on the desk considered this to be even slightly odd.

No doubt about it. Many men hate to shop, especially for shoes. Aside from the proverbial "snappy dresser" who goes for the Guccis, men don't tend to think much about what's on their feet as long as mud doesn't come through the holes, and they're not nearly as likely as women are to make shoe shopping into an involved project. For many, it's a chore; it's got to be done; and they do it as quickly and painlessly as possible. With that attitude, they're probably not going to put much effort into saving $5 on a pair, either. So it's a wonder there are even this bare handful of stores that offer discounts on men's dress shoes.

That's dress shoes. Cowboy boots are different. About these, men can become rather passionate. For information on them, see Western Wear and Cowboy Boots. And for information on stores that carry shoes for both men and women—a category that includes athletic shoes, which offer another exception to the "men-don't-care-about-shoes" rule—check the chapter entitled Shoes for Men, Women and Children.

Don Q's Walk Shop

2351 E. Evans Ave., Denver, 777-2893.

10 a.m. to 6 p.m. Monday, Friday and Saturday; til 7:30 p.m. Tuesday, Wednesday and Thursday; 11 a.m. to 4 p.m. Sunday.

Don Q isn't a discounter, but he has an anniversary sale right around the beginning of the second week of August every year, and his stock of walking shoes is marked down by 10% to 40% storewide. Brands include Rockport, Ecco, Timberland, Birkenstock, Teva, Easy Spirit, Clarks and K-Swiss. Mephisto never participates in the clearance.

Florsheim Factory Store

Loveland, (970) 962-9499.

See Factory Outlet Malls for address, hours and directions.

A broad range of Florsheim shoes are sold here at 20% to 60% off suggested retail. The outlet also carries shoe polish, slippers and socks.

Larry's Shoes

175 Fillmore St., Denver, 322-0277.

10 a.m. to 9 p.m. Monday through Friday; 11 a.m. to 7 p.m. Saturday; noon to 6 p.m. Sunday.

This Texas-based company has only one store outside of Texas—this one. It offers brand-name dress and athletic shoes for men and a regular discount of at least 10%, and it has sales during regular clearance seasons when the deals get considerably better.

Lee's Men's Store

3463 S. Broadway, Englewood, 761-7302.

9:30 a.m. to 6 p.m. Monday through Thursday; 9:30 a.m. to 8 p.m. Friday; 9:30 a.m. to 5 p.m. Saturday.

Lee's sells dress and casual shoes in brands that include Florsheim, Nunn-Bush, Bostonian, Weyenberg and others, at regular discounts ranging from 30% to 70%. They also do regular clearances.

T&C Men's Center

7400 E. Hampden Ave. (Tiffany Plaza), Denver, 770-9700.

10 a.m. to 7 p.m. Friday and Saturday; noon to 6 p.m. Sunday.

Dress shoes sold regularly at discount here include Florsheim, Adolfo, Baxter and Steeplejack.

Section 6

Personal
Accessories

Accessories and Jewelry

It's truly amazing the number of stores that survive on the sale of hair doodads, swimsuits, jewelry, slips, scarves, underwear, gloves, fashion watches, neckties, pantyhose, socks, sunglasses and small leather goods. Some are represented here, as well as several larger stores where you can find good deals on these items. These are great places to look for gifts, and you'll find some spots to replenish necessities, too, such as pantyhose and boxer shorts.

Arrow Factory Outlet

167 Meraly Way, Silverthorne, (970) 262-1742.

10 a.m. to 8 p.m. Monday through Saturday; 10 a.m. to 6 p.m. Sunday.

Besides shirts and other men's furnishings, Arrow is an outlet for Gold Toe Socks and a place where neckties are sometimes less than $10.

Barbizon Lingerie

Castle Rock, 688-5412; Silverthorne, (970) 468-7808.

See Factory Outlet Malls for address, hours and directions.

Barbizon nightwear, bras, panties, slips, camisoles, plus Vanity Fair, Eileen West and Jantzen at discounts of up to 60%.

Bruce Alan Bags

Castle Rock, 688-2920.

See Factory Outlet Malls for address, hours and directions.

This shop sells leather and vinyl bags from a variety of manufacturers, and you can usually find something for as little as $12; the upper range is around than $100. There are also wallets, luggage, small leather goods, attachés and portfolios. It also carries its own brand, Bruce Alan, which is sold only in Bruce Alan factory outlets.

Bula

145 E. Sixth St., Durango, (970) 259-1727.

See Factory Outlet Malls for address, hours and directions.

After the 1994 Winter Olympics, which showed the world clearly labeled Bula headwear on the heads of Tommy Moe and everyone else on the U.S. Ski Team, sales for this Durango-based company went sky high. Bula, which was founded 10 years ago by three college students, is now the leading ski headwear company in the United States, and Bula is the official headwear for the U.S. Ski Team. The headwear sold at this factory outlet is found at ski shops everywhere, and here factory seconds and overruns are priced just a shade more than wholesale. They take orders over the phone.

Chico's

Castle Rock, 688-2950.

See Factory Outlet Malls for address, hours and directions.

Lots of stores listed under Women's Clothing also carry accessories and jewelry. I mention Chico's because every time I tell someone I like her belt, the person says she got it at the Chico's outlet.

Also see Discount Department Stores and Membership Warehouses

Burlington Coat Factory, Marshall's, Ross, T.J. Maxx and other such stores are great sources for pantyhose; the supply seems inexhaustible. Hanes, Calvin Klein, Pappagallo, Round the Clock and other familiar brands can be found for about $2 a pair less than you'd pay at non-discount stores. These are also a good places to look for socks, slips, panties and bras. Other bins to check: purses, gloves, belts, wallets, hats and children's underwear and accessories. And be sure to examine the jewelry cases in the fronts of the stores.

We've purchased our last several watches at Sam's Club. Both Sam's Club and Price Club have cases filled with jewelry, some of it quite nice. They also carry sunglasses, underwear, t-shirts and socks. And Price Club has a rather nice selection of briefcases, daypacks and luggage.

Donna Karan Company Store

765 Anemone Trail, Dillon, (970) 262-2151.

Ski season: 10 a.m. to 8 p.m. Monday through Saturday; 10 a.m. to 6 p.m. Sunday. Off season: 10 a.m. to 6 p.m. every day.

On the day we were there, one of the better deals at this generally pricey factory outlet was on handbags, which ranged around $110-$120 for all-leather bags with that DKNY cachet.

Etienne Aigner

Castle Rock, 688-9650; Silverthorne, (970) 468-6455.

See Factory Outlet Malls for address, hours and directions.

You can buy a Etienne Aigner handbag here for between $50 and $100. The regular discount is 30% off suggested retail. They also carry billfolds and other small leathergoods.

Gap Kids

3000 E. First Ave., Denver (Cherry Creek Mall), 388-0393; 6911 S. University Blvd., Littleton (Southglenn Mall), 797-1866.

10 a.m. to 9 p.m. Monday through Friday; 11 a.m. to 8 p.m. Saturday; 11 a.m. to 6 p.m. Sunday.

Socks from The Gap are thick, all-cotton and come in great colors. Children's extra-large size socks from Gap Kids are virtually identical to adult size 9-11, and they often sell for as much as a dollar a pair less. When they hit the clearance rack, the Gap Kids socks can be as little as 99¢ a pair. There are other kids' accessories that will fit adults, too, particularly women. Gap Kids is one of the few places in Denver where you can sometimes find boys' neckties—and theirs are much funkier than Foley's. Check in whenever you're near a Gap Kids. You never know what you'll find.

Imperial Headwear

5200 E. Evans Ave., Denver, 757-1166.

See Direct and Seasonal Sales.

Imperial Headwear has manufactured cloth billed caps in Denver since 1916. When they have a warehouse sale, all kinds of hats and visors that, on average, retail for $10 or $15 apiece go for two for $10, three for $10, three for $5 or even three for $4.

Jay Feder Jewelers

910 16th St., Denver, 534-0251.

9 a.m. to 5:30 p.m. Monday, Wednesday and Friday; 9 a.m. to 8:30 p.m. Tuesday and Thursday. Closed on Jewish holidays.

Although this store is not technically a discounter, discounting is a slippery concept when it comes to fine jewelry. What does 40% off mean at a department or mall store, when 100% is 60% more than it should be? Fine jewelry is one area where suggested retail price means even less than in other merchandise categories. So you have to learn the basics and check and compare for yourself.

You'll be treated fairly here. Feder has written a book on buying diamonds that is available at his store, and he offers these suggestions for those shopping for gold or precious gems. Browse to figure out approximately what you want, then get on the phone and make some comparisons. Phone the retailer armed with specific questions about style, grams of metal weight, carat weight of gold, the four "Cs" of diamonds—cut, clarity, carat and color—and about the store's refund policies. When you think, from phone research, that you've found a good deal, go to the store and examine the item's workmanship carefully. Get the refund policy in writing.

JF Options

Denver Merchandise Mart, 451 E. 58th Ave., Denver, 292-4744.

9 a.m. to 5 p.m. Monday through Friday and by appointment evenings.

This store, which usually has some jewelry for sale, specializes in helping victims of theft settle their insurance claims on fine jewelry. They'll help establish a current replacement value and meet the insurance industry's standards. Theft isn't the only contingency that may be covered by insurance; some policies also cover loss and breakage. Going into JF Options is a good reason to visit the Merchandise Mart.

Jockey

Castle Rock, 660-0880; Loveland, (970) 669-7002; Silverthorne, (970) 262-1643.

See Factory Outlet Malls for address, hours and directions.

Underwear for men, women and children; sportswear (polo shirts, t-shirts, tank tops) for men and women; swimwear for men. There's a whole line of Jockey for Her that includes sports bras. Prices are generally 25% to 30% below those at standard retailers.

L'cessory

Castle Rock, 688-2792.

See Factory Outlet Malls for address, hours and directions.

This outlet carries costume jewelry from a variety of manufacturers (labels include Disney and Timex), plus some items from the L'cessory line. You could find a pair of earrings for less than $10. There are also fashion jewelry and watches, women's belts and hair accessories and children's gift items. Prices are usually about 40% off suggested retail. Discounts go up when there's a sale.

Leather Loft

Castle Rock, 688-5836; Loveland, (970) 593-0535; Silverthorne, (970) 262-0259.

See Factory Outlet Malls for address, hours and directions.

Six manufacturers—Leather Loft Basics, Carlo Amboldi, Exeter Ltd., Lisa Loren, Boulder Ridge, and Borelli—put the Leather Loft label on the wallets, handbags, gloves, luggage, belts, jackets and travel accessories that are sold at these outlets. The regular discount is 20%. Be sure to check the clearance wall.

Leathermode

Loveland, (970) 593-0814.

See Factory Outlet Malls for address, hours and directions.

Leather garments (skirts, dresses, vests, jackets, pants, chaps), luggage and accessories. Labels include Avirex, Beyond, Marcel Kassini, Michael Lawrence, Mr. Club, New Age, St. Dennis and U2.

L'eggs/Hanes/Bali

Castle Rock, 688-6455; Durango, (970) 385-5232; Loveland, (970) 669-3777; Silverthorne, (970) 468-9563.

See Factory Outlet Malls for address, hours and directions.

Hanes and L'eggs pantyhose, socks for all, women's lingerie, men's underwear. Discounts are usually 40%-60%; some items are slightly irregular. Although women with larger bra sizes generally have trouble finding bras at good prices at most discount places, many have good luck with Bali.

Levi's outlets

Castle Rock, 688-6711; 1316 Main Ave., Durango, (970) 247-2945; Loveland, (970) 635-9333; Silverthorne, (970) 262-0133.

See Factory Outlet Malls for address, hours and directions.

Here we found nylon wallets with Velcro® closings, which are perfect for children.

Maidenform

Castle Rock, 688-8234; Silverthorne, (970) 468-5266.

See Factory Outlet Malls for address, hours and directions.

Maidenform outlets sell previous-season merchandise and slow movers from the current line, including bras, daywear, sleepwear and accessories. Discounts start at 30% and go up when there's a sale. The average price of a bra is around $7.

Mail-order pantyhose

Showcase of Savings, L'eggs Customer Service, P.O. Box 748, Rural Hall, North Carolina 27098, (919) 744-1790. National Wholesale Hosiery Division, 400 National Blvd., Lexington, North Carolina 27294, (704) 249-0211.

If you can't get to one of the four factory outlet L'eggs/Hanes/Bali stores in Colorado, you can get pretty much the same deals by ordering through the mail. The mail-order division for L'eggs/Hanes/Bali offers "flawless" irregulars at about 30% to 60% below retail. The National Wholesale Hosiery Division also offers discounts.

Napier

Castle Rock, 688-4515.

See Factory Outlet Malls for address, hours and directions.

Napier-label fashion jewelry is sold here at 30% to 60% less than suggested retail. If you're looking for something specific that was in the stores a couple months ago, ask the clerk about it. My mother-in-law asked about a piece she'd been yearning for and found it here at a good price.

Olga-Warner

Castle Rock, 660-1495.

See Factory Outlet Malls for address, hours and directions.

Lingerie, foundations and apparel from Olga, Warner, designer brands and others are sold here at discounts of 30% to 50% off suggested retail. Discounts go deeper when there's a sale.

Sheepskin Factory

510 S. Colorado Blvd., Denver, 329-8484.

9 a.m. to 6 p.m. Monday through Saturday; 11 a.m. to 5 p.m. Sunday.

The Sheepskin Factory ships most of its products out of state. Visit this outlet to find seat covers, slippers, rugs, steering wheel covers and more. A pair of shearling slippers that might retail for $50 is $29 here.

Silverheels Jewelry

Castle Rock, 660-0886; Silverthorne, (970) 262-0872.

See Factory Outlet Malls for address, hours and directions.

These stores carry Southwestern-style sterling silver jewelry, much of it set with malachite or turquoise stones, as well as belts, clothing and gift items. Discounts vary.

Socks Galore by Hanes

Castle Rock, 688-8260; Silverthorne, (970) 468-5500; Durango, (970) 259-1727.

See Factory Outlet Malls for address, hours and directions.

These stores were recently purchased by Hanes, and labels on socks and hosiery include Thorlo, Champion, Jockey, Hanes, Instep, Classic Sole, E.J. Plum and the Socks Galore label by Hanes itself. Discounts start at 30% and may be as much as 70%.

Sunglass Broker

Silverthorne, (970) 262-1954.

See Factory Outlet Malls for address, hours and directions.

This Colorado store is actually more of discounter than a factory outlet. It sells Bollé, Serengeti, Ray-Ban and other labels at discounts starting at 15%; prices are lower on sale items.

Sunglass Hut

Loveland, (970) 669-7584.

See Factory Outlet Malls for address, hours and directions.

This Florida-based company has most of its stores in regular malls. Though it's not technically a factory outlet, it is a discounter. It guarantees it will match the lowest price you find for an identical product.

Sunglass Outlet

Castle Rock, 660-0750.

See Factory Outlet Malls for address, hours and directions.

This shop handles some two dozen labels, including, Bollé, Serengeti, Ray-Ban and other market leaders, at discounts of 20% to 50%.

Ties, etc.

Castle Rock, 660-0799.

See Factory Outlet Malls for address, hours and directions.

This is a clearance center for Alta Moda, a store for men's furnishings in Cherry Creek North. Here you can find discounted 100% silk Italian ties, suspenders, belts, bowtie and cummerbund sets, and more.

Tie the Knot

6911 S. University Blvd. (Southglenn Mall, cart in front of J.C. Penney's) 347-9107. Headquarters, 798-7789.

Southglenn: 10 a.m. to 7 p.m. Monday through Saturday; 11 a.m. to 6 p.m. Sunday. Airport: 7 a.m. to 7 p.m. daily.

This little retailer makes its reputation not on price, but on selection. If you're looking for something a little different, check Tie in a Cup; designs by M.C. Escher and Frank Lloyd Wright;

music art from the Rolling Stones, Jerry Garcia, Pink Floyd, Led Zeppelin and the Allman Brothers; Molecular Expressions, lots of sports-team ties; or whatever else may be temporarily hot when you're reading this.

Ultra Legs Hosiery Outlet

3489 S. Logan St., Englewood, 761-3705.

9 a.m. to 6 p.m. Tuesday through Saturday.

Ultra Legs Hosiery Outlet is the only local source of Ultra Legs hosiery, which is manufactured in Canada. The prices are regularly about 30% to 50% less than department store prices on comparable goods, and there are no seconds. Sizes range from petite to queen, and the store offers 40 colors and lots of patterns. The store also stocks swimwear, "naughty" lingerie and some conventional women's clothing—all at discount.

U-Trau Factory

1170 E. 49th Ave. (just north of I-70 at the southeast corner of East 49th Avenue and Nome Street), Denver, 375-9620.

8 a.m. to 5 p.m. Monday through Friday.
See Stray Factory Outlets.

U-Trau is a Denver manufacturer that makes and silkscreens a number of nifty clothing items (colorful boxer shorts in sizes toddler through men's extra large, jam shorts, pants, caps and t-shirts) that are sold mainly through college bookstores and resort town shops. You pay a fraction of retail at the factory, particularly when you buy seconds, samples or overstocks. At our house, we find that their matching t-shirts and boxer shorts make great pajamas.

Victoria Creations

Castle Rock, 660-3848.

See Factory Outlet Malls for address, hours and directions.

Fashion jewelry and accessories from Victoria Creations, Richelieu Pearls, the Design Connection, Bijoux and Givenchy at discounts of up 70%.

Villa Italia Post Office

7200 W. Alameda Ave., Denver (Villa Italia Mall), 922-8030.

10 a.m. to 6 p.m. Monday through Saturday.

Official U.S. Post Offices no longer sell those nifty pins and key rings with stamp designs on them. But you can get them at this contract post office in Villa Italia Mall. Merchandise includes inexpensive earrings, necklaces, refrigerator magnets, money clips, stationery and other stamp-related goods.

Wallet Works

Castle Rock, 660-0190; Loveland, (970) 593-0733.

See Factory Outlet Malls for address, hours and directions.

These are factory outlets for the Amity Corporation of Wisconsin, which is the world's largest leather manufacturer. Prices are anywhere from 20% to 70% off retail, depending on what's on sale. Men's and women's wallets are the outlets' bread and butter, but they also carry purses, briefcases, Jansport backpacks, laptop carriers, luggage, keychains and belts. When we checked out, we liked the way that, à la McDonald's, the clerk asked, "Would you like a wallet with that?"

Whims/Sarah Coventry

Castle Rock, 688-2690.

See Factory Outlet Malls for address, hours and directions.

Jewelry, fashion watches, hair accessories, sunglasses and other small gift items from labels that include Sarah Coventry, Alex Nicole, KMT, Kenneth Jay Lane, Rosecraft Kids and 1928. Discounts start at 10% and go up to 70%.

Wolf's Closeouts

1240 E. Colfax Ave., Denver, 832-2889.

9 a.m. to 5 p.m. Monday through Saturday.

This tiny Capitol Hill store is an outlet for several manufacturers and sells earrings, hair accessories, necklaces and other accessories at ridiculously low prices—as little as 38¢, hardly ever more than 88¢.

Cosmetics and Fragrances

OK, we confess. We don't buy many cosmetics because we wear them only on very special occasions such as White House visits or job interviews. A tube of lipstick lasts about 15 years in our house, and it's more likely to melt, break or get lost than wear down. Nevertheless, we are aware of the fact that other women wear makeup regularly and might appreciate knowing about some good sources. So here are some places to explore.

The Body Shop

3000 E. First Ave. (Cherry Creek Mall), Denver, 657-9419; 1426 Larimer St. (Larimer Square), Denver, 436-9022; 1200 Pearl St. (Pearl Street Mall), Boulder, 545-2044; 750 Citadel Drive (Citadel Mall) Colorado Springs, (719) 380-0448.

Cherry Creek: 10 a.m. to 9 p.m. Monday through Saturday; noon to 6 p.m. Sunday. Larimer Square: 10 a.m. to 7 p.m. Monday through Saturday; noon to 5 p.m. Sunday. Other locations open mall hours.

This politically correct store is dedicated to environmentalism, herbal recipes for skin and hair products and also to the proposition that too much hype and expense surround cosmetics. That means prices are lower than you're probably used to paying. For example, if you can't stand paying $35 for three ounces of facial scrub, try the four-ounce Cucumber Cleansing Milk for $4.90. However, formulations are also milder. The bath gel, frankly, doesn't do much to perfume a tub.

Colours and Scents

Castle Rock, 660-4807; Silverthorne, (970) 262-2101.

See Factory Outlet Malls for address, hours and directions.

Cosmetics sold at discounts of 20% to 40% include Borghese, Elizabeth Arden and Ultima II. There are lots of well-known fragrances at discounts of 15% to 45%, including Nina Ricci, Opium, White Shoulders, Safari, Halston and Giorgio.

Mountain Fashions

28005 Highway 74, Evergreen, 674-6220.

9:30 a.m. to 5:30 p.m. Monday through Saturday; noon to 4 p.m. Sunday.

This independent outlet sells cosmetics from Estée Lauder, Borghese and Clinique at 40% below retail. It's mostly returned merchandise, but they won't put it out if it looks as if it has been used.

Perfumania

Castle Rock, 688-9711.

See Factory outlet malls for address, hours and directions.

Florida-based Perfumania has a retail outlet in the Cherry Creek Mall. But if you're looking for discounts, not-current merchandise sells here at discounts of 5% to 50%. The store carries well-known men's and women's fragrances, including Opium, Gauche, Paris, Halston, Anne Klein, Shalimar, Oscar, White Diamonds, Giorgio, Paco Rabanne, Jazz, Polo and Barishnikov. The Jerome Privée line is exclusive to Perfumania; try the bath gels.

Prestige Fragrance

Castle Rock, 660-8697; Loveland, (970) 663-3186; Silverthorne, (970) 262-0319.

See Factory Outlet Malls for address, hours and directions.

Prestige is a sister store to Colours and Scents. It takes the middle of the road in prices; Colours and Scents is at the higher end. The store carries well-known fragrances as well as cosmetics from Charles of the Ritz and Ultima II, among others. Discounts range from 30% to 80%.

Luggage and Briefcases

We've never seen the point to matched luggage, but we don't read Emily Post much, so maybe it's in there somewhere and we missed it. Our family's luggage was purchased individually, with each member's needs in mind; it doesn't match. We don't believe that anyone should have a suitcase that's too big for its owner to carry—even if it's just from the car to the house. We've lived this long without anything bigger than a weekender. If you have a big suitcase, you'll only fill it, and then you won't be able to lift it. Better to have two small pieces, so you can balance your load. We've never owned a suitcase with wheels. Some people swear by them, but we've had enough experience with strollers that we don't want to explore the unwieldy world of wheeled luggage.

So much for philosophy. Here are some places to find deals on good luggage. By the way, luggage is one of the best gifts you can buy for graduates, newlyweds or even retirees whose old pieces are heavy, outdated and worn. More places that sell briefcases are listed under the Party, Holiday, Office and School Supplies heading. And if you *really* don't care about Emily Post, check places that sell sporting goods; many of them sell duffel bags and backpacks.

AAA (American Automobile Association)

4100 E. Arkansas Ave., Denver; 633 17th St. (downtown), Denver; 1096 S. Sable Blvd., Aurora; 1933 28th St., Boulder; 8601 W. Cross Drive, Littleton; 7400 S. University Blvd., Littleton; 1010 W. 104th Ave., Northglenn; 7770 W. 44th Ave., Wheat Ridge. (Universal phone number for metro Denver: 753-8888.) 3525 N. Carefree Circle, Colorado Springs, (719) 591-2222.

8 a.m. to 6 p.m. Monday through Friday; open til 8 p.m. Wednesday; 9 a.m. to 1 p.m. Saturday. Downtown Denver: 9 a.m. to 5 p.m. Monday through Friday.

Members often use the auto club's trip-planning and road services, but how many think of AAA when they're buying luggage or a briefcase? AAA gives members significant discounts on Samsonite. We found a 26-inch hard-sided suitcase with wheels, suggested retail $200, for $86.95.

American Tourister

Castle Rock, 660-8130; Silverthorne, (970) 468-7808.

See Factory Outlet Malls for address, hours and directions.

This store has discounts of 10% to 40% off retail prices for American Tourister luggage. Some items are from the current line, but the best discounts are on discontinued styles. As with other factory outlets, don't depend on being able to find the same item on your next visit. If you want a piece, buy it when you see it.

Atlas Luggage

2433 Curtis St., Denver, 292-0033.

9 a.m. to 5 p.m. Monday through Friday; 10 a.m. to 2 p.m. Saturday.

Atlas Luggage is the outlet for the area's seven Colorado Baggage stores and carries discontinued or irregular models of Samsonite, Boyt, Tumi, Schlesinger, Hartmann and other brands at discounts of 30% to 70%.

Bruce Alan Bags

Castle Rock, 688-2920.

See Factory Outlet Malls for address, hours and directions.

Luggage and briefcases bearing the labels Travel Pro, London Fog, Samsonite and Samboro (made by Bruce Alan) are sold at discounts of 30% to 50%.

Also see Discount Department Stores and Membership Warehouses

Burlington Coat Factory, Marshall's, Ross and T.J. Maxx may, at any time, carry briefcases and luggage. We've recently seen a rather nice selection of briefcases, day packs and luggage at Price Club, too.

Leather Loft

Castle Rock, 688-5836; Loveland, (970) 593-0535; Silverthorne, (970) 262-0259.

See Factory Outlet Malls for address, hours and directions.

Air Express, Skyway and Boulder Ridge leather luggage is sold at a regular discount of 20%; be sure to check the clearance wall.

Leathermode

Loveland, (970) 593-0814.

See Factory Outlet Malls for address, hours and directions.

Most of the luggage is of the carryon variety, including Airliner, Travel Pro, Perry Ellis, Bill Blass, Viaggo, Skywalker and Don Lapel. The latter makes all-leather small luggage and briefcases. Discounts vary; you could find a small carryon for about $70.

Samsonite

Silverthorne, (970) 262-9495.

See Factory Outlet Malls for address, hours and directions.

Samsonite and American Tourister are owned by the same parent company, but the lines of luggage are separate. The Samsonite outlet carries several different styles at discounts ranging from 10% to 60% off retail. Most is first quality; seconds are available and are more heavily discounted.

Wallet Works

Castle Rock, 660-0190; Loveland, (970) 593-0733.

See Factory Outlet Malls for address, hours and directions

Jansport backpacks are a regular item; so is luggage from Ricardo, Capezio, Travel Well, Skyway and Samsonite. On most brands, the discount is 25% to 70% off; the discounts on Samsonite aren't as deep.

Section 7

For
Children

Baby Necessities

Although it seems hard to believe when you bring home an eight-pound infant, your child is going to need an astonishing amount of stuff. But not right away. Babies *really* just need lots of love, more care and patience than the average human can provide, pacifiers, a car seat and lots of diapers. Toss out those lists of "layettes." Layettes are nearly as outdated a concept as trousseaus. Babies don't need many clothes. In the summer, we've seen babies going around in nothing more than t-shirts and diapers, and they look charming. In the winter, a newborn can get all the warmth it would get from indoor clothing by being swaddled in a receiving blanket. But parents *like* to dress up their babies; it's a perk. As for toys, child development expert Burton White doesn't think babies need toys during their first year. Young babies, in particular, just don't know how to play yet. Besides clothing, though, there are many other products that can make life a little easier and lift your spirits. Just don't go overboard. You're in this for the long haul, and you need to conserve your resources.

Also check chapters on Children's discount clothing, Children's consignment stores and Toys.

Baby Junction

2222 S. Havana St., Aurora, 751-0691.

10 a.m. to 6 p.m. Monday through Friday; 10 a.m. to 5 p.m. Saturday.

Baby Junction rents car seats, bassinets, cribs, toddler beds, strollers, high chairs, play yards, backpacks and more. Many young couples find it's cheaper to rent these items for the short time they're needed than it is to buy them and then later unload them at a garage sale.

Basic Comfort

445 Lincoln St., Denver, 778-7535.

8 a.m. to 5 p.m. Monday through Friday.

This Denver manufacturer makes fabric baby products such as adjustable head supports and pillows designed to make baby more comfortable. The products go to small baby boutiques, general merchandise stores and maternity shops throughout the country. Prices at this outlet are approximately 30% less than retail.

Bed, Bath and Beyond

2500 E. First Ave. (west of the Cherry Creek Mall), Denver, 321-0742.

9:30 a.m. to 9 p.m. Monday through Friday; 9:30 a.m. to 6 p.m. Saturday and Sunday.

Bed, Bath and Beyond is new to Colorado with this store, which, besides all sorts of linens and household goods, offers an array of children's toys and furnishings.

Burlington Coat Factory

12455 E. Mississippi Ave., Aurora, 367-0111; 3100 S. Sheridan Blvd., Denver, 937-1119; 400 E. 84th Ave., Thornton, 287-0071; 7325 W. 88th Ave., Westminster, 431-9696; 545 N. Academy, Colorado Springs, (719) 597-8505.

10 a.m. to 9:30 p.m. Monday through Saturday; 11 a.m. to 6 p.m. Sunday.

Cribs, dressers, strollers, infant clothes, bedding, car seats, swings, playpens, walkers and high chairs at discounts of 30% to 50%. Be very careful when you buy at Burlington; return policies are extremely restrictive.

Carter's Childrenswear outlets

Castle Rock, 688-0648; Silverthorne, (970) 262-2238.

See Factory Outlet Malls for address, hours and directions.

Babies cannot have too many of those little stretchy outfits with the snaps up the legs. Consider buying them all from the same source, because they all snap differently and parents three-quarters asleep at 3 a.m. can go crazy trying to figure out the snap pattern. The Carter's outlets offer theirs (called Jamikins), plus blanket sleepers, playwear, bedding, hooded towels and other baby necessities at discounts of 30% to 50%.

Lil' Things

14301 E. Exposition Ave., Aurora, 341-6612; 8055 W. Bowles Ave., Littleton, 932-9620; 9120 Wadsworth Parkway, 422-6406, Westminster.

10 a.m. to 9 p.m. Monday through Friday; 9 a.m. to 9 p.m. Saturday; 10 a.m. to 6 p.m. Sunday.

This supermarket for babies offers discounts on cribs, changing tables, strollers, chests, bath seats, bottles, high chairs—the works. There are also items for older children. Lil' Things guarantees that it will meet any advertised price.

Linens 'n' Things

8527 E. Arapahoe Road, Greenwood Village, 689-9690; 5264 S. Wadsworth Blvd., Littleton, 904-0404.

10 a.m. to 9 p.m. Monday through Saturday; noon to 6 p.m. Sunday.

This isn't a deep discounter, but we found the discounts on "Things" somewhat more impressive than the discounts on "Linens." Some of the best deals are on toys, baby equipment, children's placemats, bibs and (yes) juvenile linens.

Little Colorado

15866 W. Seventh Ave., Golden, 278-2451.

8:30 a.m. to 6 p.m. Monday through Friday.

This local manufacturer of wooden children's furniture sends toy boxes, toddler beds, rocking horses, step stools, shelves and table-and-chair sets throughout the United States and even to Japan. Seconds—items with scratches, dents or uneven paint—are sold at discounts of 10% to 25% here at Little Colorado's factory outlet.

Mothers & Others

40784 U.S. Highway 6 (Eagle-Vail business center), Avon, (970) 949-1381.

10 a.m. to 5:30 p.m. Monday through Saturday.

If they're taking the kids along on vacation, getting away just isn't what it might be for parents. But some of the strain can be alleviated. Mothers & Others rents cribs, strollers and all sorts of other baby accessories, by the week, day or month.

Stork & Bear Co.

610 Main St., Frisco, (970) 668-5937.

10 a.m. to 6 p.m. Monday through Saturday; peak season, Sundays 10 a.m. to 4 p.m.

This full-line store for children's clothing, accessories and toys also rents portable cribs at $25 a week and high chairs, strollers and backpacks at $18 a week. Good sales on previous-season merchandise and a marvelous assortment of creative toys.

Stork Town

8601 W. Cross Drive, Littleton, 933-1118; 4094 S. Parker Rd., Aurora, 690-6727; 3650 Austin Bluffs, Colorado Springs, (719) 590-7970.

10 a.m. to 7 p.m. Monday through Friday; 10 a.m. to 6 p.m. Saturday; noon to 5 p.m. Sunday.

This Denver-based discounter has more than 40 models of cribs on display at each store, more than 70 among the three stores, plus furniture, car seats, bedding, strollers, accessories and gifts.

Toys R Us

7200 W. Alameda Ave., Lakewood, 922-8697; 5684 W. 88th Ave., Westminster, 426-8697; 1801 28th St., Boulder, 442-8697; 13790 E. Mississippi Ave., Aurora, 745-8697; 5395 S. Wadsworth Blvd., Littleton, 972-8697; 4100 E. Mexico Ave., Denver, 757-8697; 3730 Citadel Dr. North, Colorado Springs, (719) 597-8697.

9:30 a.m. to 9:30 p.m. Monday through Saturday; 10 a.m. to 6 p.m. Sunday.

Everyone knows the world's largest toy-store chain, but a surprising number of people don't realize that Toys R Us is a good source for baby furniture, strollers, car seats, disposable diapers, wipes, formula, clothing and all sorts of other necessities for babyhood. Toys R Us guarantees the lowest price in town. If you see something advertised for less than what you paid for it here, take them the ad and they'll refund the difference.

Women's Exchange Ltd.

1215 E. Fourth Ave., Denver, 777-9508.

10 a.m. to 5 p.m. Monday through Saturday.

Denverite Annie Slocum makes Annie Blankets, 100% cotton flannel, oversize receiving blankets that come in a variety of prints and solids, including an Aztec design, gingham, stripes, hearts, confetti and florals. They are finished with two satin ribbons, wash nicely and cost $20. These and other well-appreciated baby gifts are sold at the Women's Exchange Ltd. The Women's Exchange is also a good source for handmade christening garments, baby clothing and bibs, and the store has a list of people who can make clothing or sweaters to order for special occasions.

Children's Clothing

For some reason, the Denver-Boulder area is blessed with a large number of children's clothing manufacturers, all of whom make cute items, most of whom use all-cotton knit fabric and many of whom have factory outlet sales. These folks include Ava Kids, Boofers, Gamine, Imagine, JNK/Birdlegs and Rocky Mountain Kids, and there are probably others that we just haven't heard about yet.

With these outlets and the many factory outlets that don't have factories anywhere in the vicinity, plus a number of creative independent retailers who sell cheap because they know how to buy even cheaper, there's really no need ever to pay retail. The stores in this listing offer both an opportunity to buy spiffy designer-quality kids' clothes on the cheap and to save on things every child must have—such as jeans or underwear. The focus is on these places because we assume you already know about Target, Mervyn's, Wal-Mart and Kmart.

Be sure to check the Sportswear for Men and Women category. Many of those shops also carry children's sizes. *Also see* Children's Shoes, Children's Consignment, Baby Necessities, and Toys. And several of the stores listed under Menswear also carry clothing in children's sizes.

Ava Kids

500 W. South Boulder Road, Lafayette, 673-9300; 17 Old Town Square, Fort Collins, (970) 493-1900; 2628 Broadway, Boulder, 447-8200.

10 a.m. to 6 p.m. Tuesday through Saturday.
Also see Direct and Seasonal Sales.

Colorful, comfortable, mostly all-cotton clothing (sizes 6 months to 14 years) is sold at below wholesale prices at the factory outlet for this Boulder manufacturer. Much of what's sold at the outlet is off-season or imperfect, and exchanges are for store credit only, so examine potential purchases carefully. Warehouse sales are also held in Denver in May, August and November.

Boofers

2350 N. 95th St., Boulder, half a mile north of Arapahoe, 666-1883, 666-1884, 442-3334; 2425 Canyon Blvd., Boulder, 388-9830; The Total Look, 2120 S. Holly St., Denver, 758-6976.

Canyon Blvd: 10 a.m. to 5 p.m. Monday through Friday; 11 a.m. to 4 p.m. Saturday. 95th St.: 10 a.m. to 6 p.m. Fridays; variable hours Monday, Wednesday and Saturday—call first. Total Look: 10 a.m. to 5 p.m. Monday through Friday; 11 a.m. to 4 p.m. Saturday.

This Hanna Anderssonish all-cotton clothing is manufactured in Boulder. It's made for comfort, with no zippers, buttons or drawstrings, and for durability, from wonderful cotton-knit fabric purchased from the Absorba mill. Sizes range from preemie through adult. A basic item of the Boofers line is flat-knit long underwear, which is available up to adult extra large. Boofers' line of adult clothing recently expanded to include items formerly manufactured by Estar, so now there is also much for women. The Total Look in Denver chiefly handles the women's line, but the people there can inform you on the kids' line. Most Boofers clothing is sold out of state for prices approximately twice what you can get it for by going to the Boulder showroom on 95th Street (the one on Canyon is chiefly for adult clothing), ordering by phone or attending one of the warehouse sales in Boulder. For information on how to get this clothing on sale, see the listing under Direct and Seasonal Sales.

Bugle Boy

167 Meraly Way, Silverthorne, (970) 468-0143; 1316 Main Ave., Durango, (970) 385-7890; Loveland, (970) 663-2213.

10 a.m. to 8 p.m. Monday through Saturday.

Merchandise includes t-shirts, sweatshirts, shorts, jeans, short sets and, of course, those great cargo pants with all the zippers and pockets. The merchandise may be off season, but these are wardrobe basics. There's never much girls' clothing, although most girls we know wear jeans, t-shirts and shorts more often than they wear skirts and dresses. The base discount is less than 30%—a $17.99 kids' polo shirt was $14.99 the day we checked prices in Silverthorne.

Carter's Childrenswear outlets

Castle Rock, 688-0648; Silverthorne, 262-2238.

See Factory Outlet Malls for address, hours and directions.

Although these outlets sell layettes and Baby Dior, all at 20% to 60% less than retail, don't pass them up if your children have outgrown blanket sleepers. Carter's lined raincoats, for example, are the most common model found on the hooks at our children's elementary school. Sizes go up to 14.

Chocolate Soup

7400 E. Hampden Ave., Denver, 741-6017.

10 a.m. to 9 p.m. Tuesday through Friday; 10 a.m. to 6 p.m. Monday and Saturday; noon to 5 p.m. Sunday.

You don't have to go to Silverthorne or Castle Rock to find factory outlets for kids' clothing. Chocolate Soup is a factory outlet for the adorable appliquéd children's clothing that bears its label (it's made in Lee Summit, Mo.), and clothing almost always sells for 40% less than the suggested retail price. Frequent sales drop prices even lower. In addition to the clothes that bear Chocolate Soup's label, the store also carries J. Hook, Baby Togs, Rosy Kids, Oshkosh B'Gosh, Schwab, Doespun and others, all at discount.

Also see Discount Department Stores and Membership Warehouses

If you aren't regularly checking the racks for children's clothing at Burlington, Marshall's, Outlet World, Ross, T.J. Maxx (even Tuesday Morning), you're missing some good bets. And, judging from the number of people we've seen with shopping carts filled with tiny clothing, Price Club and Sam's Club sometimes have phenomenal deals, too.

Donna Karan Company Store

765 Anemone Trail, Dillon, (970) 262-2151. (Take exit 205 from I-70 and go south into Dillon. The store is behind the City Market.)

Ski season: 10 a.m. to 8 p.m. Monday through Saturday; 10 to 6 Sunday. Off season: 10 a.m. to 6 p.m. every day.

Your tykes can be appropriately dressed for Christmas week in Aspen if you stop here along the way. There's a small children's section that covers (brokenly) sizes 4T to 10 in both boys' and girls'. The clothes are beautifully made—cute but not cutesy-wootsy. The kids' line is surprisingly affordable, at least here. OK, so we don't usually pay $40 for a dress for our daughter, but lots of people do. And the prestige! There's no telling how long this store will carry children's clothing; DK has put the kids' line on probation. And better bring the kids along for sizing and approval. The return policy is strict to the point of being nearly impossible.

Eagle's Eye Kids

Castle Rock, 660-9810; Loveland, (970) 593-0351; Silverthorne, (970) 262-2119.

See Factory Outlet Malls for address, hours and directions.

The Eagle's Eye label is not widely distributed in Colorado. The clothing in this store is sporty (khaki pants, cotton-knit tops), in sizes 2T to 14 for both boys and girls. Eagle's Eye started as a sweater company, so look for acrylic or cotton (no "itchy" wool) hand-knit sweaters.

Echo Field

201 Steele St., Denver, 355-1480.

9 a.m. to 7 p.m. Monday through Friday; Saturday 10 a.m. to 5 p.m.; noon to 4 p.m. Sunday.

Echo Field is a Minnesota manufacturer of 100% cotton clothing in sizes infant through 12 that used to sell clothing to such gone-but-not-forgotten retailers as Merry Simmons and Jelly Beans. Here, off-season items and seconds are well discounted.

Gamine

1014 S. Gaylord St., Denver, 722-1629.

9:30 a.m. to 3 p.m. Tuesday through Friday; 10 a.m. to 5 p.m. Saturday.

Gamine is a Denver manufacturer of children's clothing in sizes for infants to 6 for boys and infants to 10 for girls. These loose-cut, comfortable clothes are done in the best-quality fabric in both knits and wovens, with an emphasis on cute patterns.

Gap Kids

3000 E. First Ave., Denver (Cherry Creek Mall), 388-0393; 6911 S. University Blvd., Littleton (Southglenn Mall), 797-1866.

10 a.m. to 9 p.m. Monday through Friday; 11 a.m. to 8 p.m. Saturday; 11 a.m. to 6 p.m. Sunday.

Just keep your eye on those sale racks. "Seasons" at The Gap are only six weeks long, and when they're over, those colors are history. If you hit the store on the right day, you can find jeans for $9.99, dresses for around $15, socks for $1 a pair and shirts for around $6. The planets won't line up straight for you very often at The Gap, but when they do, it's pretty darn awesome.

Genuine Kids

Castle Rock, 660-1973; Silverthorne, (970) 262-2013.

See Factory Outlet Malls for address, hours and directions.

Follow this closely. These stores used to be Trader Kids, which was associated with the adult line, Boston Trader. It recently became an independent division of Oshkosh B'Gosh. Some clothing is still sold under the Trader label, but most of the merchandise has the Genuine Kids label and is sold only in these outlets. Some, however, is sold in independent boutiques. Whatever. The children's apparel sold at these outlets ranges from infants to preteens, and sells at 30% to 70% less than retail.

Huggable Kids' Wear

8601 F-7 W. Cross Drive, Littleton (just north of Southwest Plaza), 979-6447.

10 a.m. to 6 p.m. Monday through Friday; 10 a.m. to 5 p.m. Saturday.

This isn't a discount store, but rather a traditional retailer that occasionally has some terrific clearances on good labels, including Flapdoodles, Tickle Me, Ruth Scharf, Knitwaves, Sweet Potatoes, Hartstrings, Good Lad and Golden Rainbow in sizes from infant up to 7 for boys and up to 14 for girls. In the time we've been doing the Shop Smart column, we've seen at least six stores like this one go out of business, including the venerable Merry Simmons. How about giving these people a little support?

Imagine

Boulder, periodic sales at the Depot, 443-5714.

See Direct and Seasonal Sales for possible sale dates.

This local manufacturer creates cotton clothing for infants through size 12. It's all 100% cotton knit, all garment dyed, and it's both casual and dressy. Call to get on the mailing list for their direct-to-the-public sales. One is generally held in late August.

JNK/Birdlegs

1150A Speer Blvd., Denver, 436-9216.

See Direct and Seasonal Sales for possible sale dates.

Denverite Jean N. Kirol ships these adorable all-cotton clothes all over the nation, but this is the only place she sells them in the metro area (although Balizoo handles the label in Durango). The line covers sizes 2T to 7 for boys, 2T to 10 for girls. The warehouse is open to the public for sales in May and August, and if you call Kirol, she'll put you on the mailing list so you'll be notified of the next sale.

Kid's Zone

Castle Rock, 660-0212.

See Factory Outlet Malls for address, hours and directions.

This shop carries a full array of children's sizes with a surprisingly good selection of clothing for preteen girls. Lines include Bryan, Beginnings, Children's Hour and Ruth Scharf, and prices are 30% to 40% off retail.

Mackenzie James & Co.

1804 S. Pearl St., Denver, 733-1987.

This catalog company has another firm make cotton separates for them, then decorates the leggings, corduroys, rompers, sweatshirts, t-shirts and fleece dresses with colorful hand-painted balloons, teddy bears and other juvenile designs. Sizes go to 8 for boys and 12 for girls but will appeal most to younger children. Sample sales and clearances in March, May, August and December.

Oshkosh B'Gosh

Castle Rock, 660-3378; Loveland, (970) 635-9963; Silverthorne, (970) 262-2065.

See Factory Outlet Malls for address, hours and directions.

This adorable line, which has its origins in Wisconsin farm wear, is sold at the factory outlets at about 35% less than retail. If you live in Denver, check Chocolate Soup first. Its Oshkosh clothing is usually discounted by at least that much.

Pour Moi

4800 Baseline Road, Suite C-110, Boulder, 499-1774.

9:30 a.m. to 5:30 p.m. Monday through Saturday.

This store was founded by two Boulder mothers who had a hard time finding the right clothes for their preteen daughters. It's not a discount store, but they have sales. There are lots of denim, knits, party wear and dressy dresses.

Rocky Mountain Kids

Louisville, 665-4420.

See Direct and Seasonal Sales for possible sale dates.

This Louisville-produced line of clothing for children, sizes infant to 8, includes rompers for infants, leggings, screen-printed t-shirts, shorts, bike shorts, baggies and flannels. Most merchandise is exported from Colorado. What's sold in state is sold at periodic warehouse sales. At these sales, the clothing is genuinely inexpensive, ranging from $4 to $8. Call to get on the mailing list.

A Step Ahead

8200 S. Quebec St., Englewood, 694-0404.

10 a.m. to 5:30 p.m. Monday through Saturday.

In addition to its women's clothing, this store stocks good children's clothing labels—Tickle Me, Flapdoodles, Sweet Potatoes, Zoodles, Mousefeathers—at a 20% discount, and prices are reduced further when there's a sale. There's a large children's play area that includes Nintendo games.

This Is Bliss

5942 S. Holly St., Englewood, 773-8331.

10 a.m. to 5:30 p.m. Monday through Saturday.

It's not a discounter, although they do have sales, but here's a place where you can find the right clothes for preadolescent and young teen-age girls.

Children's Consignment

Children, especially babies, outgrow clothes so quickly that it just doesn't pay to buy them retail. Consignment stores are the best place to find that cute outfit you just can't bear to pay $30 for. This listing is primarily for children's clothing, but several places also carry children's furniture and accessories. Many of the shops listed in this category are not true consignment stores; they buy their merchandise outright. What this means for shoppers is that the items have been carefully screened—no shop owner wants to have inventory that she can't sell.

Baby Central

409 W. Main St., Frisco, (970) 668-5333.

10 a.m. to 5 p.m. Monday through Saturday.

When in the mountains for skiing or a trip to the factory stores, check out this store. It carries clothes in sizes infant to 10. The owner buys everything outright, so she's picky about what she carries.

Bargain Babes

7020 W. 38th Ave., Wheat Ridge, 467-1107.

10 a.m. to 5 p.m. Monday through Saturday.

The clothes in this store go from infant to size 14. Also look here for furniture and toys. The clothing is on consignment; the furniture is purchased outright.

Boomerang Baby

1419 Krameria St., Denver, 329-0570.

10 a.m. to 5 p.m Monday through Saturday; open until 7 p.m. Tuesday.

This store offers a mixture of consignment and new clothes. Look here, too, for clothing, bedding and shoes.

Busy Kids Consignment

5010 N. Academy Blvd., Colorado Springs, (719) 528-1991.

10 a.m. to 5:30 p.m. Monday through Saturday.

Clothes, furniture, toys and shoes are all available at this consignment store. Sizes go up to 14.

Children's Exchange

307 Columbine St., Denver, 321-3897.

10 a.m. to 4 p.m. Tuesday through Saturday.

Next time you're driving through Cherry Creek North, have some time and can find a parking space near this store, stop in and paw through the $1 racks. There are occasionally some great deals, and you'll never know what you're missing unless you look. Sizes range from newborn to 14.

Cotton Kids

10920 S. Parker Rd., B-10, Parker, 840-9901.

10 a.m. to 6 p.m. Monday through Saturday.

This store carries children's clothing in sizes for newborns up to adolescents as well as baby equipment.

Everything for Kids

8640 W. Colfax Ave., Denver, 274-5724.

Noon to 5:30 p.m. Monday; 10 a.m. to 5:30 p.m. Tuesday through Friday; 10 a.m. to 5 p.m. Saturday.

Owner Kristine Olsen makes consigning easier than anyone else. If you live on Denver's west side, she'll come to your home to pick up large items, such as cribs. She takes clothing in plastic bags. She goes through it to sort out what's not salable, so you don't have to stand around feeling rejected. She'll donate the rest to charity. And sometimes she pays cash. She carries, well, everything for kids.

Everything for Kids

908 N. Circle Drive, Colorado Springs, (719) 473-5224.

10 a.m. to 4 p.m. Monday through Saturday; 10 a.m. to 5 p.m. in the summer.

This store specializes in clothes newborn to size 5–6, accessories, furniture and toys.

Gumballs Kids Outlet

5524-A Prince St., Littleton, 795-6557.

10 a.m. to 5 p.m. Monday through Saturday.

When Gumballs runs a clearance, things get really cheap—like 50¢. There's lots for newborns. Sizes run up to about 10. The store also stocks toys, baby equipment and shoes, including cleats, ballet slippers and tap shoes.

Just Kids Consignment Boutique

4466 Barnes Road, Colorado Springs, (719) 570-7122.

10 a.m to 6 p.m. Monday through Friday; 9 a.m. to 5 p.m. Saturday.

This store offers clothing, furniture and accessories for infant to size 12.

Kids Again

8253 S. Holly St., Littleton, 740-7333; 9116 W. Bowles Ave., Littleton, 973-9234.

Holly: 10 a.m. to 5 p.m. Monday through Saturday (open Thursday until 7 p.m.). Bowles: 10 a.m. to 6 p.m. Monday through Friday; 10 a.m to 5 p.m. Saturday.

These stores carry children's clothing in infant to preteen. They have an especially nice selection of the "in-between" sizes for both boys and girls—those preteens who don't yet wear adult clothes but are no longer little children. Look here for clothes for sports and dance. You will also find maternity wear. And if you need a special occasion maternity dress, the store will lease it to you.

The Kids' Collection

2200 S. Monaco Parkway, Denver, 757-2512.

10 a.m. to 5:30 p.m. Monday through Friday; 10 a.m. to 5 p.m. Saturday; noon to 4 p.m. Sunday.

This store has been in the area for 14 years carrying children's and maternity clothing. The clothes are bought outright, and the store claims a large clientele from mountain towns.

Kids Quarters

511 N. Union Blvd. (across from the Olympic training center), Colorado Springs, (719) 630-3271.

10 a.m. to 5 p.m. Monday through Saturday.

You'll find baby furnishings, toys and clothing for children up to size 14 at this store.

Lil Darlins' Near New Shop

1050 S. Wadsworth Blvd., Lakewood, 935-7990.

10 a.m. to 6 p.m. Monday through Thursday; 10 a.m. to 4 p.m. Friday; 10 a.m. to 5 p.m. Saturday; noon to 4 p.m. Sunday.

Lil Darlins' carries children's clothing, used baby equipment and a selection of new craft items, including quilts, handmade toys, crocheted blankets and hand-painted onesies that make nice baby-shower gifts. Lil Darlins' is child-proof, has a play area and is wheelchair accessible.

Lil Duds

6470 W. 120th Ave., unit D-1, Broomfield, 465-1228.

9:30 a.m. to 5:30 p.m. Monday and Wednesday through Saturday.

This store is clean and large—2,500 square feet. The owner accepts only the best, stain-free maternity and children's clothing. Children's clothing ranges in size from newborn to size 12. There's also baby furniture.

Pockets

2862 Bluff, Boulder, 444-3554.

9:30 to 5:30 p.m. Tuesday through Friday; 10 a.m. to 5 p.m. Saturday.

This consignment store offers boys' clothing up to size 10 and girls' sizes up to 12, as well as toys.

Tatters for Tots

5720 W. Coal Mine Rd., Littleton, 933-7667.

10 a.m. to 6 p.m. Monday through Saturday.

You'll find all sorts of baby equipment and lots of clothes in sizes newborn to 12-14. As with other consignment stores, look for good clearance sales in the spring and fall.

Teddy Bear's Trunk

967 N. Park St., Castle Rock, 660-2120.

10 a.m. to 6 p.m. Monday through Friday; 10 a.m. to 4 p.m. Saturday; 12:30 to 4 p.m. Sunday.

A pair of Oshkosh B'Gosh overalls generally goes for around $7; some get marked down to $3.50. The store is in the shopping center behind the McDonald's.

Twice Nice

1646 Pearl St., Boulder, 443-9042.

10 a.m. to 6 p.m. Monday through Saturday; noon to 5 p.m. Sunday.

This store has children's and women's casual clothing including jeans, sweaters and shoes. The clothes have been bought outright; look for good-quality current merchandise.

Twice Upon a Time

8166 S. Holly St., Littleton, 220-5075.

10 a.m. to 5 p.m. Monday through Saturday; til 6:30 p.m. Thursday.

This children's consignment store accepts and sells only items that are perfect and current. They pay cash for children's clothing and toys, or you could consign those things for a chance of getting somewhat more. Maternity clothing, baby equipment and children's furniture are taken only on consignment.

The Wright Place

109 Kiva Rd., Security, (719) 392-3584.

10 a.m. to 6 p.m. Monday through Friday; 10 a.m. to 4 p.m. Sunday. Closes an hour earlier from April through October.

In addition to women's clothing, the Wright Place carries clothing for infants to preteens as well as baby furniture and accessories.

Children's Shoes

Children's shoes provide parents with a shopping nightmare. We're told that it's vital that shoes fit right or our children will walk funny all their lives. We're told that children have different walking patterns that create different wear patterns on shoes, so children should always have new, not used, shoes. Then we figure out that kids outgrow shoes once every six months or so and that they need several pairs at a time (unless they're going to wear sneakers to their uncle's wedding, never go out in the snow and refuse to participate in ballet, tap dance, soccer or basketball). An average pair of kids' shoes will cost about $40 full price—figure a kid needs three pair at a time twice a year, and you're spending $240 per child per year on shoes alone. No wonder so many parents put their kids into $2 plastic sandals all summer long.

But here's a trick. Try to schedule shoe replacement to coincide with clearances. Clearances are at predictable times—January, spring and late summer. Don't wait until your kids' toes are at the end of their sneakers. Buy when the shoes are cheap, and try holding out until they're cheap again. None of the stores listed below are regular discounters, but they all have sales, and they all offer a few pairs of clearance shoes all the time. Besides these independent places, keep J.C. Penney's in mind. It sells Stride Rite, Reebok and several other good children's brands, and it has sales. And be sure to check the Shoes for Men, Women and Children chapter. Women, in particular, should also ask whether children's shoe stores have anything in their size, especially during clearances.

The Bear Foot

3000 E. Third Ave., Denver, 321-8721.

10 a.m. to 5:30 Monday through Saturday; 1 p.m. to 4 p.m. Sunday.

This store carries a wide variety of labels, including Capezio, Rachel, Sam and Libby, 9 West Kids, Keds and Eastland, and although it's not a discounter, there's always a rack of shoes marked down by 20% to 40%. There are also clearances in

January and February and in late summer, associated with the Cherry Creek Arts Festival and the Cherry Creek Sidewalk Sale.

Feet First

2525 Arapahoe Road, Boulder, 939-9618.

10 a.m. to 6 p.m. Monday through Saturday.

This store, an authorized Stride Rite dealer, carries a variety of other brands of children's shoes. In 1994, it claimed to have sold the largest number of Stride Rite shoes in the state. Stride Rite shoes go on sale throughout the year, and there are also always a few pairs that have been marked down for clearance.

Kicks

7400 E. Hampden Ave., Denver, 220-1952.

10 a.m. to 7 p.m. Tuesday through Friday; til 7 p.m. Saturday; noon to 5 p.m. Sunday.

This store has a broad selection of children's shoes including Stride Rite and has clearances periodically through the year. Kicks has a whole room filled with clearance shoes.

Little Feet and More

275 Clayton St., Denver, 388-9535.

10 a.m. to 6 p.m. Monday through Saturday.

This store has a nice selection (brands include Keds, Reebok, Nike, LA Gear, Jumping Jacks and Miss Capezio) and sales for seasonal clearances. If you're not there during a sale, be sure to ask what's on clearance.

Planet Shoe Zone

9116 W. Bowles Ave., Littleton, 933-2900; 7175 W. 88th Ave., Westminister 420-6200.

10 a.m. to 8 p.m. Monday through Friday; 9 a.m. to 6 p.m. Saturday; 11 a.m. to 5 p.m. Sunday.

Planet Shoe Zone claims to be the largest shoe store in the state for either children or adults, with some 16,000 pairs at each outlet. Brands include Reebok, Minnetonka, Mootsies Tootsies, Converse, Jumping Jacks, Durango Boot, ChildLife, Bass, Nike, Fila, LA Gear, Little Capezio, Toddler University and Keds. The stores have storewide clearances at seasonal transitions, and even when there's not a sale, check the Blue Zone for clearance items.

Stride Rite

6911 S. University Blvd., Littleton (Southglenn Mall), 795-3241.; The Citadel (Hwy 24 and Chelton Rd.), Colorado Springs, (719) 591-1213.

Littleton: 10 a.m. to 9 p.m. Monday through Friday; 10 a.m. to 6 p.m. Saturday; 11 a.m. to 5 p.m. Sunday.

Stride Rite has sales throughout the year (be sure to check in the spring, when you'll be in the market for dress shoes for Easter and Passover), and there are always a few pairs that have been marked down for clearance.

Toys

Toys are the tools of childhood, perhaps as necessary as clothing if you want your children to *do* something. And developmentally appropriate toys are outgrown nearly as quickly as clothing is. But parents don't need to go broke keeping children properly supplied. Try these places, as well as the listings in the Children's consignment chapter; many of those stores carry toys in addition to clothing. Also check the Museum Shops chapter; children's museum shops throughout the state stock inexpensive, educational toys. Many of the stores listed under Housewares, Gifts and General Merchandise sell toys, too, as well as several listed under Discount Department Stores and Membership Warehouses. Finally, check, too, in the chapters for Baby Necessities and Children's Clothing.

The Bookies

4315 E. Mississippi Ave., Glendale, 759-1117.

10 a.m. to 6 p.m. Monday through Saturday; noon to 5 p.m. Sunday.

Everything at this store sells 15% off the suggested retail price. That includes toys, and The Bookies has quite a few, many of which are somehow thematically connected to children's books. And don't miss Bookies annual sidewalk sale, which is always held on a Saturday and usually is in early August. Lines form early, and toys, books, games and educational items go cheap.

Gund

Castle Rock, 660-4863.

See Factory Outlet Malls for address, hours and directions.

Gund, founded in 1898, is the oldest toy company in America. This is the only factory outlet in the western United States for the New Jersey–based company, and it's also the largest. Gund makes 700 different models of stuffed toys, and this outlet will have 500 of them at any given moment. Discounts range from 30% to 60% off suggested retail, and there are always a few things at the front rack near the door that are marked down to $10 or $12. The store ships.

Kazoo & Company

2930 E. Second Ave., Denver, 322-0973; 3000 E. First Ave., Denver (Cherry Creek Mall), 329-3043.

10 a.m. to 8 p.m. Monday through Friday; 10 a.m. to 5:30 p.m. Saturday; noon to 5:30 p.m. Sunday.

Kazoo & Company isn't a traditional discounter, but it runs sales. September brings the annual birthday store sale, for which everything in the store (with, according to one irate shopper, some exceptions) is marked down by 15%. Deals are also good at the Cherry Creek sidewalk sale, usually held in late July.

Kiddieland

316 S. Broadway, Denver, 744-3325.

9:30 a.m. to 5 p.m. Monday through Saturday.

Evelyn and Saul Shafner, who have owned Kiddieland since 1947 (making it the oldest independently owned toystore in Denver), have been in the process of closing it for almost a year. It's been a slow process, though, and if you're reading this before summer 1995, it may still be open. Give it a try. When we last checked, everything in the store was reduced by 20%.

Playnix

1375 N. Academy Blvd., Colorado Springs, (719) 596-7529; 759 S. Colorado Blvd., Denver, 744-8406; 3530 S. Logan St., Englewood; 761-5630; 4950 S. Yosemite St., Greenwood Village, 694-6434; 5066 S. Wadsworth Ave., Littleton, 972-1713.

9:30 a.m. to 7 p.m. Monday through Friday; 9:30 a.m. to 5:30 p.m. Saturday; noon to 5 p.m. Sunday in Denver. Hours vary; call each store.

Playnix is a wonderful toystore, although it's not really a discounter. It does, however, hold several sidewalk sales during the summer, as well as other sales throughout the year, including the anniversary sale in September and October. The Belcaro and Englewood stores have clearance corners where the conscientious parent or grandparent can usually find a good deal. And kids love the Toy of the Month Club, which entitles members to get a cheap toy free once a month. Members of the Birthday Club receive a $3 gift certificate.

Russ

Silverthorne, (970) 468-5036.

See Factory Outlet Malls for address, hours and directions.

All the Russ trolls, stuffed toys, mugs and novelty items sold at this factory outlet are half the price of suggested retail.

Smiley Toy Library

Inside the Smiley Branch of the Denver Public Library, 4501 W. 46th Ave., 477-3622.

6:30 p.m. to 7:30 p.m. Tuesday; 10 a.m. to noon Thursday; 11:30 a.m. to 1:30 p.m. Saturday.

Any child who has a current Denver Library card may use it to check out toys from this library.

Toy Exchange

12354 W. Alameda Parkway, Lakewood, 986-5546.

Noon to 5 p.m. Monday; 10 a.m. to 5 p.m. Tuesday through Saturday.

The Toy Exchange buys and sells used toys for children up to the age of 8, with occasional items for older children and adult collectors. Merchandise includes riding toys, stuffed animals, dolls, action figures, baby and toddler toys, puzzles, games, musical tapes, books and bicycles.

Toy Liquidators

Castle Rock, 660-9481.

See Factory Outlet Malls for address, hours and directions.

This store puts together under one roof all the toys that you see red-tagged at Toys R Us because they've been discontinued by the manufacturer, as well as good deals that the buyer finds on overstocks and liquidations.

Section 8

Sporting Goods

Sporting Goods

We're Coloradans. We ski, sail, run, golf, tube, sky-dive, swim, play tennis, fence, snowboard, fish, play softball, canoe, practice martial arts, ice skate, bungee-jump, river raft, snowshoe, hike, ice-fish, lift weights, dive, camp, Rollerblade, hunt, kayak, bike, ride horses, bobsled and rock climb. And if we don't, we want to look like we do. So we buy fitness equipment, hiking boots, backpacks and "expedition quality" khaki shorts. Do we want to pay full price for this stuff? Heck, no! That's for tourists. We're Coloradans!

All About Fitness

2520 S. Colorado Blvd., Denver, 759-1711.

10 a.m. to 8 p.m. Monday through Thursday; 10 a.m. to 7 p.m. Friday; 10 a.m. to 6 p.m. Saturday; noon to 5 p.m. Sunday.

This place offers a 12,000–square foot showroom, and it delivers, sets up, services and will take exercise equipment back within 30 days, provided it's in like-new condition. The owner says he'll meet any advertised price on identical equipment.

Arvada Surplus

5701 Olde Wadsworth Blvd., Arvada, 424-5434.

8 a.m. to 8 p.m. Monday through Friday; 8 a.m. to 6 p.m. Saturday; 10 a.m. to 5 p.m. Sunday.

Coleman camping equipment is always discounted at this military surplus store, as a sort of loss leader, as are Levi 501s, which sell regularly for $23.99. Arvada Surplus is a great place to browse for any sort of hunting, fishing or camping equipment.

Bicycles, used

Someone else's outgrown bike always seems to be available at a garage sale, but if you'd like to be sure that your "new" bike has been checked for safety, trade your old one in at a store that handles used bikes and get one that's been professionally reconditioned. Some places that provide this service include:

All Bicycles, 3821 S. Broadway, Englewood, 761-4158.
American Cyclery, 2140 S. Albion St., Denver, 756-1023.
Collins Bicycles, 3217 E. Colfax Ave., Denver, 322-1786.
Greentree Cyclery, 1549 S. Pearl St., Denver, 777-4518.
Project Earth Bicycles, 1004 S. Gaylord St., Denver, 777-6158.
Sports Plus, 1055 S. Gaylord St., Denver, 777-6613.

Boulder Sports Recycler and Boulder Sports Paddle Shop

1727 15th St. and 1729 15th St., Boulder, 786-9940.

11 a.m. to 6 p.m. Tuesday through Thursday; 11 a.m. to 7 p.m. Friday; 10 a.m. to 5 p.m. Saturday; noon to 5 p.m. Sunday.

These consignment shops sell new and used adventure gear and clothing. Here you might be able to pick up a used snowboard for $20. The Paddle Shop offers kayak and rafting equipment at below retail and consignment prices, as well as discounted whitewater trips.

Cabela's

Interstate 80 to Exit 59, Sidney, Nebraska, (800) 237-4444.

8 a.m. to 8 p.m. Monday through Saturday; noon to 5 p.m. Sunday.

Sporting-goods fanatics think nothing of driving three or four hours to their Mecca, the Cabela's store in Sidney. The store offers more than 60,000 necessities for hiking, camping, fishing and hunting displayed over 52,000 square feet. Cabela's is primarily a catalog company, and if you don't feel like looking at lots of scenic southern Wyoming, call to request a free catalog. While you're on the phone, ask when they're having their annual sidewalk sale.

Camping equipment rental

Virtually anyone with access to a reliable car can afford a camping vacation. Fees are nominal. No equipment, you say? Several sporting goods stores rent camping equipment, including tents, sleeping bags, lanterns and stoves. Try:

EMS-Eastern Mountain Sports, 1616 Welton St., Denver, 446-8338.

Mountain Sports, 821 Pearl St., Boulder, 443-6770.

REI-Recreational Equipment Inc., 4100 E. Mexico Ave., Denver, 756-3100; 8991 Harlan St., Westminster, 429-1800.

Sports Rent, 8761 Wadsworth Blvd., Arvada, 467-0200; 560 S. Holly St., Denver, 320-0222.

Christy Sports

2563 Kipling, Lakewood, 237-0475; 8100 W. Crestline Ave., Littleton, 972-0432; 5926 S. Holly St., Englewood, 740-7055; 201 University Blvd., 321-3885; 5225 W. 80th Ave., Arvada, 427-1166.

10 a.m. to 8 p.m. Monday through Friday; 10 a.m. to 6 p.m. Saturday; 11 a.m. to 5 p.m. Sunday.

Christy is not a discounter, and we've never been very impressed with the prices on their clearances. But they deserve mention because a friend bought a pair of skis there, used them, found that they weren't good skis for her, took them back, and they refunded her money.

Colorado Mountain Club

710 10th St., Golden, 279-5643.

9 a.m. to 5 p.m. Monday through Friday.

The Colorado Mountain Club operates a small bookshop specializing in mountaineering, and if you're a member, you'll be notified of the semi-annual sale of used mountain-sports equipment.

Colorado Recycled Sports

133 County Line Road, Littleton, 797-1825.

10 a.m. to 6 p.m. Monday through Saturday.

This discount-oriented sporting goods store carries about 70% used and 30% new stuff, with an emphasis on individual sports (skiing, golf, biking, tennis), rather than team sports.

Colorado Ski and Golf

2680 S. Havana St., Aurora, 337-1734.

9 a.m. to 8 p.m. Monday through Friday; 9 a.m. to 5 p.m. Saturday; noon to 5 p.m. Sunday.

Colorado Ski and Golf was named the top ski retailer by *Snow Country Magazine* in 1993 and 1994. The store will match the lowest price advertised on any item, always has a few things on clearance and runs sales at seasonal transitions. The emphasis, however, is on having service personnel who know how to help beginners or experts find the right equipment.

Colorado Springs Army Surplus

355 N. Circle Drive, Colorado Springs, (719) 389-0468.

9 a.m. to 5:30 p.m. Monday through Saturday.

This store in the middle of Colorado's biggest military town sells new and used military surplus clothing and insignia; field equipment; camping, fishing and hunting supplies and equipment; and lots of boots, socks, canteens, belts, berets, sunglasses and camp stoves.

Cycle Logic

2525 Arapahoe Ave., Boulder, 443-0061; 6336 Leetsdale Drive, Denver, 399-2453; 5670 W. 88th Ave., Westminster, 650-2430; 3820 W. 10th St., Greeley, (970) 356-3663.

10 a.m. to 7 p.m. Monday through Friday; 9 a.m. to 6 p.m. Saturday; 11 a.m. to 4 p.m. Sunday. Later during daylight savings time.

Bicyclists mark their calendars for Cycle Logic's semi-annual super sales, which take place in late March and late July or early August. Prices at these clearances may be cut by as much as 75% on bike clothing, and there are also good deals on bikes and accessories.

Denver Sports and Colorado Springs Sports

7848 County Line Road, Englewood, 792-3374; 9219 Sheridan Blvd., Westminster, 426-0202; 4285 N. Academy Blvd., Colorado Springs, (719) 594-4998.

9 a.m. to 9 p.m. Monday through Saturday; 11 a.m. to 6 p.m. Sunday.

Sports and Recreation, a national firm based in Tampa, Florida, has more than 60 of these stores nationwide, each going by the name of the town where the store is located. (Perhaps the chambers of commerce of Westminster and Englewood should have a word with headquarters.) These huge stores make a low-price guarantee and have frequent sales.

Discount Fishing Tackle

2645 S. Santa Fe Drive, Denver, 698-2550; 5550 Wadsworth Bypass, Arvada, 421-4025; 4000 S. Parker Road, Aurora, 699-3400.

9 a.m. to 8 p.m. Monday through Friday; 9 a.m. to 7 p.m. Saturday; 9 a.m. to 5 p.m. Sunday.

You can get discounts here on closeout, seconds, discontinued and surplus tackle and hiking boots.

Exercise Equipment Outlet

1812 Wazee St., Denver, 293-3858.

10 a.m. to 6 p.m. Monday through Saturday; noon to 5 p.m. Sunday.

When you buy, ask about free trial periods and return policies. Exercise Equipment Outlet offers a 30-day return policy.

Factory Surplus

2300 Walnut, Denver, 825-2003

8 a.m. to 5:30 p.m. Monday through Friday; 8 a.m. to 5 p.m. Saturday.

Clothing, fishing, paint, hardware, boots, socks and anything you might need for camping are sold here at discount prices.

Fishing equipment rental

You get a rod, I'll get a pole, honey. And if you can't afford to buy, rent:

Angler's All, 5211 S. Santa Fe Drive, Littleton, 794-1104.
Sports Rent, 8761 Wadsworth Blvd., Arvada, 467-0200; 560 S. Holly St., Denver, 320-0222.

Gart Sports Final Markdown

2875 S. Santa Fe Drive, Englewood, 761-3043.

10 a.m. to 8 p.m. Monday through Friday; 10 a.m. to 6 p.m. Saturday; 11 a.m. to 5 p.m. Sunday.

This is a clearance center for all the Gart stores, which means you'll find an unpredictable assortment of stuff that hasn't moved or has been discontinued. It was winter the last time we visited, and the emphasis was skiing. There were some ski boots for only $19.99, although the majority were $150 to $200. There were also lots of parkas for kids and adults, skis, ski poles, sweaters, bibs, long underwear, goggles, gloves, turtlenecks and hats. They also had a few bicycles, pieces of exercise equipment and sunglasses. Don't forget to consult the Direct and Seasonal Sales section for details on Gart's annual blowout sale, Sniagrab.

Gart Sports

See "Sniagrab," under Direct and Seasonal Sales.

Gates Tennis Center

100 S. Adams St., Denver, 355-4461.

9 a.m. to sundown daily.

People in the know, such as tennis instructors, say the pro shop here is a good place to buy tennis racquets, because prices are reasonable and the people who work there will help determine your needs, then string a racquet to meet them. If you're just getting started, you can demo as many racquets as you like ($4 for each racquet) and all charges can be applied to the purchase of the one you finally decide to buy.

Glenn's Surplus

114 E. Mill St., Colorado Springs, (719) 634-9828.

8 a.m. to 6:30 p.m. Monday through Thursday; 8 a.m. to 5:30 p.m. Friday and Saturday.

Besides military surplus, you can stock up here on sleeping bags, backpacks, backwoods cooking equipment and supplies for camping and hunting. Glenn's also has paintball supplies.

Jax Mercantile

1200 N. College Ave., Fort Collins, (970) 221-0544.

9 a.m. to 8 p.m. Monday through Friday; 9 a.m. to 6 p.m. Saturday; 9 a.m. to 5:30 p.m. Sunday.

Hunters who come to northern Colorado from Nebraska and Wyoming make this 39-year-old institution a regular stop. Prices are competitive, the selection is comprehensive, there's usually some merchandise on clearance, and there are also sales. The emphasis at Jax is on mountain sports, and in addition to sporting goods, the store also has books, maps, sportswear, footwear, a gourmet kitchen area, a hardware section, work clothes and government surplus.

Lowe Alpine Systems

620 Compton, Broomfield, 465-3706.

See Direct and Seasonal Sales.

This Broomfield manufacturer offers seconds, overstocks and discontinued sleeping bags, fleecewear, jackets, technical climbing gear, backpacks, tents, outdoor clothing and raw material at an annual sale in late spring. (In 1994 it was May 6-7.) The sales are usually advertised in *Westword* and the *Boulder Daily Camera*. There's no mailing list, and they won't tell you anything much on the phone, but you might try calling in April to find out when the next sale is due.

Madden Mountaineering

2400 Central Ave., Boulder, 442-5828.

8:30 a.m. to 5:30 p.m. Monday through Friday.

This is an outlet for this local manufacturer of backpacks, travel packs, fanny packs, duffel bags and similar equipment. Everything in the outlet is discounted, and there are deeper discounts on seconds and discontinued models.

Nordic Track Factory Outlet

Castle Rock, 660-0100.

See Factory Outlet Malls for address, hours and directions.

The price of first-quality equipment is same here as it is at Nordic Track's mall stores. (There's one in the Cherry Creek mall.) There are discounts, though, on accessories, electronics for the machines, clothing, videos and scratch-and-dent equipment.

The North Face

2490 S. Colorado Blvd., Denver, 758-6366; 629K S. Broadway, Boulder, 499-1731.

Denver: 9 a.m. to 6 p.m. Monday through Saturday; til 9 p.m. Wednesday; noon to 5 p.m. Sunday; 758-6366. Boulder: 10 a.m. to 8 p.m. Monday through Friday; 9 a.m. to 6 p.m. Saturday; 11 a.m. to 5 p.m. Sunday.

The North Face is not a discounter, but its clearances can be very worthwhile. At one such clearance, we found women's pleated canvas pants for just $9.99, and a friend still brags about the deal he got on children's skis. If you think you might be interested in their sales, call and ask to be put on the mailing list.

Play It Again Sports

7651 W. 88th Ave., Arvada, 431-6585; 653 S. Broadway, Boulder, 499-2011; 8601 W. Cross Drive, Littleton, 979-3379; 6518 S. Broadway, Littleton, 798-8824; 1090 S. Sable Blvd., Aurora, 337-2737; 3977 E. 120th Ave., Thornton, 280-9520.

10 a.m. to 6:30 p.m. Monday through Friday; 10 a.m. to 5 p.m. Saturday; noon to 4 p.m. Sunday.

These stores carry about a 50-50 mix of new and used equipment and have a full array of equipment, with goods for team—especially hockey and football—as well as individual sports.

Pro Golf Discount

8025 Sheridan Blvd., Arvada, 650-5454; 290 W. Hampden Ave., Englewood, 761-2847; 850 Wadsworth Blvd., Lakewood, 233-4935; 1440 S. Colorado Blvd., Denver, 759-9783; 1155 S. Havana, Aurora, 695-6222; 2525 Arapahoe, Boulder, 939-8555; 9635 E. Arapahoe Road (Denver Tech Center), Englewood, 799-6133; 8501 W. Bowles Ave. (Southwest Plaza), Littleton, 973-4580; 6949 N. Academy Blvd., Colorado Springs, (719) 260-7193.

10 a.m. to 6 p.m. Monday through Friday; 10 a.m. to 5 p.m. Saturday; 11 a.m. to 4 p.m. Sunday.

Anything to do with golf is sold here at discount (golf balls at near to cost), and they have a low-price guarantee on any advertised equipment.

Skis, used

If they're going to serve their customers, ski-rental shops have to have the latest equipment. In late February and early March, the shops start to sell off the equipment that they bought new the previous fall. The oldest or most frequently rented equipment is cheapest. These clearances are right up there with garage sales as sources for unsophisticated gear for getting started; a basic set of skis with bindings can be as low as $60. The high-performance stuff is out there, too, at about half of its original price, but it goes fast. Check the *Yellow Pages* under Skiing Equipment, Rental and Sales.

Sports Plus

1055 S. Gaylord St., Denver, 777-6613.

10 a.m. to 6 p.m. Tuesday through Friday; til 8 p.m. Wednesday and Thursday; 10 a.m. to 5 p.m. Saturday; noon to 5 p.m. Sunday.

Sports Plus carries about half new and half used, reconditioned equipment. The emphasis is on individual sports, although it carries kids' soccer supplies, and we found very good prices there on cleats. Try it when you're looking for something your children will outgrow quickly, like a bicycle or skis. Sports Plus rents Rollerblades for use in nearby Washington Park.

Sports Rent

8761 Wadsworth Blvd., Denver, 467-0200; 560 S. Holly St., Denver, 320-0222.

7 a.m. to 8 p.m. daily.

Sports Rent rents nearly any kind of equipment you might need for individual outdoor sports, from fishing boats to picnic baskets. They sell the used summer equipment in September and the used winter equipment in March.

Surplus City

2732 W. Colorado Ave., Colorado Springs, (719) 634-1264.

9 a.m. to 7 p.m. Monday through Friday; 9 a.m. to 6 p.m. Saturday; 10 a.m. to 5 p.m. Sunday.

Surplus City offers discounts on equipment for fishing, hunting, camping, backpacking, rafting and paintball, and also carries tools, books, maps and military insignia.

Western Trading

3524 S. Broadway, Englewood, 789-1827.

8 a.m to 9 p.m. Monday through Saturday; 10 a.m. to 5 p.m. Sunday.

If you've got some gaps in your camping equipment, you can fill them inexpensively at this army-navy surplus store. There's everything from the mundane (stainless steel forks, 48¢) to the exotic (Israeli paratrooper bags, $17.95). And Levi's 501s sell regularly at a good discount.

Sports Team Paraphernalia

Is there a resident of the state of Colorado who doesn't own at least one Rockies baseball cap? Well, maybe a few. But we're a sports-fan kind of state, and we've got the stuff to prove it. If you want to find out where to find some of that stuff cheap, read on.

Burlington Coat Factory

12455 E. Mississippi Ave., Aurora, 367-0111; 3100 S. Sheridan Blvd., Denver, 937-1119; 400 E. 84th Ave., Thornton, 287-0071; 7325 W. 88th Ave., Westminster, 431-9696; 545 N. Academy, Colorado Springs, (719) 597-8505.

10 a.m. to 9:30 p.m. Monday through Saturday; 11 a.m. to 6 p.m. Sunday.

Burlington Coat Factory stores generally carry a decent selection of coats and jackets for various NFL teams, including the Broncos. Most Burlington Coat Factory discounts are in 30% to 50% range. Make sure you want what you buy. Burlington Coat Factory has a very restrictive policy on returns.

Also see Discount Department Stores and Membership Warehouses

Price Club and Sam's Club almost always have special deals on something or other with a Broncos, Rockies or Nuggets logo on it.

Fan Fair

Castle Rock, 688-6665.

See Factory Outlet Malls for address, hours and directions.

This is a clearance center for Fan Fair stores in the Westminster, Southwest Plaza and Villa Italia malls. Overstocked items from those mall stores are sold at moderate discounts. For example, a pullover Broncos jacket that sells for $99.99 in the malls would be $89.99 here.

307

Mile High Flea Market

7007 E. 88th Ave., Henderson, a few miles north of Denver on Interstate 76, 690-3542.

6 a.m. to 5 p.m. Wednesday, Saturday and Sunday. Admission costs $1.50.

Did you realize that about a third of the stuff sold at the flea market is new merchandise? There are some 600 retailers with permanent shops at the flea market and some four miles of temporary booths. A sting operation left the public with the impression that many of the sports-team items sold here are not licensed. In fact, many small booths are operated by salespeople getting rid of their samples or by someone who's going out of business. The merchandise you're considering is probably completely legitimate, and the discounts can be wonderful.

Mr. K's Sportsworld

10556 Melody Drive (Northglenn Mall), Northglenn, 456-2025; 8770-N Wadsworth Blvd., Arvada, 456-2025.

Northglenn: 10 a.m. to 9 p.m. Monday through Friday; 10 a.m. to 7 p.m. Saturday; 11 a.m. to 6 p.m. Sunday. Arvada: 10 a.m. to 6 p.m Monday through Friday; 10 a.m. to 4 p.m. Saturday.

Mr. K's has been a family-owned business in the Denver area for 17 years. Prices are competitive, the selection is very good (they claim to have the best selection of caps in the area), and they have an annual inventory-reduction clearance sale in January and February.

Mr. Mike's Pro Sports Outlet

15493 E. Hampden Ave., Unit F, Aurora, 699-6330; Mile High Flea Market, units H 20, 22, 24 and 26, Henderson.

Aurora: 10 a.m. to 7 p.m. Monday through Friday; 10 to 6 Saturday; 11 a.m. to 5 p.m. Sunday. Mile High: Flea market hours. Hours extended during the holidays.

For discount licensed Broncos, Rockies, college or pro team t-shirts, hats, jackets, and so on, try Mr. Mike's Pro Sports Outlet. If you hunt, you may find prices that are similar or cheaper than

Mr. Mike's but not with this kind of selection. There are infant sizes, children's sizes—even items for dogs—carrying logos for 150 different sports teams. Colorado Rockies t-shirts are as low as $6.99, and hats range from $4.99 up to $15.99 for the same style the players wear; popular fitted Proback hats, $20-$25 elsewhere, are $12.99.

U.S. Olympic Training Center Gift Shop

One Olympic Center, Colorado Springs, (719) 578-4792.

9:30 a.m. to 6 p.m. Monday through Saturday; noon to 5 p.m. Sunday.

This is the spot to buy a wide variety of items displaying the Olympic torch logo of the U.S. Olympic Training Center, including sweatshirts, t-shirts, hats, mugs, polo shirts, jackets, kids clothes, pins, watches, hats and backpacks. They also carry a few shirts for specific sports (not for ice skating because skaters have a separate organization) and some souvenirs of Olympics past, present and future.

Index

Impo Glaztile, 40, 112.
Interior designers, 113.
International Villa, 86.
Irene's, 226.
Izod/Gant, 18, 23, 31, 163.

Jax Mercantile, 303.
Jay Feder Jewelers, 250.
J. Crew, 31, 164.
Jerry's Nut House, 40, 120.
JF Options, 251.
JH Collectibles, 31, 195.
JNK/Birdlegs, 47, 278.
Jockey, 18, 26, 31, 164, 251.
John Henry & Friends, 18, 31,
    181.
Jonathan Logan, 18, 196.
Jones NY Factory Finale, 18, 26,
    31, 196.
Junk-Tique, 87.
J-Rat Performance, 40, 164.
Just A Second, 23, 164.
Just Kids Consignment Boutique,
    209, 283.
Just Samples, 48, 181, 196.

Kacey Furniture Clearance Center,
    73.
Kazoo and Co., 292.
Keyston Bros., 100.
Kicks, 288.
Kiddieland, 292.
Kids Again, 209, 283.
The Kids' Collection, 209, 284.
Kids Quarters, 284.
Kid's Zone, 18, 279.
King Soopers, 63.
Kitchen Collection, 18, 26, 87.
Kmart, 5.
Kogle Cards, 148.
Koret, 18, 197, 205.
Kuppenheimer Men's Clothiers,
    182.

La Cache, 80.
Lakewood Crafts, 100.
Larry's Shoes, 244.

L'cessory, 18, 251.
Leanin' Tree, 40, 58, 148.
Leather Loft, 18, 27, 31, 173, 252,
    263.
Leathermode, 27, 252, 263.
Lee's Men's Store, 182, 244.
L'eggs/Hanes/Bali, 18, 23, 27, 32,
    252.
Le Grue's, 100.
Lenox, 27, 87.
Leslie Fay, 19, 32, 197.
Levi's, 19, 23, 27, 32, 164, 252.
Lil Darlins Near New Shop, 209.
Lil Duds, 209, 284.
Lili Marlene, 80.
Lil' Things, 269.
Linda Lebsack Books, 140.
Linens 'n' Things, 100, 269.
Little Colorado, 41, 269.
Little Feet and More, 288.
Liz Claiborne, 32, 165, 197.
Loehmann's, 197.
London Fog, 24, 27, 32, 165, 173.
Love You Fashions, 63.
Lowe Alpine Systems, 48, 303.
Luxury Furniture Rental, 73.

MacFrugal's Bargains and Close-
    outs, 5, 87.
Mackenzie James & Co., 48, 279.
Madden Mountaineering, 41, 304.
Mad Dog & the Pilgrim Bookshop,
    141.
Madison Exchange, 48.
Mail-order furniture, 74.
Mail-order pantyhose, 253.
Maidenform, 19, 32, 253.
Marc Jeffries, 182.
Marie Diamond, 19, 198.
Marika, 32, 198.
Marisa Christina, 32, 198.
Marshall's, 6.
Maternity Works, 209.
McKinzey-White, 130.
McMillan Sales Corp., 113.
Media Play, 130.
Meininger's, 101.